3

SPACETIME FUNDAMENTALS

INTELLIGIBLY (RE)LEARNT

Special Relativity's Cosmographicum

BRIAN COLEMAN

BCS

Website: https://spacetimefundamentals.com

PUBLISHED BY BCS
bjc.sys@gmail.com
VELCHRONOS, Ballinakill Bay
Moyard
County Galway H91 HFH6
Ireland

Licensed under the Apache License, Version 2.0
(⇒tufte-latex.googlecode.com)
Templates modified by author

THIRD PRINTING *March 2021*

Preface

"The history of cosmic theories... may without exaggeration be called a history of collective obsessions and controlled schizophrenias."
Arthur Koestler   *The Sleepwalkers* 1955

[1] Spacetime theory's arduous ongoing evolution was recently landmarked by the epochal detection of gravitational waves precipitated thirteen hundred million years ago, by coalescing black holes over eighty million million times more distant than our sun. Surprisingly, physicists worldwide seem unaware of the *original* prediction of such waves well before Einstein's profound general relativity insights on the matter, by *Henri Poincaré*: *"Propagation of gravitation is not instantaneous, but occurs at the speed of light."*[2,3]. Many may discount such 'post-truth' heedlessness as mere academic nonchalance, yet few will have grasped that such a global scholastic debacle is uncannily mirrored by parallel endemic misapprehensions not alone with regard to other historical precedences, but also involving *some* of relativity's actual theory as still propagated. Commenced over a decade ago in a quest for a more coherent understanding of basic spacetime theory, this book shows how basic school trigonometry and elementary calculus suffice to provide deep insights into the 'macroscopic' nature[4] of our universe's *largely* 'special relativity' background. Several of its novel minimalistic approaches have been partly expounded in four papers in the *European Journal of Physics* and several recent papers in the *Results in Physics* research journal.

As a help towards bridging the yawning chasm in relativity theory between mathematical erudition and physical intuition, special software[5] has been developed for creating a series of spacetime geometry models which hopefully will find favour among general readers and also be of special interest to relativity physicists. Their insightful graphics diminish a 1907 relativity sacred cow: *overgeneralised* Minkowski spacetime. They also resolve the six decades old *'Bell's string paradox'* question: *How does an accelerating medium 'expand'?*

[1] Arthur Koestler. *The Sleepwalkers*. Hutchinson / Penguin, 1959

[2] *"...la propagation de la gravitation n'est pas instantanée, mais se fait avec la vitesse de la lumière.":*
[3] Henri Poincaré. Sur la dynamique de l'électron. Académie des sciences, Paris, 1905

[4] As distinct from the 'microscopic' world of quantum mechanics and intriguing dark matter issues.

[5] Using *PoVRay* freeware: *Persistence of Vision*, Raytracer Ltd. Victoria, Australia. http://www.povray.org

The *Prologue chapter 0 provides an overview of the book mainly for the benefit of physicists accustomed to conventional approaches to spacetime theory. It could actually be bypassed (at least on first reading) by novices unburdened by still pending controversies.[6] Chapters 1–7 deal with the relativity of *nonaccelerating objects*. Chapters 8–10 are concerned with relativistic acceleration and, in particular, the iconic yet *improperly formulated* $E = Mc^2$ equation.[7] Chapters 11–14 present innovative, seemingly wholly overlooked, spherical geometry insights into the physics of *unchanging own-acceleration*.[8] Although quite elementary, this basic geometry will no doubt appear strange to those who have learnt relativity in the traditional manner. Chapter 15 examines in detail the intricate 'shutdown' scenario of accelerating twin rockets. Chapter 16 repeats the inter-rockets radar formulae derivations in the 2016 *Results in Physics* [9] paper—curiously (and ominously) a 'nontopic' even in current textbooks.

Chapters 17 and 18 put the generally misappropriated 'Minkowski metric' equation in a new light in the context of relativity literature's important yet notoriously convoluted topic of an extended medium's 'rigor mortis' acceleration.[10] An equivalent *real variables*[11] 'rigor mortis' metric is introduced at an elementary level hopefully self-explanatory even to those unfamiliar with metrics and basic vector equations, together with its *visualisable* ('own-') metric surface which has the remarkably simple shape of a hand-held fan.

Chapters 19–21 deal with the long wrangled over *Bell's string paradox* (in dispute since 1959). The surprisingly simple solution involving *a nonpresent tense 'own-length'*, was briefly 'aired' at a 2012 symposium in Göttingen[12] and has been expounded in depth in the mentioned 2017 research journal paper. Chapter 21 shows how radar trajectories projected onto the uniformly expanding medium's 'own-surface' fully comply with necessary conditions.[13]

The concluding Epilogue chapter presents a brief historic background on the Minkowski metric saga and the related enigmatic Bell's string paradox. It also outlines experiences with hesitant editors, reviewers and other book authors many of whom have proven highly reluctant to come to terms or even take issue with conclusions irreconcilable with their own accustomed view of things. Physicists such as *David Bohm* have in the past attempted to remonstrate against such prevailing lethargies, with limited success:[14]

> *"Just because of the very breadth of its implications...the theory of relativity has tended to lead to a certain kind of confusion in which truth is identified with nothing more than that which is convenient and useful."*

Koestler's 1955 assessment of the cosmic theories saga still rings true.

---

[6] Chapters and sections preceded by an asterisk (*) may be skipped without loss of continuity.

[7] Which should, as even Einstein later agreed, be $E = m\gamma c^2$.

[8] Conventionally misnamed *'proper' acceleration*.

[9] Much of the contents of chapters 15–17 have already appeared in that paper.

[10] Traditionally known as 'rigid motion' which however has a *different meaning* in differential geometry.

[11] As opposed to the Minkowski metric's *complex variables*.

[12] B.C. Relativity Acceleration's Cosmographicum and its Radar Photon Surfings—A Euclidean Diminishment of Minkowski Spacetime, February 2012. URL http://www.dpg-verhandlungen.de/year/2012/conference/goettingen/part/gr/session/4/contribution/4

[13] In addition to presenting the contents of this book's chapter's 19 and 21, the author's 2017 journal paper shows how, without relativistic preconditions, the real metric own-surface is established purely mathematically as a unique laterally expanding surface.

[14] David Bohm. *The Special Theory of Relativity*. Routledge, 1965, 1996

Special note

A physics background is not assumed for this book[15],[16] which is devoted exclusively to special relativity in one dimension and focuses on essentials. Only school level calculus and trigonometry are needed, and, in the final chapters, readiness to come to grips with easily explained vectors. As well as referencing literature sources, sidenotes take issue with entrenched misleading aphorisms such as *'a moving rod contracts'* or *'a moving mass increases'*, and dysfunctional misnomers such as *'proper time'* which needs to be replaced by *'own-time'*. Such unorthodox terminologies are included in the book's *Glossary*.

Although perhaps contrary to some physicists' initial impressions, the book's contents are fully in accord with enlightened special relativity theory. This also applies to its final chapters which address the concept of an accelerating extended medium's 'non-inertial own-length'—a much discussed topic not, in the present author's opinion, hitherto appropriately dealt with in relativity literature. Very surprisingly, the straightforward solution emerges in the context of entirely overlooked yet easily visualised spherical geometry.

Acknowledgements

During the prolonged writing of this book, difficulties encountered on submitting offshoot papers to academic journals[17] were alleviated by encouragements from several people. These included *David Mermin*,[18] *Wesley Mathews*,[19] *Dragan Redžić*,[20] *Lev Okun*,[21] *Robert Brehme*,[22] *Changbiao Wang* (Yale), *Volker Bach* (Gauß Institut, Braunschweig), *Gerhard Wortmann* (Paderborn), *Masud Chaichian* (Helsinki), *Valery Morozov* (Russian Academy of Sciences)[23] and Dublin academics *Ian Elliott*, *Roy Johnston*, *Gerald O'Sullivan*, *Annraoi de Paor* and *Kevin Hutchinson*. Also helpful were *Liam* and *Maura Connolly Little*, *Rory Harrington*, *Hugh Evans*, *Victor Hamilton* (Belfast relative of *Joseph Larmor*), and *Nikolai Demidenko* for Russian translations.

Although a 2009 correspondence with Russian physicist *Stanislav Podosenov*[24] (born in *Archangelsk* and a member of both the *Russian Academy of Sciences* and the *New York Academy of Sciences*), was inconclusive, he has now kindly proposed joint cooperation on the accelerating frames topic—as described in this book's final Epilogue. Further details on this will be provided on this book's dedicated website:[25]   https://spacetimefundamentals.com .

Special thanks are due to LATEX pioneers *Donald Knuth* and *Leslie Lamport* for their excellent desktop publishing program and to *Edward Tufte* for his exemplary book design. *Tibor Tómác's* bookcover templates and *Kevin Godby's* 'workaround' advice were likewise invaluable. The *PoVRay* graphics software proved to be an excellent synergetic tool for the geometric modelling of relativistic acceleration scenarios.

[15] A German version of this book has also been published:

[16] Brian Coleman. *Raumzeittheorie Elementar Neu Begriffen*. BCS, 2018

[17] As outlined in the book's *Prologue and Epilogue.

[18] David Mermin. Relativity Without Light. *American Journal of Physics*, 52:119–124, 1984

[19] Wesley Mathews. Relativistic velocity and acceleration transformations from thought experiments. *American Journal of Physics*, 73: 45–51, 2004

[20] Dragan Redžic. Relativistic Length Agony Continued. *Serb. Astron. J.*, 188:55 – 65, 2014

[21] Lev Okun. *Energy and Mass in Relativity Theory*. World Scientific, 2009

[22] F Sears and R Brehme. *Introduction to Special Relativity*. Addison Wesley, 1968

[23] *Lebedev Physical Institute*

[24] S. A. Podosenov, J. Foukzon, and E. Menkova. *Difficulties in the Interpretation of the Einstein's Relativity Theory*. Lampert Academic Publishing, 2017b

[25] Under development as this book is being launched.

About the author

When completing an engineering degree in *University College Dublin* in the 1960's, the author became intrigued by Maxwell's equations of electromagnetism, yet remained perplexed by the literature's 'treatment' of basic space-time issues. As in the nature of things, he turned to other matters over the following decades. Working for *Siemens* in the 1970s, he developed process control programs for steel plants in Germany, Austria, Russia and Norway, and, in the mid 1980s (then with own company *BC Systems GmbH, Erlangen*), designed and commissioned the logistics software for a *Bosch* machine tool complex in Moscow. Vivid recollections of the importance in artificial intelligence systems of *conceptual clarity* have motivated the book's treatment of relativity as 'a spatio-temporal process'. Its structuring and didactic approach also owe much to the experience in the 1990s of authoring a whole series of medical manuals for Siemens' *Somatom Computed Tomography* scanners. Ex-colleagues to whom the author was indebted for crucial personal support during those decades include *Brian Sweeney* (Dublin), *Reinhard Fleischer* (*Oberingenieur*, Erlangen) and *Anthony Mason* (Siemens Medical Division).

Returning to Ireland in 1998, he rekindled his interest in relativity and, unexpectedly, published a series of papers in the *European Journal of Physics* (2003, 2004, 2005, 2006). A paper on a much disputed 'Sagnac effect' issue appeared in 2015.[26] The two recent papers in the *Results in Physics* research journal, which have attracted several thousand downloads in the US alone, introduced the innovative material of this book's three final sections.

[26] B.C. Orbiting Particles' Analytic Time Dilations Correlated with the Sagnac Formula. *Vixra.org*, May 2015. http://vixra.org/pdf/1505.0041v8.pdf

Dedications

This book is dedicated to the treasured memory of my parents *Liam* and *Noelle* and to the future of my granddaughter *Méabh*. Special tribute is due to four departed Dublin friends: *Ian Elliott* who generously provided a decade of helpful advice and patient encouragement; *Roy Johnston*, a physicist of outstanding political courage; *Noel Cummins*, an inspiring maestro of the aptly germane (also to this book) art of minimalist theatre; and *Liam Little* whose intense curiosity, enthusiasm and manifold support have proven decisive for the book's initial conception and its ultimate completion.

B.C. *VelChronos*, Ballinakill Bay, Moyard, County Galway
November 2017

Contents

PREAMBLE   1

0   *Prologue   3

    Special relativity's scope   5
    The redundant 2nd postulate   5
    Encountering the limit speed   6
    Isaac Newton's 3rd law reformulated and 'vindicated'   6
    Dormant Islamic relativistic geometry   7
    Time lost and gained—*À* la recherche du temps perdu   7
    Equations that did not bark in the light   8
    A useful Gedankenexperiment   9
    The REAL variables metric surface   9
    Solving the Bell's string paradox enigma   9
    An À LA CARTE Pandora's box   10
    Prevailing problems of comprehension   11

I   T FOR TWO   13

1   An elegant spacetime underlay   15
    1.1   Spacetime charts' 'where-lines' and 'when-lines'   16
          Elimination of 'background space'   17
    1.2   A spatio-temporal swiveling—'chronosity'   18
          Differing red and blue spacestation reference frames   18
    1.3   Mating where-lines and when-lines   19
    1.4   A boundary, perhaps 'limit', cosmic speed   20

2   Spacetime charts and world-lines   21
    2.1   Boundary speed rescaling   22
    2.2   The general chronosity-velocity relationship   23
    2.3   The dual reference frames chart   24

WORLD-LINES and EVENTS 25

The home reference frame chart and a variant 26

2.4 A universal constant with many rôles in Nature 26

2.5 *An alternate initial postulate: SPATIAL ISOTROPY 27

3 **Mirages of 'length' and time**   **29**

3.1 Events and their reference frames' intervals 30

The scaled velocity/chronosity velchronos angle 30

3.2 The MIRAGE of 'length contraction' 32

Contrasting 'length' experiences 33

3.3 Larmor time dilation factor γ 33

3.4 Meaninglessness of the present tense in relativity 34

3.5 Time travel—the simple twin paradox 35

II   **SPACETIME TRINITIES**   **37**

4 **Larmor-Lorentz transformations and velocity composition**   **39**

4.1 A simple derivation 39

4.2 Relativistic velocities of a triplet of reference frames 41

4.3 A further historical note 42

5 **The limit speed identified**   **43**

5.1 Establishing the boundary speed by starlight 43

5.2 The 'second postulate' is redundant 45

5.3 The 'contagious' limit speed 46

5.4 *A reference frames quartet 46

6 ***Measuring the Cosmic Limit Speed**   **49**

6.1 The arbitrary active signal return interval ratio 50

A crucial equation 51

6.2 Ω as a conglomerate of tandem response time ratios 51

Verifying the explicit limit speed formula 53

The question of a difference between λ and c 53

6.3 Ignatowski's tragic fate and legacy 54

7 ***Doppler relationships**   **55**

7.1 The relativity Doppler factor 55

The Doppler inter-frames signal interval ratio 56

7.2 Cosmology—Evidence of an expanding Universe 57

III FORCE, MASS AND ENERGY   **59**

   Prelude to a 2005 physics journal publication 60

8 Three acceleration perspectives   **61**
   8.1 An accelerating rocket scenario 61
        Rocket launch 61
        Rocket rendezvous 61
        A 'comoving' reference frame's parameters 62
   8.2 The primary acceleration relationships 63
        'Retroperspective' comoving frames' acceleration 63
        The home frame acceleration value 64
   8.3 The 'apocalyptic' dynamics identities 65

9 Diversifying momentum and force   **67**
   9.1 Classical momentum and classical force 68
   9.2 Dropping the 'relativistic mass' oxymoron 68
   9.3 Momentum diversified—spatial and temporal 69
   9.4 Force diversified—object-frame and observer-frame 69
        'Also Spuke Zerothruster' 70
        Newton's 3rd law 'upgraded' 70
        The four forces of the apocalyptic identities 71

10 The $E = m\gamma c^2$ pentagon   **73**
   10.1 Kinetic energy—imparted and acquired 73
         Nuclear energy 74
         Cosmic boundary speed limitation 74
   10.2 *Some thermodynamics 75
   10.3 *A five-fold equivalence 77
   10.4 *Non-elastic collisions 77

IV SPHERICAL GEOMETRY SURPRISES   **79**

11 The unit thrust rocket   **81**
   11.1 Unit own-accleration interrelationships 82
         The velchronos angle differential 82
         Velocity as a function of rocket own-time 82
         Unit thrust home time and distances 83
         Unit thrust home frame world-lines 84
   11.2 A unit thrust courier's multi-spacestation deliveries 84
         The single 'home' reference frame chart 84
         Staggered dual frame charts 85
   11.3 The unit acceleration rocket's equations summarized 86

12 Relativity's <u>real</u> spherical triangles   **87**

12.1 The spherical triangle sines and cosines laws 88

12.2 Unit sines law ratio spherical triangles 89

    The triple gammas velocity formulae 90

12.3 Spherical triangles' hitherto missed relativity connection 91

    Direct portrayals of relativity velocity composition 92

12.4 *Relativity spherical triangle volume and area relationships . . 92

12.5 *Spherical cosines and sines laws in global navigation 93

13 Spacetime's and Geometry's missing 'HEMIX'   **95**

13.1 Cascaded relativity tetrahedra 95

    *A relativity Doppler polyhedron 96

13.2 The differential relativity spherical triangle 97

13.3 The hemix: a 'transcendental OWN-HISTORY-LINE' 98

    Hemix vector coordinates 99

13.4 *The hemix's 16th century sibling: THE LOXODROME 100

14 A Spacetime Odyssey   **101**

14.1 Time travel ovoidal projections 102

    A coherent ovoids framework 102

    Hemix 'distance ray' stereographic projections 102

    Seventeen time travel relativistic parameters 102

14.2 An outgoing and return spacetime itinerary 104

V   AN OCCAM STEEPLECHASE   **107**

15 'Time dispersal' and 'retro-separation'   **109**

15.1 Two rockets' rendez-vous with two spacestations 109

    Home/spacestation frames' world-lines 110

15.2 Shutdown time and distance 'dispersals' 111

    A finishing post time gap 111

    Shutdown 'time gap re-synchronization' frame 113

    The 'event horizon' case 113

15.3 Front rocket's 'retrospective' separation $\mathcal{L}$ 114

16 Two curious radar intervals   **115**

16.1 The unit own-thrust home frame 'world-surface' 116

16.2 Emitted photon transit times 116

16.3 Unit thrust rockets' asymptotic horizon 118

16.4 Returning photons 118

    Re-emitted photons 119

16.5 Unit thrust inter-rocket radar intervals 120

16.6 Evidence unwittingly 'withheld' 120

A fallacy's domino effect 121

16.7 A photon's unit thrust medium-timed crossing rates 121

Photon crossing rates in the limit 122

VI THE RELATIVITY CURATE'S EGG   123

17 Rigor Mortis acceleration   125

17.1 Non-unit fixed own-thrust relationships 125

17.2 A one-off single frame world-surface 126

17.3 Corresponding fixed thrust radar intervals 126

17.4 The 'rigor mortis' scenario 128

Rigor mortis fixed radar intervals 128

Rigor mortis space and time dispersals 129

17.5 The 'rigor mortis' home frame world-surface 130

Fixed velocity 'rigor mortis' world-surface loci 131

The rigor mortis accelerations condition 131

17.6 The good-in-spots bad egg 131

18 Two real—Euclidean—metric own-surfaces   133

18.1 Increment curves and medium curves 134

18.2 The simple nonaccelerating own-surface 134

18.3 The rigor mortis medium's own-surface 135

A shortcut to chapter 17's rigor mortis condition 135

Characteristics of the rigor mortis metric own-surface 136

18.4 The 'hemicised' rigor mortis own-surface 137

18.5 Migrants on a rigor mortis gravity train 138

A rigor mortis gravitational field 139

18.6 The rigor mortis 'real metric' 139

18.7 Relativity's pseudo-Euclidean Minkowski metric 140

VII ROLLER-COASTING SPACETIME   141

19 The unit thrust medium own-surface   143

19.1 A further perpetuated error in relativity literature 143

19.2 Intrinsic own-surface criteria for a unit thrust medium 144

A simple question 144

19.3 The missing own-surface Υ 145

Own-surface Υ's helices and hemices 147

19.4 The medium's 'lengths' in four reference frames 148

19.5 Non-inertial 'present tenses' 150

20 A Relativity Cosmographicum's real spacetime metrics   **151**

   20.1 Kepler's 16th century 'Mysterium Cosmographicum' 151

   20.2 The relativity helicoidal sextet 152

        Pseudo-expansion/pseudo-contraction helicoids Γ and K 153

        Ruled surface helicoids Θ, Ψ and Δ 154

   20.3 *Extrinsic* and *intrinsic* parameters 154

   20.4 The unit thrust medium's gravity train 155

   20.5 *The uniform thrust medium's real metric 156

        The awkward mixed differentials variable coefficient 157

21 *Radar mappings from inertial home frame onto own-surface Υ   **159**

   21.1 Radar photon trajectories 159

        Outgoing photon paths 159

        Returning photon paths 160

   21.2 Shared radar curves' crossing angles and geodesic curvatures . 162

        A 'retrospective' insight 163

   21.3 Validations of the unit thrust medium's own-surface Υ 164

22 Epilogue   **165**

   22.1 "A glorious non-entity" 165

        Twistings and turnings 166

   22.2 Groves of Academe 166

        A Dutch drawbridge 167

        The Ante Portas 'invitation' 167

        Mistrodden ground 168

   22.3 Two Russian overtures 169

   22.4 The Emperor's New ~~Mind~~ Clothes 170

Glossary   **173**

Bibliography   **175**

Index   **181**

List of Figures

1   Albert Einstein and Charlie Chaplin   3
2   1st Solvay Conference 1911—Einstein and colleagues   4
3   John Lighton Synge, 1897-1995 Irish physicist   11

1.1   A French railway daily schedule   16
1.2   Spacetime chart of respective train compartments   16
1.3   Classical spacestations' spacetime chart   17
1.4   Zero velocity   17
1.5   Moderate velocity   17
1.6   High velocity   17
1.7   Near infinite velocity   17
1.8   Dual frame's chronosity   18
1.9   Low velocity   18
1.10 Moderate velocity   18
1.11 High velocity   18
1.12 Dual reference frames chart at some 'boundary' speed   19

2.1   Henri Poincaré, 1854-1912   21
2.2   Dual reference frames chart at SCALED boundary speed   22
2.3   Dual reference frames chart at arbitrary scaled speed   24
2.4   Enrique Loedel, 1901-1962   24
2.5   General world-line trajectories of a dual reference frames chart   25
2.6   Hans Freudenthal, 1905-1990   27

3.1   Reciprocal mirages of relativistic perception   30
3.2   Spacestations' left and right end trajectories.   31
3.3   So-called 'length contraction   32
3.4   Time dilation   33
3.5   Simplified time travel chart   35

4.1   Joseph Larmor, 1851-1942   39
4.2   Larmor-Lorentz transformations   40

4.3 George FitzGerald, Dublin physicist 1851-1901   42

5.1 William of Ockham, 1285-1349   43
5.2 Star-photon-Earth reference frames triplet   44
5.3 Ole Rømer, 1644-1710   44
5.4 Classical physics and relativity physics velocity triad surfaces.   46
5.5 Relativistic velocity triad surface for speeds above limit speed   47
5.6 A reference frames quartet   47

6.1 Equation of motion mathematical citation   49
6.2 Signal response times ratio   50
6.3 Triplet signal exchanges   52
6.4 Vladimir Ignatowski, 1875-1942   54

7.1 Christian Doppler, Austrian physicist 1803 - 1853   55
7.2 Limit speed signal response ratio   57
7.3 Vesto Slipher, U.S. physicist, 1875 - 1969   58

8.1 Home and Rendezvous acceleration schematic   62
8.2 An accelerating rocket's coordinates   63
8.3 Retrospective acceleration frames triplet   64

9.1 Jean Buridan, French philosopher 1295-1356   67
9.2 Isaac Newton, English scientist 1643-1727   68

10.1 Precollision reference frames and relative velocities   75
10.2 Postcollision reference frames and relative velocities   76

11.1 Home frame hyperbolic world-line of a rocket and spacestations   85
11.2 Cascaded dual reference frames charts of rocket and spacestations   85

12.1 Abul Wafa Buzjani, 940-998 Persian mathematician   87
12.2 Spherical triangle sine law proof   88
12.3 Spherical triangle cosines law proof   89
12.4 Regiomontanus, German astronomer 1436-1476   89
12.5 Unit sines ratio spherical triangles   90
12.6 Velocity addition visualized   92
12.7 Determining surface distance between ships   93

13.1 Alice chatting about physics and epistemology   95
13.2 A relativity tetrahedron's radar trajectories   96
13.3 Cascaded relativity triangles/tetrahedra   96
13.4 Relativity acceleration visualized   97
13.5 Differential dual reference frame charts   98

13.6 Loxodromes of Pedro Nuñes 1502-1578   100

14.1 Astronomy Ireland 2005 lecture web graphic.   102
14.2 Mercator projection. Image uploaded Sept. 2015 to Wikipedia by *Daniel R. Strebe.*   102
14.3 Rocket acceleration parameters   103
14.4 A time travel return trip   104
14.5 A *longer* time travel return trip   105

15.1 Home frame hyperbolic world-lines of uniformly accelerating rockets   110
15.2 Loedel chart with rocket and spacestation world-lines   112

16.1 Home frame world-surface of a uniformly accelerating medium   117

17.1 Home frame world-surface of a non-uniformly accelerating medium   127
17.2 1895 Punch magazine cartoon "True Humility"   130

18.1 A nonaccelerating medium's metric own-surface   134
18.2 Rigor Mortis own-surface—the egg's good spots   136
18.3 The 'hemicised' rigor mortis own-surface   138

19.1 The unit thrust medium's hemicoidal metric own-surface Υ.   146
19.2 Various 'lengths' between uniformly accelerating rockets.   148
19.3 The unit thrust mediums' non-inertial 'proxy' frames.   149

20.1 Johannes Kepler's 'Mysterium Cosmographicum'   152
20.2 Johannes Kepler, 1571-1630   152
20.3 A relativity cosmographicum and its helicoid sextet   154
20.4 Cylindrical coordinates differential   156

21.1 Home frame world-surface of a uniformly accelerating medium   160
21.2 Own-surface increment and medium curves with radar trajectories   161

PREAMBLE

Overleaf: *Abstract graphic* of a
mathematical surfaces mapping.

The *optional* *Prologue chapter outlines why this book has been written and
gives a broad overview of special relativity as treated in its seven main parts.

Readers who have already 'acquired' some knowledge of the subject may
be surprised to learn that some of its exposition as presented in books and
papers—both popular and academic—is not only in several ways cumbersome, but often quite misleading. On the other hand, novices not wishing
to become unnecessarily entangled in such historical mixups, or those impa-
tient to 'get on with it', might prefer to go directly to the Part I—T FOR TWO
initial chapter An elegant spacetime underlay, which 'starts at the beginning'.

.

0
*Prologue

LESS WHO SAID WHAT, MORE WHAT THERE IS TO SAY.

"Euphoric in our ivory towers,
How blissful we, the ancients' heirs;
The intellect rests oft abroad,
Yet ever there—the solemn word…
Who dares to verse his gruesome yarns,
Our grimmest retribution earns.
And should he rudely truthful be,
We'll damn him for Eternity."

Documents of a Life's Pathway
(Extracts translated by present author.)

"Froh in hoher Halle wohnen,
Glücklich wir, die Epigonen.
Bleibt der Geist auch meistens fort,
Fehlt doch nie das grosse Wort…
Wer da Greuelmärchen dichtet,
Grimmig wird von uns gerichtet.
Wenn er gar die Wahrheit spricht,
Dann verzeihen wir's ihm nicht."

Dokumente eines Lebenswegs
Albert Einstein

[1]To mark his 1933 exit from the tragically usurped *Prussian Academy of Sciences*, ALBERT EINSTEIN poetically satirised reactionary opposition to the revolution in physics in which HENRI POINCARÉ and he had played primary rôles. The main conclusions of their new spacetime theory, whose nongravitational basis is known as FLAT SPACETIME or SPECIAL RELATIVITY, have nevertheless now been consolidated by a century of observation and experiment.

The discerning mathematician Poincaré and the outstandingly intuitive physicist Einstein, who appeared together at the 1911 *Solvay Conference* in Belgium, had a better inkling than most of challenges and misunderstandings afflicting relativity theory. Most unfortunately, although highly appreciative of each other's contributions to physics, the two were hardly on speaking terms.

Figure 1: Albert Einstein with fellow satirist Charlie Chaplin

[1] Albert Einstein. *Dokumente eines Lebenswegs/Documents of a life's pathway.* WILEY-VCH, 2005

©BCS IRELAND 2017 ISBN 978-1-9998410-1-0
Brian Coleman SPACETIME FUNDAMENTALS INTELLIGIBLY (RE)LEARNT

Figure 2: 1st Solvay Conference. Hotel Metropole Brussels 1911. *Albert Einstein* behind *Henri Poincaré* and *Marie Curie*, *Hendrik Lorentz* seated 4th left, *Arnold Sommerfeld* standing 4th left.

[2] A A Logunov. Henri Poincaré and Relativity Theory, 2005. URL http://arxiv.org/pdf/physics/0408077.pdf

[3] Louis Essen. *The Special Theory of Relativity: A Critical analysis.* Clarendon Press Oxford, 1971
[4] Essen recklessly referred to a 'thought experiment' as *'a contradiction in terms'.*
[5] Georg Galeczki and Peter Marquardt. *Requiem für die Spezielle Relativität.* Haag and Herchen Frankfurt, 1997
[6] The present author however does not concur many of that book's contentions.
[7] Ambrose Bierce. *The Devil's Dictionary.* Neale, New York, 1911

At the time perplexed by initial lack of recognition of several ground-breaking papers and also under considerable personal stress, Einstein in his 1905 paper had omitted—most untypically—to refer to important insights earlier expounded by his French colleague.[2] He later often expressed profound admiration of Poincaré who however tragically had succumbed to illness in 1912.

Ironically, had the two pioneers been in proper communication, modern day comprehension of relativity theory might not still be partly compromised by the confusions alluded to in this book's preface. Groundless dismissals of special relativity such as by the co-developer of the world's first practical atomic clock *Louis Essen*,[3,4] have long been deservedly consigned to the history bin. On the other hand, how muddled *some* matters still remain is chronicled in a somewhat polemic yet interesting 1997 book entitled *Requiem für die Spezielle Relativität*.[5,6]

The present book's several unorthodox approaches to the subject arose from the impression that, as special relativity's 2005 centennial symposiums unwittingly testified, the theory's engrossing GENESIS—unravelling—of its underlying *'flat spacetime' theory*, continues to be propagated in a manner oddly reminiscent of how AMBROSE BIERCE'S *Devil's Dictionary* defined EDUCATION:[7]

"THAT WHICH DISCLOSES TO THE WISE AND DISGUISES FROM THE FOOL- ISH, THEIR LACK OF UNDERSTANDING."

Paradoxically, not all who deem themselves wise in the matter appear to be aware of some of the theory's still prevailing inconsistencies.

Special relativity's scope

Although some relativity formulations and approaches of Austrian-born physicist *Wolfgang Rindler* are seriously contested both in this book as well as by other authors, his erudite textbooks are often insightful. One example is his apt description of *the domain of special relativity*:[8]

> "Special relativity is the theory of an ideal physics referred to an ideal set of infinitely extended gravity-free inertial frames ... [The theory] would exist even if light and electromagnetism were somehow eliminated from nature. It is primarily a new theory of space and time, and only secondarily a theory of the physics in that new space and time..."

This points to a pure 'spacetime continuum' theory potentially compatible even within conceivable 'parallel' universes.[9] For purposes of clarity, in this book we 'evolve' such a theory *purely on a one-dimensional basis* and confine our deliberations to nongravitational special relativity—'child's play' as Einstein called it, compared with its highly mathematical gravitational counterpart *general relativity*.

The redundant 2nd postulate

A major hurdle denying a school maths literate public—and many physicists—an *achievable* grasp of special relativity, is an endemic mindset known as 'PRESENTISM', a legacy of Newtonian physics. The assumption that physical phenomena must somehow be explainable from *a present tense standpoint*, the subconsciously self-imposed scourge of many relativity texts even by accomplished authors, has led to relativity theory being generally introduced by a 'forced fed' actually superfluous imposition—*postulation* of the speed of light being a limit speed. Nevertheless, and contrary to general consensus, the *single* assumption of cosmic spatial homogeneity ('sameness') as propounded in Poincaré's classic 1902 *La Science et l'hypothèse*,[10] alone suffices to deduce a hypothetical finite limit speed (λ).[11] The theory's core equations can then be far more elegantly established than by the 'normal' path, as was realised already in 1909 by the ill-fated Georgian born Russian physicist VLADIMIR IGNATOWSKI:[12,13]

> "The Relativity Principle [as] set up by Albert Einstein has achieved such profound significance, both physical as well as epistemological, that it seems appropriate to reconsider its foundations and as precisely as possible examine the consequences which produce it: firstly to get a clear picture of this principle, about which much arbitrariness prevails, and secondly to establish a guideline for obtaining confidence in not underestimating, but also not overestimating it."

[8] Wolfgang Rindler. *Introduction to Special Relativity.* Oxford Universtiy Press, 1982, 1991

[9] Not necessarily 'a fantasy', given the extraordinarily esoteric nature of current speculations regarding 'dark matter'.

[10] Henri Poincaré. *La Science et l'hypothèse.* Flammarion, Paris, 1902

[11] David Mermin. Relativity Without Light. *American Journal of Physics*, 52:119–124, 1984

[12] Vladimir Von Ignatowski. Das Relativitätsprinzip. *Arch. Math. Phys.*, 17/18:1/17, 1910

[13] ⇒the present book's section 6.3 Ignatowski's tragic fate and legacy extract from Aleksander Solzhenitsyn's *The Gulag Archipelago*.

In the book's *Part I*—T FOR TWO, a symmetrical chart world-lines approach imagining that spacetime intrinsically incorporates a disparity of simultaneities increasing with velocity, leads to the heart of the matter. A mutually perceived distance-rated *'speed of time dissimultaneity'* ('chronosity' ψ[14]) emerges as equal to a mutually perceived time-rated *'speed of spatial distance'* (velocity v) divided by the square of an initially unquantified *causality boundary speed* λ (lambda). Mutual *'mirage'* perceptions of length 'contraction' and time 'dilation' are *consequences* of this simple relationship. Their proper interpretation as subjective *perceptions* rather than objective phenomena, underlines the futility of conventional 'presentism' approaches still frequently encountered in the literature. A key parameter here is the *'velchronos'* (velocity/chronosity) angle ϕ whose *sine* reflects scaled relative velocity i.e. $\sin\phi = v/\lambda = \psi\lambda$.

Encountering the limit speed

Part II—SPACETIME TRINITIES uses the straightforward *physically kernel* velocity/chronosity relationship to immediately establish the *'Larmor-Lorentz' transformations* as well as special relativity's important *velocity composition relationship*. Using this velocity equation, a little 'lateral thinking' suffices to *logically identify* an instance of the limit speed λ—the speed of light c. Moreover, a resulting *arbitrary signal speed* 'Doppler' equation involving clocked radar signals between a trio of relatively moving spacestations,[15,16] yields an actual explicit formula for *measuring* (at least in theory) the λ/c ratio, without having to assume that λ and c are the same. This places the speed of light on a par with now evidenced gravitational waves *as an instance* of the cosmic limit speed.[17,18] The equivalent more simple *limit speed signal* Doppler equation allowed *Edwin Hubble* to deduce that our universe continually expands.

Isaac Newton's 3rd law reformulated and 'vindicated'

Ironically, as even Einstein—to little avail—emphasized in 1948, relativity's iconic $E = Mc^2$ equation is actually inappropriate,[19] a matter widely misunderstood even in academic circles. This is due both to the presentism mindset as well as to dominance of the (epistemologically speaking) ill-chosen 'relativistic mass' concept ($\Rightarrow$ section 9.2 Dropping the 'relativistic mass' oxymoron), aptly condemned[20] by *Lev Okun* as "*...a kind of pedagogical virus which very effectively infects new generations of students and professors and shows no signs of decline.*". Flaunted at length in a popular work by *Richard Feynman* whose renowned intuition and legendary thoroughness both failed him in this matter, the anachronism's widespread acceptance led a standard textbook[21] to wrongly conclude: "*...ideas of momentum conservation fail [in relativity]...[the correct equations] must be guessed.*"

[14] Greek letter ψ—*psi*—is chosen deliberately since it resembles a 'crossed' v.

[15] B.C. A dual first-postulate basis for special relativity. *European Journal of Physics*, 24:301–313, May 2003

[16] B.C. An elementary first-postulate measurement of the cosmic limit speed. *European Journal of Physics*, 25:L31–L32, 2004

[17] As explained in detail in chapter 6 *Measuring the Cosmic Limit Speed.

[18] http://www.zb math.org/?q =an%3A1046.83001

[19] Correct is:
$$E = mc^2 / \sqrt{1 - \frac{v^2}{c^2}}.$$

[20] Lev Okun. The mass versus relativistic and rest masses. URL http://isites.harvard.edu/fs/docs/icb.topic1214842.files/11lev-okun-on-mass.pdf

[21] James H Smith. *Introduction to Special Relativity*. Dover, 1965, 1996

[22],[23],[24]Purging the relativistic mass misnomer also clears the path[25],[26] towards redeeming, *if appropriately reformulated*, the full validity of Newton's action/reaction principle whose role in relativity has been generally misinterpreted, as for example in [27] (page 11): *"Logical as the third law is, there is a loophole in it…".*

Part III—FORCE, MASS AND ENERGY focuses on two sets of equations of paramount importance. The *primary acceleration relationships* associate an object's (possibly varying) *own-acceleration* (α)[28] in its own ever changing *comoving reference frame*, with the object's retrospectively perceived acceleration (β) of successive comoving frames' anchored objects. Conversely, a home frame anchored object's perception (a) of the accelerating object then emerges. Secondly, two also known though little appreciated 'apocalyptic identities', derived using elementary calculus, crucially yield—with little further effort—the all important generally misinterpreted force relationships. With the relativistic mass impediment discarded, Newton's landmark yet generally wrongly assessed third law—*action equals reaction*—can then be placed in an entirely new and proper light, yielding the core $E = m\gamma c^2$ equation where γ (Greek *gamma*) equals $1/\sqrt{1 - v^2/c^2}$.

Dormant Islamic relativistic geometry

The remainder of the book focuses on objects under *fixed thrust* such as a constant 'own-acceleration' rocket which, as it turns out, has *twelve* relativistic parameters which are all functions of the velchronos angle whose sine reflects the rocket's scaled velocity. In 2004 the present author was surprised to discover an extraordinary connection between relativistic velocity composition in terms of such velchronos angles, and the angles of a special category of spherical triangles. Described in the book's *Part IV*—SPHERICAL GEOMETRY SURPRISES, this insight—which has its origin in *10th century Islamic spherical geometry*—permits what are to all appearances unprecedented visual insights into the intriguing mathematics of velocity composition, relativistic acceleration and the 'time travel' scenario involving an *accelerating* rocket (as opposed to the simplistic 'twin paradox' case where a rocket just reverses velocity[29]).

Although uncannily resembling the early 16th century LOXODROME yet apparently unknown,[30] a remarkable spherical 'HEMIX' curve traces the own-time clock of a unit (scaled) thrust rocket whose velocity ('velchronos') angle is reflected by the curve's meridianal inclination. This truly basic geometry plays a further profound role in the book's final *Part VII*.

Time lost and gained—À la recherche du temps perdu

[31]As two identically accelerating rockets increase in velocity, coincidentally

[22] Richard Feynman. *Six Not So Easy Pieces - Einstein's Relativity, Symmetry, and Space-Time.* Addison-Wesley, 1997

[23] However appealing they may be, Feynmann's less philosophical approaches ("The only sensible way is what is the *most convenient way…*"), are disparaged in Lange's 2002 book preface:

[24] Marc Lange. *An Introduction to the Philosophy of Physics.* Blackwell, 2002

[25] B.C. Special relativity dynamics without a priori momentum conservation. *European Journal of Physics*, 26:647–650, 2005

[26] B.C. A five-fold equivalence in special relativity one-dimensional dynamics. *European Journal of Physics*, 27:983–984, 2006

[27] Bernard Schulz. *Gravity from the ground up.* Cambridge University Press, 2003

[28] Traditionally mislabelled 'proper' acceleration.

[29] Spending most time just 'cruising' on the outwards and on the return journies.

[30] The author is open to correction on this.

[31] *In search of lost time* is a classic novel by *Marcel Proust.*

passing home frame observers would simultaneously record both rocket clocks as also having identical readings. Observers coincidentally stationary with the two rockets in each rockets' comoving frame, would however insist that home frame observers recorded the rocket clock *at different times*. What 'happens' if the rockets *cease* accelerating simultaneously,[32,33,34] is analysed using the symmetrical spacetime chart, in the 'Time dispersal' and 'retro-separation' chapter of *Part V*—AN OCCAM STEEPLECHASE. In the shutdown frame, first the front rocket is seen to stop, but the rear rocket continues *backwards* until it slows down to a stop. Shutdown reference frame observers would *ultimately* record the rockets' own-clocks as *out of synchronism* i.e. as 'time dispersed'.

The curious case of equations that did not bark in the light

Part V's second chapter Two curious radar intervals, is concerned with an *extended* medium comprising an infinite number of infinitesimal increments between two rockets. All increments having fixed though possibly differing fixed own-thrust, are represented by home frame hyperbolic world-lines which together form a single reference *home* frame 'world-surface'. A notable insight, rarely addressed, directly emerges: *A rocket permanently accelerating faster than 1g, never sees an event over a light year away—its 'asymptotic horizon'.*[35]

Unit thrust inter-rocket radar intervals, strangely absent in relativity textbooks, are then derived in the same chapter for *identical thrust* rear and front rockets. Very significantly, BOTH INTERVAL PERIODS ACTUALLY VARY.[36] Having diligently acknowledged a submitted paper's[37] straightforward radar equations as "essential... and correct", a mainstream research journal reviewer however then prevaricated with a non sequitur:

> "...the paper is based on special-relativistic equations, and therefore on the second postulate. Imposing at the end a condition violating the second postulate will trivially lead to a contradiction, of course, but would anybody feel compelled to accept the author's conclusions on the basis of such reasoning?"

[38]Clearly, relativists remain transfixed by the naive illusion that the inertial frames limit speed principle must also apply to identical fixed thrust rockets whose radar intervals are thereby supposed to be constant. A similar related impasse is wide lack of awareness that what is known as *Minkowski spacetime* (dealt with later in this book's final *Part VII*), is *overgeneralised*. Such post-truth intransigences in basic physics in the face of plain evidence to the contrary, have a four centuries old precedent: the legendary refusals by geocentric academics in Pisa to accept Galileo's invitation to look through his telescope. On the demise of one of the former, the latter wryly remarked:[39]

> "Never having wanted to see the moons of Jupiter on Earth, perhaps he'll see them on the way to heaven."

[32] As judged in the home frame. A scenario discussed in:

[33] F Sears and R Brehme. *Introduction to Special Relativity*. Addison Wesley, 1968

[34] Dragan Redžic. Note on Dewan&Beran Bell's spaceship problem. *Eur.J.Phys.*, 29:N11–9, 2008

[35] By coincidence the asymptotic horizon happens to be *just under* one light year distant.

[36] ⇒ page 116's section The unit own-thrust home frame 'world-surface'.
[37] Springer reference PLUS-D-15-01123, submitted August 2015. The paper was accepted for publication in January 2016, in Elsevier's *Results in Physics*.

[38] The unquestionably sincere reviewer's nevertheless inconsequential rhetorical question, is in itself a reflection of how deeply this simple *fundamental* radar intervals misapprehension has remained anchored among physicists.

[39] Galileo. *Le Opere di Galileo Galilei*, volume XI. Firenze, Tip. di G. Barbera, 1900

A useful Gedankenexperiment

Likewise treading into normally considered general relativity physics terri-
tory, the same chapter deals with a *thought experiment* ('Gedankenexperiment')
where a rear rocket-emitted photon crosses the continuous medium's scaled
unit thrust increments, each of which is labeled in accordance with its scaled
original launch distance l from the rear rocket and possesses a clock showing
its own-time τ.

The REAL variables metric surface

The book's *Part VI*—THE RELATIVITY CURATE'S EGG's first chapter Rigor
Mortis acceleration, deals with an extended medium between two rockets,
whose individual constituent 'increments' have in general *differing* fixed thrusts.
Inter-rocket radar intervals derived for this general case immediately point
to the key equation for a special 'RIGOR MORTIS' ACCELERATION SCE-
NARIO known in relativity as *'rigid motion'*. The subsequent chapter Two
real—Euclidean—metric own-surfaces presents a simple *real variables metric
approach* to this scenario whose 'own-surface' is *visualisable*—in the surprisingly simple shape of a hand-held fan. The scenario is further elaborated upon
in the context of a rigor mortis *'gravity train'* where passengers can choose to
age differently from their co-passengers.

In hindsight, the rigor mortis scenario is not at all complicated, yet it has
been obscured in contemporary textbooks both by unnecessary mathematics
as well as by *misleading* 'presentism' formulations. The present book's radar
approach published in 2016[40] is short, does not involve an obfuscating complex variables 'metric',[41,42] and epitomises the quite neglected area of relativity radar physics whose surprising straightforwardness seems to have es-
caped the notice of relativists.

Solving the Bell's string paradox enigma

Part *VII*—ROLLER-COASTING SPACETIME's first chapter The unit thrust medium
own-surface answers the question first posed in 1959 and inconclusively treated
in *John Bell's* 1976 paper:[43]

> HOW ARE INDIVIDUAL PARTS OF A HOMOGENEOUSLY ACCELERATING
> EXTENDED MEDIUM *'separated'* ?

Pondering in 2008 on this enigma and wary (and weary) of inconsistent attempts in papers claiming to have resolved the issue, the author turned to the
2004 discovered spherical geometry insights (treated in *Part IV*). The surprising solution emerged:[44] a *unit pitch helicoid* generated by an accelerating point
object's 'hemix' curve, a conclusion far simpler than efforts in the literature
seemed to suggest possible.

[40] B.C. Minkowski spacetime does not apply to a homogeneously accelerating medium. *Results in Physics*, 6:31–38, January 2016

[41] A historical account of Minkowski's contributions to relativity theory appears in:

[42] Scott Walter. Minkowski, Mathematicians, and the Mathematical Theory of Relativity. *Einstein Studies*, 7:45–86, 1999

[43] John Bell. *Speakable and Unspeakable in Quantum Mechanics*, chapter How to teach special relativity (1976), pages 67–68. Cambridge University Press, 1987

[44] B.C. Bell's twin rockets non-inertial length enigma resolved by real geometry. *Results in Physics*, 7:2575–2581, July 2017

[45]This geometry is epitomised in the pinnacle chapter of the book—A Relativity Cosmographicum's real spacetime metrics. The relativity helicoidal sextet section describes a *'pseudo expansion' helicoid*, a *'pseudo contraction' helicoid* and a *'hemicoid' own-surface* which are 'searchlight beamed' by a *'distances ruled surface'* whose pivot angle represents the sine of the medium's home frame scaled velocity. The 'beam' intersects the hemicoid along lateral *helix* curves crossing the respective hemices. The helices' curved lengths correspond to the accelerating medium's expanding non-inertial own-length. The surface's 'metric' equation's incompatibilty with the Minkowski metric points to the latter's *general invalidity even in special relativity*.

In the (optional) *Radar mappings from inertial home frame onto own-surface ϒ chapter, forwards and reverse radar trajectories are 'mapped' (with the help of elaborate graphics software) from the accelerating medium's *home frame world-surface*—standard hyperbolic world-lines crossed by upwards and downwards unit limit speed radar diagonals—onto the new real own-surface *'hemicoid'*. Crucially, as well as matching conditions for medium-timed 'asymptotic' photon crossing rates, trajectory path lengths *metrically* reflect the derived inter-rocket radar intervals exactly. A parallel here would be a backwards projection of the familiar Mercator map onto a metrically correct world globe.

An À LA CARTE *Pandora's box*

Just before the accelerating extended medium topic came into prominence in the 1950s, a world-renowned Dublin physicist *John Lighton Synge*[46] completed two classic relativity books. In the second work[47] he remonstrated narrowness of approach among physics colleagues:

> "When, in a relativistic discussion, I try to make things clearer by a spacetime diagram, the other participants look at it with polite detachment and, after a pause of embarrassment as if some childish indecency had been exhibited, resume the debate in their own terms."

Nevertheless, in his earlier book[48] Synge expounded Minkowski spacetime as kernel to special relativity without explicitly dealing with extended accelerating media—an unwitting omission common to most relativity literature then as now. Further compounding matters, formally correct but obtuse textbook treatments of the so-called 'rigid motion' accelerating medium, have afforded Minkowski spacetime an unwarranted *general* justification, with fatal results for the theory of extended media in relativity physics. Minkowski's pseudo-Euclidean postulated—*à la carte*—metric is not only inapplicable in general relativity (as occasionally acknowledged), where an extended accelerating medium is concerned it is valid *only* for the so-called 'rigid motion' case.

Physicists surprised by this may wish to read the author's 2016 and 2017 *Results in Physics* journal papers or the final Epilogue chapter, before proceeding with the book.

Prevailing problems of comprehension

Notwithstanding his own succumbing to Minkowski's overgeneralisation, Synge himself, in the same first chapter of his special relativity book, eloquently pinpointed the presentism impediment which still today continues to obscure several important aspects of relativity theory.

> "In modern works on theoretical physics axiomatisation has been largely abandoned. Instead, the entry to a new subject is by what may be called the "cuckoo-process". The eggs are laid, not on the bare ground to be hatched in the clear light of Greek logic, but in the nest of another bird, where they are warmed by the body of a foster mother, which, in the case of relativity, is the Newtonian physics of the nineteenth century. The student is first indoctrinated with Newtonian physics, and he accepts its concepts as true to physical reality. Then, step by step, the concepts are modified, until finally he bites off the head of his foster mother and flies from the nest a full-fledged relativist.

Figure 3: John Lighton Synge, 1897-1995 Irish physicist

> This cuckoo-process follows the true order of historical development in science and it has the advantage that at every stage of the transformation the learner has the comforting support of familiar surroundings. As each support falls away, it is replaced by another, constructed to the new pattern. But it is confusing. The concepts of Newtonian physics interlock with one another (e.g. force, acceleration, inertial mass and gravitational mass), and until one has finally reviewed all Newtonian concepts, there is always present a suspicion that the same word is being used with meanings which differ with the context. Into this void we admit at once the whole body of *pure mathematics*, or at least those portions of pure mathematics which we may have occasion to use later. *Applied* mathematics on the other hand is excluded, for almost all applied mathematics deals with Newtonian physics, and the words used in it evoke Newtonian concepts and these we are prepared to admit only singly under scrutiny. ...

> This embargo on applied mathematics is serious,[49] for it excludes the dynamics of particles and rigid bodies, celestial mechanics, Lagrangian and Hamiltonian methods, hydrodynamics, elasticity and electrodynamics.

[49] Underlinings by the present author.

> The trouble with these subjects is that they all involve the Newtonian concept of time, and that ... is one of those Newtonian concepts which we shall not take over into relativity."

The present book's chapters 8–16 deal with the dynamics topic in an epistemologically and analytically unambiguous manner, as already partly described in 2005 and 2006 *European Journal of Physics* papers. 'Rigid motion', discussed at length in a 2016 *Results in Physics* paper, is treated in chapters 17 and 18. The 'elasticity' issue, expounded in the 2017 sequel paper in the same journal, is addressed in chapters 19–22.

The following main initial chapter of the book explains how, by envisaging right from the start that TIME MIGHT POSSIBLY BE DIFFERENTLY SHARED, much of the 'trouble' referred to by Synge can simply be bypassed.

I

T FOR TWO

[50] In 1881 in Potsdam, Berlin and in 1887 in Cleveland, Ohio with *Edward Morley.*

[51] In 1899/1900 in Dublin, with *Frederick Trouton*

[52] Michel Janssen. The Trouton Experiment and E = mc2

[53] before Dutch physicist *Hendrik Lorentz* independently came up with the same idea.

[54] ⇒chapter 4, Larmor-Lorentz transformations and velocity composition.

[55] Originally spelt 'chronocity' in:

[56] B.C. A dual first-postulate basis for special relativity. *European Journal of Physics,* 24:301–313, May 2003

In the last two decades of the 19th century earnest attempts to measure our Earth's speed through the 'aether', were made by Polish-born American *Albert Michelson* (optically)[50] and Irish physicist *George FitzGerald* (electrodynamically)[51,52]. It was considered certain even then that observable variations of coherent light wave interference 'fringes' should result from velocity changes due to the Earth's axial rotation and its orbiting around the Sun. Yet, to the consternation of most physicists, no appreciable fringe shifts could be detected and the experiments were considered to have failed. As a possible explanation, FitzGerald himself in 1889 conjectured[53] that moving objects 'contract'. This suggestion however overlooked the crucial phenomenon of *relativistic 'time dilation'* which, ironically, was referred to a decade later in 1898 by a Belfast friend of FitzGerald—*Joseph Larmor.*[54]

By coincidence during that same period, a graphical trains schedule appeared in French railway stations which happens to be a perfect starting point towards resolving the dilemma. Modifying this chart, *Part I's* first chapter An elegant spacetime underlay points to a *possible* simple yet fundamental property of Nature. Two spatially apart but relatively stationary *nonaccelerating* 'home frame' observers would indeed, at *their* same time, record that clocks of two passing likewise nonaccelerating objects are out of synchronism—even though the observed objects are relatively stationary in their particular reference frame and consider their own respective clocks to be sychronised. Such a TIME SCHISM, which we label 'CHRONOSITY',[55] [56] turns out to have an extraordinary yet inescapable *consequence*: a 'causality' *boundary relative speed* which governs the relative movement of all objects in our Universe. The Spacetime charts and world-lines chapter shows how, on the basis of assumed homogeneity of space and time, this *natural phenomenon* may be expressed by what is arguably relativity's most fundamental kernel relationship: 'CHRONOSITY' EQUALS VELOCITY DIVIDED BY A BOUNDARY SPEED SQUARED.

The Mirages of 'length' and time chapter deals with that ratio's direct ramifications: mutual *perceptions* of so-called 'length contraction' and time dilation registered by relatively stationary observers in one inertial (nonaccelerating) frame of reference who measure relative distance between passing spatially apart objects' as well as the latters' perceived clock times' rate of change. The chapter concludes with a simple time travel scenario.

1

An elegant spacetime underlay

'...δῆλον γὰρ ὡς ὑμεῖς μὲν ταῦτα (τί ποτε βούλεσθε σημαίνειν ὁπόταν ὂν φθέγγησθε) πάλαι γιγνώσκετε, ἡμεῖς δὲ πρὸ τοῦ μὲν ᾠόμεθα, νῦν δ' ἠπορήκαμεν νν ...'
Πλάτων   Σοφιστής

...Apparently you are long familiar with what you actually mean when you use the expression BEING, *we however once thought we understood it, but now find ourselves at a loss...*
Plato SOPHISTES 340 BC   (Foreword to Heidegger's BEING AND TIME 1927)

THE THEORY OF MOVEMENT IN WHAT WE INSTINCTIVELY THINK OF AS OUR UNIVERSE'S 'EXISTENTIAL BACKGROUND'—a gravity-free 'space/time continuum'—is known as 'flat spacetime' or *special relativity*. Although the limelight has shifted even beyond the gravitational arena of its offspring *general relativity* ('curved spacetime'), to the esoteric quantum mechanics of subatomic particles and—as yet—unresolved mysteries of 'dark matter', special relativity's profound relevance is vividly reflected in the ever ominous threat to mankind of thermonuclear conflagration, no less than by its now indispensable use in global positioning by satellite.

Notoriously referred to by one of its foremost pioneers Albert Einstein as 'child's play', special relativity is assumed by most people to be incomprehensible. Partly responsible for this *avoidable* state of affairs is the conventional adoption of our universe's cosmic limit speed as *a starting point* for coming to grips with the theory. Yet Providence has elegantly arranged such a limit as AN INEVITABLE CONSEQUENCE OF AN UNDERLYING INTRINSIC PROPERTY OF NATURE WHICH IS EASILY FORMULATED.

©BCS IRELAND 2017 ISBN 978-1-9998410-1-0
Brian Coleman SPACETIME FUNDAMENTALS INTELLIGIBLY (RE)LEARNT

Figure 1.1: A French railway
daily schedule showing twenty
five trains connecting thirteen
stations between Paris and Lyon.
As mentioned in an *Edward Tufte*
book, this diagram appeared in *E.J.
Marey's* 1885 book *La méthode
graphique* and is attributed to
French engineer *Ibry*.

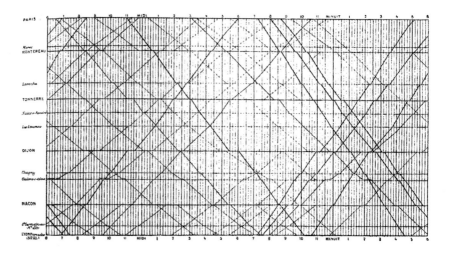

Figure 1.2: Spacetime chart of
respective train compartments

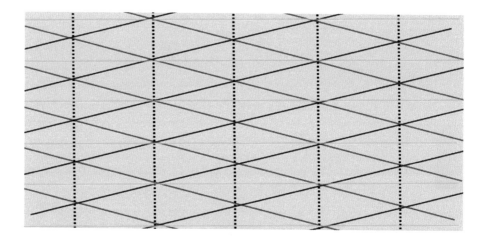

1.1   *Spacetime charts' 'where-lines' and 'when-lines'*

In the early 1880's train schedules such as in Figure 1.1 appeared in French
railway stations. A simpler spacetime chart is shown in Figure 1.2 which de-
picts a red train and an identical blue train continually moving at the same
fixed speed in opposite directions. Their individual compartments are represented by equally spaced and *symmetrically* tilted red and blue 'where-lines',
each train thus having its 'own-space' where compartment where-lines are
viewed by their respective passengers as local and stationary.

The horizontal solid green where-lines indicate 'background' space—the
passing landscape. Vertical black dotted 'when-lines' represent individual
time instants for all space (one-dimensional) and are therefore *lines of time simultaneity*.

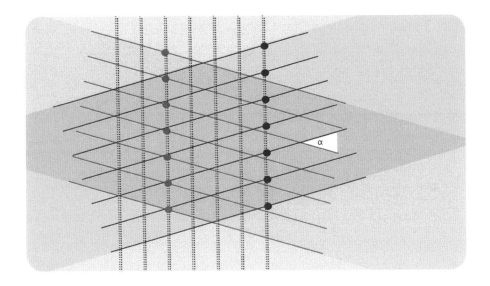

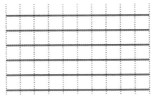

Figure 1.3: Spacetime chart of spacestations' classical perception of each other's compartments in 'empty space'

Figure 1.4: Zero velocity

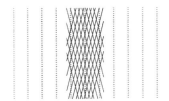

Figure 1.5: Moderate velocity

Figure 1.6: High velocity

Figure 1.7: Near infinite velocity

Elimination of 'background space'

We now change the scene to two long nonaccelerating identical *spacestations* passing one another in a region of space which is remote from all stars and planets. The spacestations experience background space only as *an invisible 'conceptual vessel' which has no anchor points*. In Figure 1.3's chart we dismiss such 'absolute space' simply by omitting the background landscape green where-lines of the earlier chart. As the vehicles may have come from different time zones, we replace the black vertical when-lines with *superimposed* red and blue when-lines which *separately* mark simultaneous events for the two spacestations. Both spacestations consider themselves to be 'stationary' in their respective *own* relatively stationary reference frame, and view the other spacestation as 'moving' at a fixed relative velocity.

Each set of spacestation compartments' where-lines is *a mirror image* of the other set. Figure 1.3's chart thus constitutes a classical *symmetrical* spacetime chart, with the red and blue where-lines intersecting at an angle α (Greek *alpha*) proportional to their relative velocity. The margin charts show how respective where-lines would become ever more congested with increasing relative velocity. Although these simple diagrams merely map the movement of spacestation compartments of one spacestation relative to those of another, they also visually prompt a straightforward crucial question:

> What characteristic 'property' in Nature's 'scheme of things' might conceivably prevent velocity from increasing without limit, but at the same time not violate the equivalence—i.e. the sameness—of space and time as experienced by nonaccelerating objects stationary with respect to one another ?

Figure 1.8: Dual frame's chronosity

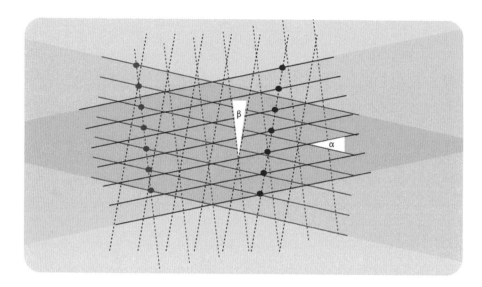

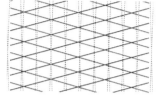

Figure 1.9: Low velocity

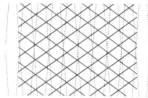

Figure 1.10: Moderate velocity

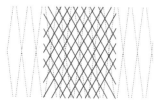

Figure 1.11: High velocity

1.2 A spatio-temporal swiveling—'chronosity'

THE SURPRISINGLY SIMPLE ANSWER lies in Providence's 'arrangement' of an extraordinary yet easily described 'natural phenomenon': a divergence of *time disparity over distance* which is 'tied in' with relative velocity—divergence of *distance displacement over time*. As indicated in Figure 1.8's chart and as we shall later *prove*, if relative speed between two reference frame 'platforms' is nonzero, then as well as their where-lines diverging, *their respective when-lines will also be at an angle to one another.* The latter tiny but nonzero angle β (Greek *beta*) will be *somehow proportional* to the velocity angle α between respective red and blue where-lines, but so minimally that we normally do not notice it.

Differing red and blue spacestation reference frames

Passengers in the red reference frame now no longer share when-line time simultaneities with the blue reference frame passengers. EACH REFERENCE FRAME'S PRESENT TENSE IS STRICTLY EXCLUSIVE—except *momentarily* for passengers of both reference frames as they pass one another.

'Events' simultaneous in the blue reference frame such as Figure 1.8's blue dot events along one blue when-line but on separate blue where-lines, if viewed from the red reference frame show *disparities of simultaneity* which increase the wider the spatial distance between such events. This *reciprocally observed* distance-rated disparity of temporal simultaneity is the spatio-temporal *converse* of velocity which itself is a time-rated disparity of spatial position. We assign this traditionally side-lined relativity of simultaneity concept a central rôle and give it a long overdue label—'CHRONOSITY':[1] a spatial separation-proportioned divergence of temporal simultaneity.

[1] Alluding to THE GREEK GOD OF TIME Χρόνος (Chronos).

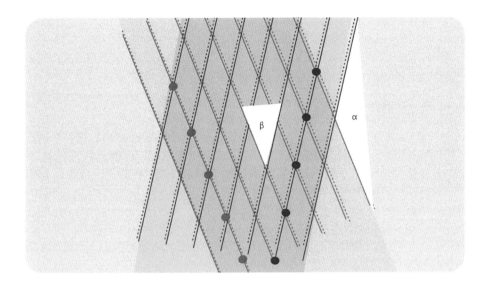

Figure 1.12: Dual reference frames chart at some 'boundary' speed

[2] Such a time divergence between reference frames we denote by the variable ψ (Greek *psi*[3] which *conveniently resembles the letter v with a stroke through it*). Chronosity will be *in some way* proportional to velocity v, always *increasing* with increasing velocity i.e. the relationship will be *monotonic*.

1.3 *Mating where-lines and when-lines*

FINALLY WE FOCUS ON AN 'EXTREME' SITUATION. As demonstrated in Figures 1.9-1.11, as angles α and β together increase, the angle between red when-lines and red where-lines *decreases*, as does likewise the angle between blue when-lines and blue where-lines. Regardless of the actual angles involved of course, red spacestation where-lines and when-lines remain respective mirror images of blue spacestation where-lines and when-lines. Figure 1.12 shows the case where respective where-lines and when-lines actually *overlap*. Relative velocity v will then have some as yet unknown BOUNDARY value we assign a special symbol to—λ (*lambda*).

Due to chronosity, red compartments generally observe opposite passing blue compartments as 'out of synchronism'. At boundry speed $v = \lambda$ as each blue compartment passes from one red compartment to the other, each red compartment passenger would report that passing blue train compartment passenger clocks *consecutively* showed the same 'blue'-time i.e. blue when-lines would 'overlap' blue where-lines. Blue spacestation's time *would appear to be frozen*. Such perceptions of course *would be reciprocal* by virtue of the two reference frames' sameness (homogeneity) i.e. red where-lines would likewise be perceived by blue spacestation passengers to overlap red when-lines at this boundary speed.

[2] Note: 'chronosity' (a term introduced in the author's European Journal of Physics 2003 paper but there spelt as 'chronocity') is not to be confused with the medical term 'chronicity'.

[3] Strictly speaking Greek χ—chi—as in Χρόνος, would be more appropriate, but we later use χ to denote an object's 'retrospective' distance.

Each reference frame's observers would thus perceive individual passing objects of the other reference frame to be APPARENTLY TIMELESS. Such *perceptions* would of course be *subjective* since for neither reference frame's 'inhabitants' would *their* respective time stand still.

1.4   A boundary, perhaps 'limit', cosmic speed

Although we do not at this point presume to know what value such a boundary speed λ might have, we may assume *it does not have to be infinite*. Our reasoning by the way also allows for the case where chronosity would be *nonexistent* i.e. $\lambda = \infty$ and hence angle β would be always zero. Should, within the context of special relativity, a relative speed *greater* than λ be actually somehow attainable, red and blue passengers would (according to our scheme of things) perceive one another's passing watches to consecutively register *a backwards time direction* !

We do not as yet however declare λ to be an *uncrossable* 'limit' speed. The actual value of λ, what sort of objects ('entities') might propagate at such a speed, and the question whether any objects might even propagate at speeds even beyond λ, are separate matters we will deal with in the next *Part II* of the book and in the later chapter 10: The $E = m\gamma c^2$ pentagon.

For now we just note that should our boundary speed turn out to be both finite and in itself actually an *unattainable* limit speed, then red where-lines and blue where-lines will never be 'all on top of one another' (as would be the case were the limit speed infinite). Providence will then have very neatly avoided the inevitable chaos of entities moving about in our Cosmos with unrestricted relative speeds, *simply by incorporating chronosity as an inherent universal property of relative movement*.

> **1.1.**
>
> BY IMPOSING CHRONOSITY ON NATURE,
> PROVIDENCE VERY NEATLY INCORPORATES
> A COSMIC *boundary* SPEED INTO OUR UNIVERSE.

How Providence manages to weave disparities of simultaneities between respective spatially separate object pairs in relatively moving spacetime reference frames, is naturally beyond our present means of comprehension. As we shall soon see however, the questions regarding the chronosity phenomenon's *verification* as well as its extraordinary ramifications, are not at all difficult to resolve.

2
Spacetime charts and world-lines

"... treatises on mechanics do not clearly distinguish between what is experiment, what is mathematical reasoning, what is convention, and what is hypothesis. This is not all.

1. There is no absolute space, and we only conceive of relative motion; and yet in most cases mechanical facts are enunciated as if there is an absolute space to which they can be referred.

2. There is no absolute time. When we say that two periods are equal, the statement has no meaning [in the 'absolute' sense], and can only acquire a meaning by a convention.

3. Not only have we no direct intuition of the equality of two periods, but we have not even direct intuition of the simultaneity of two events occurring in two different places. I have explained this in an [1898] article entitled "Mesure du Temps"...."

Henri Poincaré *Science and Hypothesis* 1902

POINCARÉ'S 1902 INSIGHTS FORMED THE BASIS OF OUR PREVIOUS CHAP-TER'S OCCAM'S RAZOR APPROACH IN EVOLVING THE CONCEPT OF SPACE-TIME'S POSSIBLE TEMPORAL DIVERGENCE. The present chapter is concerned with how 'chronosity' of spatially apart events such as nonaccelerating red and blue compartment passengers' momentary observations of one another in their respective reference frames, could relate to their relative velocity.

©BCS IRELAND 2017 ISBN 978-1-9998410-1-0
Brian Coleman SPACETIME FUNDAMENTALS INTELLIGIBLY (RE)LEARNT

Figure 2.1: Henri Poincaré, 1854-1912.

Figure 2.2: Dual reference frames chart at SCALED boundary speed

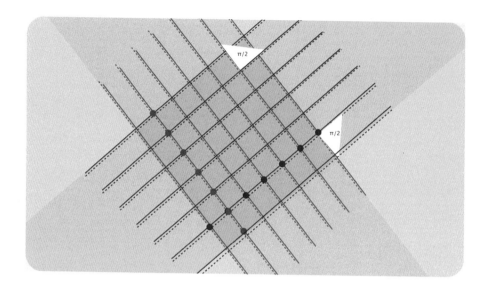

2.1 Boundary speed rescaling

[1] A *thought experiment* does not have to be *physically* achievable. Important are possibly resulting concepts and *'limit case conclusions'*.

Recalling page 19's Figure 1.12 boundary speed *Gedankenexperiment*,[1] we now imagine our time scale *stretched by our as yet unknown boundary speed factor* λ so as to make our boundary speed chart both vertically and horizontally *symmetrical*. Significantly, as velocity angle α and chronosity angle β are now both *right angles* ($\pi/2$ radians), THEIR SINE VALUE OF *one* WILL REFLECT UNIT SCALED BOUNDARY SPEED. Overlapping red when-lines and where-lines would then cross overlapping blue when-lines and where-lines *perpendicularly*, in both cases at ± 45 degrees to the horizontal, as shown in Figure 2.2. As well as our stations' blue-red *left-right* symmetry, we now have also an *up-down* spatio-temporal symmetry—scaled boundary chronosity is also one.

Observers of each reference frame would view the other frame as a 'boundary reference frame' whose passing passenger clocks continually show the *same* unchanged time. Every blue where-line crossing the red reference frame at boundary speed extends over a red frame when-line segment distance *which geometrically overlaps* an identical red frame where-line segment time interval—and vice-versa. Since scaled boundary speed therefore equals *one*, unscaled boundary speed v_λ *divided* by time scale factor λ also equals one i.e. $v_\lambda/\lambda = 1$. Moreover scaled unit boundary chronosity equals unscaled boundary chronosity[2] ψ_λ *multiplied* by λ i.e. $\psi_\lambda.\lambda = 1$.

[2] By ψ_λ and $v_\lambda(=\lambda)$ we mean respective chronosity and velocity values at boundary speed λ.

This gives us our first key—so far 'hypothetical'—result:

2.1.

BOUNDARY CHRONOSITY UNSCALED EQUALS BOUNDARY

SPEED UNSCALED, DIVIDED BY ITS OWN SQUARE:

$$\psi_\lambda = \frac{1}{\lambda} = \frac{\lambda}{\lambda^2} = \frac{v_\lambda}{\lambda^2}.$$

Naturally, velocity and chronosity values at zero relative speed are $v_0 = 0$ and $\psi_0 = 0$ respectively since zero velocity implies zero chronosity. Therefore we may also note for zero relative speed that:

$$\psi_0 = 0 = \frac{v_0}{\lambda^2}. \qquad (2.2)$$

2.2 *The general chronosity-velocity relationship*

The previous two equations relate chonosity ψ for relative boundary speed and for relative zero speed. Should[3] the same equation *not* happen to apply at any specific relative scaled velocity between an observer and an observed body in relative motion i.e. for any distance interval over any scaled time interval and hence for any ratio of such intervals, this would violate the principle of *spatial homogeneity*—sameness of nature over all regions of empty space, special relativity's traditional 'first postulate'.[4] We may therefore reasonably assume that equations (2.1) and (2.2) hold for every *intermediate* velocity. An 'informal' mathematical proof of this conclusion was outlined in the author's 2003 EJP paper *in the context of the Larmor-Lorentz transformations* which, as we show later, are *equivalent* to our chronosity-velocity relationship.[5]

[3] in the absence of gravitational mass effects.

[4] The *'second postulate'*—constancy of the limit speed of light in all inertial frames—we do not require.

[5] Ω is Greek upper case *Omega*.

2.3.

SPECIAL RELATIVITY'S KERNEL KINEMATICS RELATIONSHIP:

FOR ANY TWO BODIES IN RELATIVE UNIFORM MOTION, MUTUALLY PERCEIVED

CHRONOSITY EQUALS RELATIVE VELOCITY DIVIDED BY THE LIMIT SPEED SQUARED:

$$\psi = \frac{v}{\lambda^2}.$$

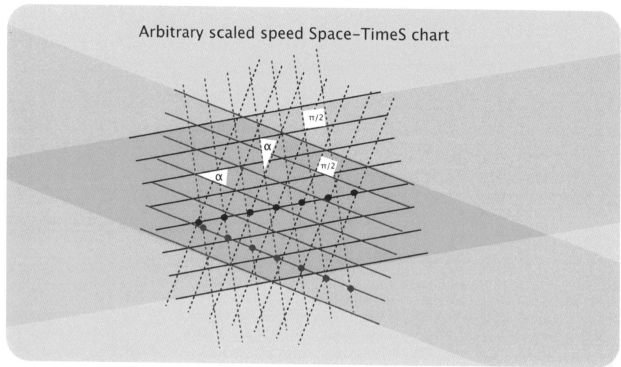

Figure 2.3: Dual reference frames
chart at arbitrary scaled speed

Figure 2.4: Enrique Loedel, 1901-
1962.

Photo kindly supplied by *Cecilia
von Reichenbach*, director, *Museo
de Física*, Universidad Nacional de
La Plata, Argentina, where he had
been professor.

[6] Enrique Palumbo Loedel. Aberración y Relatividad. *Anales de la
Sociedad Científica Argentina*, 145:
3, 1948

2.3   *The dual reference frames chart*

Figure 2.3 shows the GENERAL DUAL REFERENCE FRAMES CHART where
red where-lines are perpendicular to blue when-lines and *blue where-lines are perpendicular to red when-lines*. This follows since at zero scaled velocity angle α, red
and blue where-lines are parallel and at right angles to parallel red and blue
when-lines, and with increasing velocity/chronosity angle α when-lines and
where-lines are rotated in equal but opposite directions *symmetrically*.

An *equivalent* spacetime chart first appeared in a 1948 paper *Aberración y
Relatividad* in the Argentinian physics journal *Anales de la Sociedad Cientiífica
Argentina*[6]. It was written by *Enrique Loedel Palumbo*, a Uruguay-born physicist
who had studied in Berlin. Surprisingly the Loedel chart concept is seldom
deployed in textbooks. (Exceptions: *Sears&Brehme* (1968), *Shadowitz* (1988)
and *Sartori* (1996).) The symmetrical dual reference frames charts used in this
book—which differ from the Loedel chart only in that space and time axes are
interchanged—will be our main tool for analysing the relativistic interrelationships between objects in relative motion from the *combined* viewpoints of two
single spatial dimension reference frames.

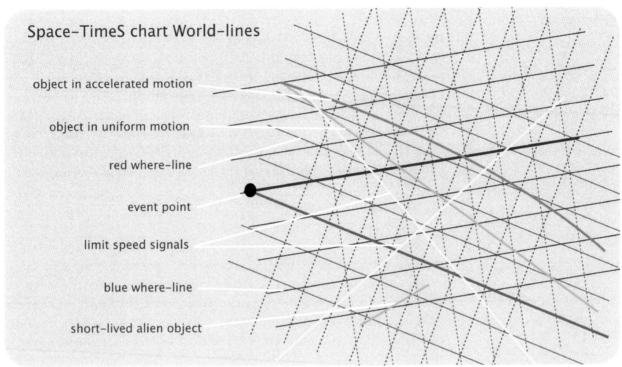

Figure 2.5: General world-line trajectories of a dual reference frames chart

WORLD-LINES *and* EVENTS

[7]Our dual reference frames chart where-lines represent fixed locations of each respective reference frame. What are called *world-lines* portray the 'history' of point objects generally not stationary in either inertial reference frame. Also each frame would consider the *other frame's where-lines* as world-lines. As shown in Figure 2.5, an accelerating ('non-inertial') point object or *'particle'* has a *curved* world-line, whereas a nonaccelerating inertial object's world-line (which also may represent a uniformly moving *signal*) will be straight. An 'event' such as the coinciding of blue and red world-lines of the respective spacestation reference origins (shown as a black point), is a single point on the chart.

Other examples shown are: a uniformly moving object and a 'short-lived' object (both in green), an accelerating object (brown) whose world-line is curved. Also included are two scaled unit boundary speed i.e. limit speed world-lines (in yellow) which, due to symmetry of the chart's when-lines and where-lines, are always *diagonals* at $\pi/4$ radians (45 degrees) inclination to the horizontal.

[7] The term *world-line* ('Weltlinie') was coined in 1907 by *Hermann Minkowski*. 'Welt' in the original German roughly means 'living space'. It also suggests *the world 'over time'*.

The home reference frame chart and a variant

Later we make use of an important *single 'home' frame* spacetime chart to portray world-lines exclusively from the perspective of observers stationary with respect to a rocket launching pad. A very commonly used variant of such a chart is the asymmetrical *dual reference frames 'Minkowski chart'*. However such a dual frames chart involves *different scaling* of its inwards inclined time and distance axes representing the second inertial frame, in contrast to the Loedel type *symmetrically scaled* dual reference frames chart. The asymmetrical Minkowski *dual frames* chart variant is deliberately avoided in this book.

2.4 *A universal constant with many rôles in Nature*

Equation (2.3) constitutes SPECIAL RELATIVITY'S MOST FUNDAMENTAL KERNEL RELATIONSHIP and is clearly *the most basic possible equivalent* to the familiar more elaborate *Larmor-Lorentz transformation* and *velocity composition* equations we will meet in the following chapters. It is the basis for *all* of the material of this book. THE CHRONOSITY/VELOCITY RATIO which we denote as $\Omega \overset{\Delta}{=} 1/\lambda^2 = \psi/v$, is the sole kernel parameter distinguishing special relativity from classical uniform motion physics where it would be zero. Having dimensions of inverse velocity squared, Ω may be said to 'govern' the entire theory of flat spacetime i.e. special relativity—a standpoint which radically eases our subject's understanding. This constant incorporates multiple 'personalities' intrinsic to our Universe:

- *The inverse square of a boundary speed of our Cosmos*—a logical deduction from the chronosity hypothesis'. *For the moment*, we denote this speed value not by one of its measurable *instances*—its traditional 'impersonator'[8] *the speed of light* c, but by the Greek letter lambda—λ. A further instance of this boundary speed which has recently emerged is *the rate of propagation of gravitational waves*.

- *The sum of the cyclic velocities of three bodies in relative straight line motion (which in classical physics is zero) divided by their negative product.*[9] This velocity composition 'triad ratio' follows from the chronosity/velocity relationship.

- [10]*The ratio of an observer's t-time rated change of a particle's 'spatial momentum'* (itself equal to mass by its own-time τ-rated change of observer-perceived distance x i.e. $m \cdot dx/d\tau$) *to the observer's distance-rated change of 'temporal momentum'* (mass by its own-time τ-rated change of observer perceived time t i.e. $m \cdot dt/d\tau$). [11]This mass by 'a speed of time', concept is very confusingly often referred to as 'relativistic mass'.

[8] *Conceptually* speaking.

[9] As established in the The limit speed identified chapter.

[10] As established in later in chapter 9; Diversifying momentum and force.

[11] Lev B Okun. The concept of Mass in the Einstein Year. pages 31–36, June 2005

- *The (so-called) 'rest' mass to energy ratio*—the theoretical basis of nuclear energy and the atomic bomb.[12] This follows directly from the previous momenta relationships.

- *Last but not least* (but outside the scope of this book), as far as currently measurable Ω equals the inverse product of the electromagnetic constants ϵ_0 and μ_0, as well as the inverse square of 'the speed of light' c.

Note: These relationships are well validated for special relativity's 'flat spacetime' continuum, but only down to space and time intervals of the order of $10^{-23}m$ and $10^{-23}s$ respectively. Intervals below that belong to the domain of *quantum theory*.

2.5 *An alternate initial postulate:* SPATIAL ISOTROPY

2.4.

> IN ALL DIRECTIONS AND FROM EVERY 'STANDPOINT',
>
> NATURE ALWAYS BEHAVES THE SAME.
>
> IN GENERAL 'SPACE' HAS NO PREFERRED DIRECTION.

The assumption of 'spatial isotropy'—sameness of nature in all *directions* of empty space[13]—brings with it *as a consequence* sameness of nature over all regions of empty space—'*spatial homogeneity*', special relativity's traditional 'first postulate'. As argued by *Georg Süssmann* in 1969[14], a little appreciated argument of the German-Dutch mathematician *Hans Freudenthal*[15] explains why:

> "If all directions from a particular point have the same geometrical anchor, no two points can be differently geometrically anchored, otherwise the connecting lines to each fixed point would differ in character."

The spatial isotropy assumption itself allows us to generally view matters *on a one spatial dimensional basis*. Poincaré's relativity principle 'upgraded' by Freudenthal's[16] spatial isotropy insight is thus sufficient to theoretically establish special relativity's kernel equation 2.3 without decreeing what value the boundary speed parameter might have—or of course whether or not it is finite. This we will sort out later in the The limit speed identified and *Measuring the Cosmic Limit Speed chapters.

Figure 2.6: Hans Freudenthal, 1905-1990. Photo kindly provided by *Ivonne Vetter, Mathematisches Forschungsinstitut Oberwolfach.*

[12] The topic of chapter 10, The $E = m\gamma c^2$ pentagon.

[13] Unaffected by gravitational bodies.

[14] Georg Süssmann. Begründung der Lorentz-Gruppe allein mit Symmetrie- und Relativitäts-Annahmen. *Z. Naturforscher*, 24a: 495–498, 1969

[15] Hans Freudenthal. Lie groups in the foundations of geometry. *Advances in Mathematics*, 1: 145–190, 1965

[16] Son of a German Jewish teacher, Freudenthal survived the second world war incognito in Holland. The above photo shows him lecturing in the 1970's in the German town of Erlangen where mathematician *Emmy Noether* was born and *Felix Klein* developed his 'Erlanger Programme' approach to geometry. Coincidentally, this book's author lived in Erlangen 1971-1998.

3
Mirages of 'length' and time

"The laws of motions and the effects..., and theorems containing the proportions and calculations for the same for the different configurations of the paths, likewise for accelerations and different directions, and for mediums resisting in greater or less degree, all these hold without bringing absolute motion into account. As is plain from this that ... since according to the principles of those who introduce absolute motion we cannot know by any indication whether the whole frame of things is at rest, or is moved uniformly in a direction, clearly we cannot know the absolute motion of any body....It must be admitted that in this matter we are in the grip of serious prejudices."

George Berkeley   *De Motu* 1721

[1]We now examine the *consequences* chronosity must have with regard to how one reference frame's observers perceive objects stationary in the other reference frame. 'Common sense' rules of 'when' and 'where' no longer apply, so we shall need to wean ourselves from our Newtonian space and time instincts and adjust our 'TERMS' and 'IDEAS' somewhat to accommodate the *'mirage-like'* unfamiliar and nonintuitive phenomena and concepts which emerge. Later in chapter 5 we explain how the limit speed λ's actual value may be identified as the speed of light. For the moment we assume only that it has a *finite* value.

The previous chapter's spacestations scenario is schematically portrayed in Figure 3.1. The dual reference frames chart of Figure 3.2 resembles the previous Figure 2.3, with time likewise scaled by factor λ, but it shows only the spacestations' respective left and right end where-lines.

[1] George Berkeley. *De motu: Sive; de motu principio et natura, et de causa communicationis motuum.* Berkeley's Philosophical Writings, New York: Collier (1974), 1721

©BCS Ireland 2017 ISBN 978-1-9998410-1-0
Brian Coleman SPACETIME FUNDAMENTALS INTELLIGIBLY (RE)LEARNT

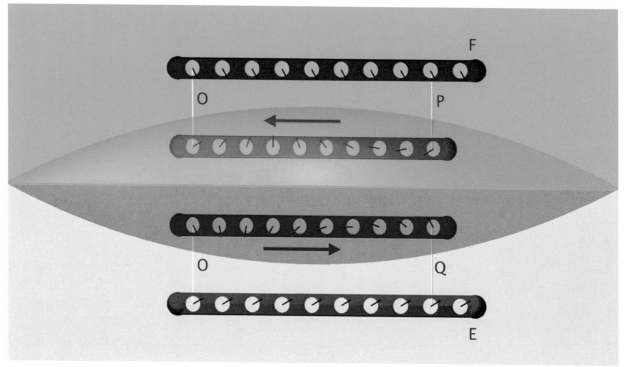

Figure 3.1: Reciprocal mirages of relativistic perception (at about half limit speed)

3.1   Events and their reference frames' intervals

Points on Figure 3.2's dual spacetimes chart are EVENTS. The blue and red stations' left ends pass each other at *event O*. Simultaneous in blue-time to event O, the red station's right end at event P is some distance from the blue station's right end (event F—also simultaneous to O in blue-time). Likewise, blue station's right end is simultaneous to O in red-time at event Q which is also some distance from the red station's right end event E simultaneous to event O in red-time. Although event O is simultaneous to P and F in the blue reference frame and to Q and E in the red-reference frame, yet E *precedes* Q in the blue reference frame and P *precedes* F in the red reference frame.

The scaled velocity/chronosity velchronos angle

When-lines of each reference frame are lines of simultaneity and, paradoxically,[2] when-line *segments.* correspond to intervals of own-length. Where-lines of each reference frame are lines of fixed position and where-line *segments* correspond to intervals of own-time. As viewed in the red spacetime frame, blue world-line[3] segment OJ represents the blue station's left end's progression from event O to event J which is simultaneous in red-time to event P.

[2] In any x/t chart for example, the 'x-axis' marking *distances* is a reference line of *fixed time*

[3] We recall that a world-line is the same as a where-line *but only in its own reference frame.*

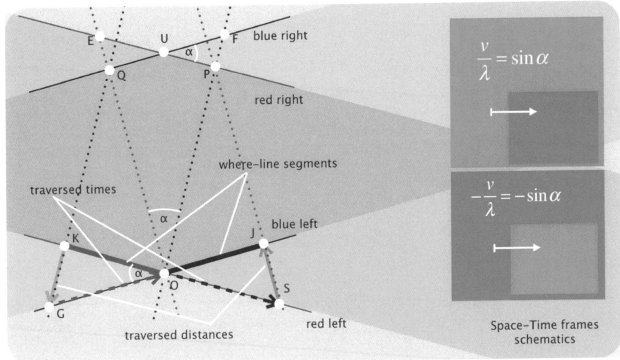

Figure 3.2: Spacestations' left and right end trajectories.

OJ extends over red-distance SJ (a red <u>when-line</u> segment) and red-time interval OS (a red <u>where-line</u> segment). The blue station thus has scaled velocity $SJ/OS = \sin\alpha = v/\lambda$ in the red frame. Similarly, as viewed in the blue frame, red world-line segment KO represents the red station left end's progression from event K to the *later* event O as it passes the blue station's left end. KO extends over a blue-distance KG and a blue-time interval GO. The red station therefore has scaled velocity $KG/GO = -\sin\alpha = -v/\lambda$ in the blue reference frame.

The frames' reciprocal scaled velocities are each denoted schematically[4] by an arrow indicating the velocity of the *observed* reference frame containing the arrow head. We call 'dimensionless' angle α the *velocity-chronosity—* 'VELCHRONOS ANGLE'—a KERNEL PARAMETER OF RELATIVITY.

Recalling equation 2.3:

3.1.

THE SCALED VELOCITY AND SCALED CHRONOSITY OF A DUAL REFERENCE FRAMES CHART, BOTH EQUAL THE SINE OF ITS VELCHRONOS ANGLE: $v/\lambda = \psi \cdot \lambda = \sin\alpha$.

[4] For a negative velocity, actual movement is in the direction opposite to that indicated by the arrow.

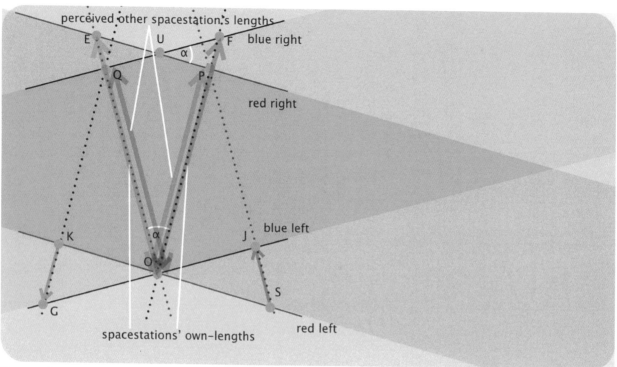

Figure 3.3: So-called 'length contraction'

3.2 The MIRAGE of 'length contraction'

At event P simultaneous in blue-time to event O (Figure 3.3), a blue station passenger a blue-distance OP away and passing red station's right end, would wrongly conclude (ignoring the reality of chronosity) that the red station has length $OP = OE \cos \alpha$. The red station's actual own-length however, equals *the longer* red when-line segment length OE.

Likewise at event Q simultaneous in red-time to event O, a red station passenger at a red-distance OQ away observing the passing blue station's right end, mistakingly assumes the blue station has length equal to distance OQ. The blue station's own-length when-line segment OF crossed by its end where-lines, *is longer* than distance $OQ = OF \cos \alpha$ perceived in red frame time.

3.2.

RECIPROCALLY <u>PERCEIVED</u> LENGTH 'CONTRACTION' EQUALS THE VELCHRONOS ANGLE'S COSINE.

$$\cos \alpha = \sqrt{1 - \sin^2 \alpha} = \sqrt{1 - v^2 / \lambda^2}.$$

YET IN NEITHER REFERENCE FRAME DOES ANY ACTUAL PHYSICAL CONTRACTION OCCUR.

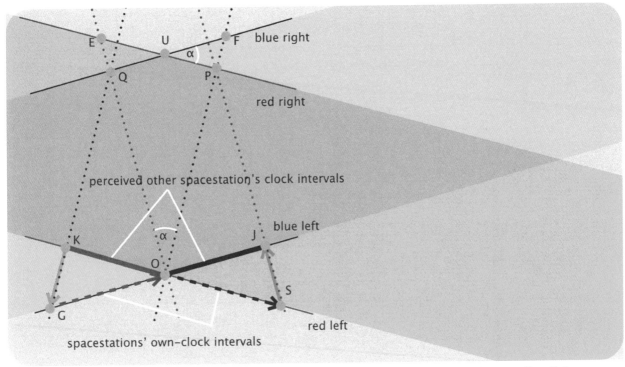

Figure 3.4: Time dilation

Contrasting 'length' experiences

In an analogous scenario, the owner of an open doors garage reports that a longer car passing through at speed was *at one instant* fully inside the garage. Yet the driver would say that as its rear end entered the garage, its front had *already* passed the exit i.e. the vehicle did *not* 'contract'. The driver would claim the garage itself 'had become shorter'. Relative velocity v is always zero for an observer comoving with an object such as a rod and certainly the rod itself will not *in any way* contract merely because it is passively observed by *another* observer to be 'moving'—as made clear by a simple rhetorical question:

> Is there a 'preferred' observer among differently relatively moving nonintrusive observers, who should be assigned the right to decide to what degree an inertial rod itself is supposed to be contracted ?

3.3   Larmor time dilation factor γ

Figure 3.4 shows the scaled time interval between the two events of the red left end passenger's where-line segment KO, from two perspectives. Events K and O are at one position in the red reference frame and the time interval on the red station's clock corresponds to red where-line segment KO. But in the blue reference frame events K and O are spatially apart, and extend over the *larger* blue-time interval $GO = KO/\cos\alpha$. The 'moving' red passenger's clock—viewed by passing blue passengers—seems to progressing more slowly in time i.e. stretching out or 'dilating'.[5] Paradoxically we reach the same conclusion regarding the blue left end where-line segment OJ i.e. $OS = OJ/\cos\alpha$, but in this case it is blue time which seems to be dilating. Notably, 'inhabitants' of neither reference frame would *in any way* be conscious of or experience i.e. *sense* any kind of physical 'time stretching'. What one might reasonably designate the LARMOR TIME DILATION FACTOR γ—*for reasons explained in the next chapter*—is the inverse of the above 'pseudo-contraction' factor $\cos\alpha$ which we define as γ (Greek *gamma*).

[5] Such perceived time stretching is manifested by *smaller* red station clock intervals.

3.3.

RECIPROCAL MUTUALLY <u>PERCEIVED</u> TIME DILATION—THE LARMOR TIME DILATION 'GAMMA FACTOR'—EQUALS THE INVERSE COSINE OF THE VELCHRONOS ANGLE:

$$\gamma \triangleq 1/\cos\alpha = 1/\sqrt{1 - \sin\alpha^2} = 1/\sqrt{1 - v^2/\lambda^2}.$$

3.4 *Meaninglessness of the present tense in relativity*

The tendency to at least subconsciously insist on *the present tense* as a mode of 'understanding' relativity physics is still extant. A renowned current textbook[6] *inappropriately* claims: "[Generally] the length L of a body in the direction of its motion with uniform velocity v is reduced by a factor $\sqrt{1 - v^2/c^2}$. ... This length contraction is no illusion, no mere accident of measurement or convention. It is real in every sense. A moving rod is really short! It could really be put into a hole at rest in the lab into which it would not fit if it were not moving and shrunk."[7] Only the last sentence, *excluding* its two final words, is fully correct. In its own frame the rod does <u>not</u> shrink, even though in the moving observer's frame it is *perceived and experienced* as if it were shrunk. The crucial point is that WHAT IS REAL IN AN OBSERVER REFERENCE FRAME, IS *not* REAL IN THE REFERENCE FRAME OF AN OBSERVED ROD. Ironically, the above mentioned widely respected author *correctly and explicitly* explained this in a textbook *two decades earlier* ([8] p. 28) in 1982: "But of course nothing at all has happened to the rod itself.".

Often referred to *improperly* by the maxim 'moving clocks to go slow', *perception* of time dilation is genuine, as is *perception* of 'length contraction'. Yet a clock does not 'dilate' in its own reference frame just because it happens to be observed from another reference frame. Time 'dilation' becomes 'real' i.e. *a fait accompli* only <u>after</u> a 'clock carrier' has changed back and forth between inertial reference frames. It is not—strictly speaking—'a present tense' phenomenon.

[6] Wolfgang Rindler. *Relativity, Special, General and Cosmological.* Oxford Universtiy Press, 2001, 2006

[7] Note: In the rod's own frame *it is not contracted*, even though in the observer frame *it would be experienced as being shorter.*

[8] Wolfgang Rindler. *Introduction to Special Relativity.* Oxford Universtiy Press, 1982, 1991

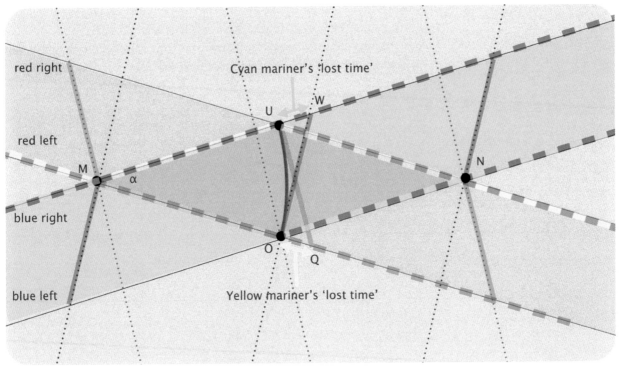

Figure 3.5: Simplified time travel chart

3.5 *Time travel—the simple twin paradox*

One of time dilation's immediate simple consequences is 'time travel', as shown in Figure 3.5. A red station's left end *'yellow' twin passenger* jumps across into the blue station's right end as it passes at event M. At the same event a blue station's right end *'cyan' twin passenger* jumps across into the red station's right end. The two mariners subsequently jump back again into their previous stations as they pass one another's respective other end at events U and O respectively. As where-line segments correspond to respective own-time intervals, each twin will note that, compared with his or her fellow passengers who did not jump, his clock's 'lost' time will equal $(1 - \cos\alpha)$ times[9] the stations' identical clock intervals between jumps. THUS WE CANNOT EXTEND OUR OWN-TIME, WE CAN ONLY OBSERVE OTHERS' OWN-TIME ADVANCING FASTER THAN OURS.

Indeed every time we make a return journey we age less than those who do not travel, but to a for us unnoticeable degree. The expression $(1 - \cos\alpha)$ is called *a versed sine*. We will encounter it again in the later chapter The unit thrust rocket where we explore further 'mechanisms' of time travel.

[9] $MO = MW \cos\alpha$ and $MW = MQ$ i.e. $OQ = (1 - \cos\alpha)MQ$.

Misunderstandings still plaguing much of the literature have severely handicapped general understanding of basic relativity, in particular also with regard to the long confused question of an accelerating *extended* medium's length expansion, the central topic of this book's final *Part VII*.

THROUGH A SPACETIME LOOKING GLASS (Anon.)

Two witches on their brooms afly, tho' neither sensed her stick ashrinking,
Did warily each other eye; "yer rod's gone short" each cackled blinking.
"Perceiv-ed length contraction—'TWERE CRAFTY DÆMONOLOGIE !"
They wailed in consternation (KNOWING NOT EPISTEMOLOGIE).

II

SPACETIME TRINITIES

Overleaf: Velocity composition computer graphic adopted from the author's 2003 EJP paper

The Larmor-Lorentz transformations and velocity composition chapter derives the equations expressing how time and distance intervals of an object or signal moving relative to both frames of our spacestations scenario relate in terms of the dual spacetime chart's respective where-line time intervals and when-line distance segments. These directly lead to the triplet velocities interrelationship—*relativistic velocity composition*. A special world-lines angle equation is then derived which is used later in chapter 6. The chapter concludes with a brief pertinent historical discussion.

The limit speed identified chapter describes how the 'speed of light' can actually be *identified* (at least as far as current measurement techniques indicate) as an 'instance' of the cosmic limit speed λ, *without* being postulated as such. Some special properties of the limit speed are then described.

The subsequent optional *Measuring the Cosmic Limit Speed chapter derives a *general* 'Doppler formula' for the ratio of consecutive response times for signals of *arbitrary* speed exchanged between relatively moving nonaccelerating pairs of spacestations. Contrary to common practice, this Doppler formula does *not* assume that signal speed s equals limit speed λ. From this equation an expression for the cosmic limit speed in terms of the response times ratio then emerges. This formula would allow the limit speed's actual value to be *independently measured* (at least in theory) as a function of signal speed c and a triplet of such response ratios, even in the (highly improbable) case where c and λ might actually differ.[10]

The likewise optional *Doppler relationships chapter discusses the *standard* Doppler formula case where signal speed and limit speed are identical, and explains how it was used around a century ago to conclude that our Universe is actually *expanding*.

[10] As already expounded in the the author's 2003 EJP paper

4

Larmor-Lorentz transformations and velocity composition

"Now write...dt_1 for $\epsilon^{-\frac{1}{2}} dt''$...where $\epsilon = (1 - v^2/c^2)^{-1}$; and it will be seen that the factor ϵ is absorbed, so that the scheme of equations...is identical in form with the Maxwellian scheme of relations for the aetherial vectors referred to fixed axes. This transformation...signifies an elongation of the space of the problem in the ratio $\epsilon^{\frac{1}{2}}$ along the direction of the motion..."

Time and space interrelationships anticipated in 1898 by Irish Huegenot Joseph Larmor

4.1 A simple derivation

Traditionally viewed as the central equations of special relativity, the *Larmor-Lorentz transformations*, which describe how own-distance and own-time intervals between any two separate events relate in respective inertial frames, may be directly established geometrically from the dual reference frames chart. Initially incorrectly put forward by Dutch physicist *Hendrik Lorentz*, their first *explicit* presentation in proper form was by Poincaré who generously labelled them *'the Lorentz transformations'*. They had previously appeared (as above) *implicitly* in a 1898 publication by *Joseph Larmor* ($\Rightarrow$[1], pp. 173-174) who was the first to point to the kernel relativity phenomenon of *'time dilation'*.

Figure 4.1: Antrim born Joseph Larmor, 1851-1942.

[1] Joseph Larmor. *Aether and Matter, Adams Essay*. Cambridge University Press, 1898/1900

©BCS Ireland 2017 ISBN 978-1-9998410-1-0
Brian Coleman Spacetime Fundamentals Intelligibly (Re)Learnt

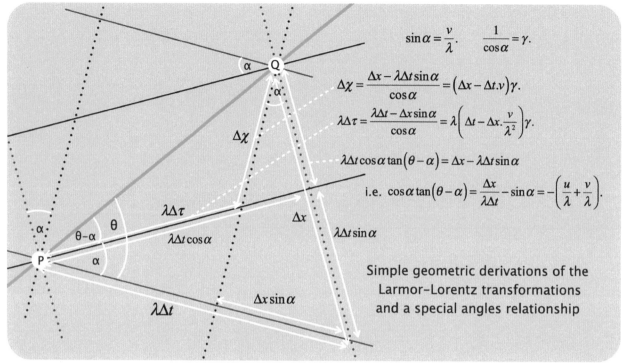

Figure 4.2: Larmor-Lorentz transformations

The equations shown in the figure:

$$\sin\alpha = \frac{v}{\lambda}. \qquad \frac{1}{\cos\alpha} = \gamma.$$

$$\Delta\chi = \frac{\Delta x - \lambda\Delta t \sin\alpha}{\cos\alpha} = (\Delta x - \Delta t.v)\gamma.$$

$$\lambda\Delta\tau = \frac{\lambda\Delta t - \Delta x \sin\alpha}{\cos\alpha} = \lambda\left(\Delta t - \Delta x.\frac{v}{\lambda^2}\right)\gamma.$$

$$\lambda\Delta t \cos\alpha \tan(\theta - \alpha) = \Delta x - \lambda\Delta t \sin\alpha$$

$$\text{i.e. } \cos\alpha \tan(\theta - \alpha) = \frac{\Delta x}{\lambda\Delta t} - \sin\alpha = -\left(\frac{u}{\lambda} + \frac{v}{\lambda}\right).$$

Simple geometric derivations of the Larmor-Lorentz transformations and a special angles relationship

[2] Such a signal need *not* necessarily be a light signal.

[3] Greek *chi, tau*

Figure 4.2's dual frames chart shows the green world-line of a nonaccelerating point object or signal[2] crossing two arbitrary events P and Q. We denote event coordinates in the red reference frame as $[x, \lambda t]$ and in the blue frame as $[\chi, \lambda\tau]$,[3] and express intervals between events as *difference* values $\Delta x, \Delta t, \Delta\chi$ and $\Delta\tau$, since we will often deal with world-lines *not necessarily crossing a chart's reference origin.*   Simple geometry gives us, with $\gamma = 1/\cos\alpha = 1/\sqrt{1 - v^2/\lambda^2}$:

4.1.

THE LARMOR-LORENTZ TRANSFORMATIONS

$$\Delta\chi = (\Delta x - \Delta t.v)\gamma; \qquad \Delta\tau = (\Delta t - \Delta x.v/\lambda^2)\gamma.$$

[4] $\Delta\chi + \Delta\tau.v = [\Delta x - \Delta t.v + \Delta t.v - \Delta x.v^2/\lambda^2]\gamma = \Delta x/\gamma$ etc.

Adding (4.1)-ii multiplied by v to (4.1)-i yields equation (4.2)-i.[4] Similarly, adding (4.1)-ii to (4.1)-i multiplied by v/λ^2 yields (4.2)-ii.

4.2.

THE INVERSE LARMOR-LORENTZ TRANSFORMATIONS

$$\Delta x = (\Delta\chi + \Delta\tau.v)\gamma; \qquad \Delta t = (\Delta\tau + \Delta\chi.v/\lambda^2)\gamma.$$

4.2   *Relativistic velocities of a triplet of reference frames*

We represent triplet scaled velocities *cyclically*. $\frac{v}{\lambda} = \sin \alpha$ is our inter-frames scaled velocity i.e. the blue frame's speed in the red frame. $\frac{w}{\lambda} = \frac{\Delta \chi}{\lambda \Delta \tau}$ represents the signal's scaled velocity in the blue frame and $\frac{u}{\lambda} = \frac{-\Delta x}{\lambda \Delta t}$ is red frame's backwards *negative* scaled velocity relative to the signal itself. Hence the signal's *forward velocity* in the red frame will be $\frac{-u}{\lambda}$. To obtain the formula for how these three velocities relate together, we merely divide equation (4.1)-i across by $\Delta \tau$:

$$w = \frac{\Delta \chi}{\Delta \tau} = \frac{(\Delta x - \Delta t.v)\gamma}{(\Delta t - \Delta x.v/\lambda^2)\gamma} = \frac{\Delta x/\Delta t - v}{1 - (\Delta x/\Delta t)v/\lambda^2} = \frac{-u - v}{1 + uv/\lambda^2}. \qquad (4.3)$$

This equation has three variants:

4.4.

> TRIAD CYCLIC VELOCITIES SUMMATION $v + w + u + \dfrac{vwu}{\lambda^2} = 0.$

The classical physics cyclic velocities equation[5] $v + w + u = 0$ is thus modified solely by the addition of the single term vwu/λ^2 !

4.5.

> TRIAD VELOCITIES RATIO $\Omega = \dfrac{1}{\lambda^2} = \dfrac{v + w + u}{-vwu}.$

4.6.

> THE FORWARD RELATIVISTIC VELOCITY EQUATION $(-u) = \dfrac{v + w}{1 + vw/\lambda^2}.$

Equation (4.6) follows from (4.4) which has the same form as (4.3)—because we have deliberately chosen *cyclic* velocity directions.

[6]Figure 4.2's simple geometry also yields a formula we use later in chapter 6. It expresses the object's *velocity increase* in the red frame over the blue station's velocity in the red frame, in terms of the angle θ between the green and red world-lines and the chart's velchronos angle α:

4.7.

> THE VELOCITY INCREASE WORLD-LINE ANGLES FORMULA $\left(-\dfrac{u}{\lambda}\right) - \dfrac{v}{\lambda} = \cos \alpha \tan(\theta - \alpha).$

[5] In classical physics for example, three cars racing at their top speeds would have *cyclic relative velocities* which together would add up as zero.

[6] Were our 'object' a limit speed signal, its diagonal world-line would be at an angle $\theta = \pi/4 + \alpha/2$ with the red station's world-line. Equation (4.7) would then reduce to $-u/\lambda = 1$.

4.3 A further historical note

The somewhat ambivalent relativity 'contraction' concept was first conjectured in 1889 (sometime before Hendrik Lorentz came up with the same 'idea') in the American journal *Science* by Irish physicist *George FitzGerald*—as a *hypothesis*:[7]

> "I have read with much interest Messrs. Michelson and Morley's wonderfully delicate experiment...I would suggest that...the length of material bodies changes...by an amount depending on the square of the ratio of their velocity to that of light."

Ironically it was FitzGerald's friend Larmor who later concretely introduced (likewise hesitantly) *time dilation* into spacetime theory, an idea leading to the *time dissimultaneities* concept which affords the expression 'contraction' a more insightful context. A moving rod is indeed 'perceived' by a relatively moving observer as *apparently* contracted, yet in its own spacetime reference frame the rod itself does *not* shrink in any way.[8]

FitzGerald[9] had also markedly contributed towards revising and reinterpreting the Scottish *James Clerk Maxwell's* pioneering equations in relativity's parallel domain of electromagnetism.[10] In addition he correctly identified important earlier 'optical ether' equations as in part analogous to those of Maxwell, which had been presented in the 1830s by fellow Irish physicist *James MacCullagh*.[11,12]

As early as 1878 FitzGerald had actually intuitively forecast another fundamental aspect of relativity theory with respect to 'material' space—the so-called *'aether'*:[13] [14,15]

> "If [it] induced us to emancipate ourselves from the thralldom of a material aether, [Maxwell's theory of electromagnetic waves] might possibly lead us to most important results in the theoretical interpretation of nature."

Moreover, in 1894 FitzGerald pointed to the essence of *general relativity theory* which emerged two decades later:

> "Gravity is probably due to a change in the structure of the aether produced by the presence of matter".

Sadly FitzGerald's untimely 1901 demise occurred before he could experience and perhaps have constructively elaborated upon Poincaré's and Einstein's subsequent ideas on spacetime.

[7] George FitzGerald. The Ether and the Earth's Atmosphere. *Science*, 13(328):390, 1889

Figure 4.3: George FitzGerald, Dublin physicist 1851-1901

[8] In spite of entrenched consensus to the contrary among many physicists.

[9] together with *Oliver Heaviside, Heinrich Hertz* and others:

[10] Bruce Hunt. *The Maxwellians.* Ithaca: Cornell University Press, 1991

[11] Olivier Darrigol. James MacCullagh's ether: An optical route to Maxwell's equations? *The European Physics Journal H*, 35: 133–172, 2010

[12] James Cushing. *Philosophical Concepts in Physics.* Cambridge University Press, 1998

[13] Joseph Larmor. *The Scientific Writings of the Late George Francis FitzGerald.* Hodges Figgis Dublin, 1902

[14] Nicholas Whyte. *Science, Colonialism and Ireland.* Cork University Press, 1999

[15] Denis Weaire (Editor). *George Francis FitzGerald.* Living Edition Austria, 2009

5

The limit speed identified

Entities must not be multiplied beyond necessity.
Occam's razor edge principle

Non sunt multiplicanda entia sine necessitate.
A 13th century *Dun Scotus* formulation.

5.1   Establishing the boundary speed by starlight

In the subsequent *optional* chapter we describe a theoretical experiment which would allow us to actually *measure* the relationship between λ and the speed of light c, if they might have proven to differ very minutely. A little 'lateral thinking'[1] however will allow us to actually *identify* limit speed factor λ by using forward velocity equation (4.6) to *logically confirm* light waves as a particular *instance* of the boundary speed..

Referring to Figure 5.2, a light photon emitted from a distant star[2,3] at an unknown relative velocity w, always appears to approach Earth with the same speed c, regardless of whatever velocity u the star itself might have relative to Earth. Putting $v = -c$ in[4] equation (4.6):

$$(-u) = \frac{-c + w}{1 - cw/\lambda^2}. \tag{5.1}$$

Clearly however, there is no *physical* connection between velocity $-u$ on the left side of equation (5.1) and the velocity parameter w on that equation's right side. Whatever the speed of a light wave leaving a star might be, it is physically unrelated to the relative speed between the star and our Earth. Yet equation (5.1) does define a *mathematical* i.e. *logical* relationship.

Figure 5.1: English philosopher William of Ockham, 1285-1349

[1] As explained in the author's 2003 *European Journal of Physics* paper.

[2] The first precise measurements of stellar light speed were performed in 1924 by R.Tomaschek.

[3] Rudolf Tomaschek. Über das Verhalten des Lichtes ausserirdischer Lichtquellen. *Annalen der Physik*, 378(1-2):105–126, 1924

[4] The photon 'sees' the Earth coming towards it at backwards velocity $v = -c$.

©BCS IRELAND 2017 ISBN 978-1-9998410-1-0
Brian Coleman SPACETIME FUNDAMENTALS INTELLIGIBLY (RE)LEARNT

Figure 5.2: Star-photon-Earth
reference frames triplet

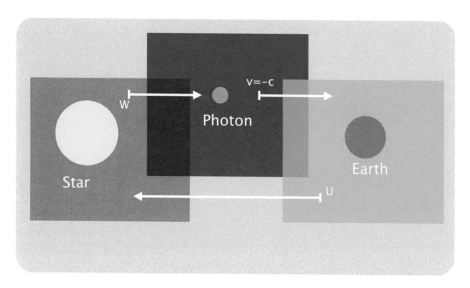

Figure 5.3:
  Ole Rømer, 1644-1710
  Danish astronomer who first
obtained a rough value for the
speed of light from apparent
variations in the orbital periods of
Jupiter's moons.

[5] We may exclude the unrealistic
only other alternative of a ratio of
infinities.

It may be assumed that light waves' velocity w relative to their emitter will always have the same value. Moreover *in at least two cases* among numerous observations, the particular stars' respective velocities u with respect to Earth may be expected to *differ* significantly, since our Earth rotates about its own axis and orbits a sun moving relative to the centre of a galaxy itself in motion relative to other galaxies. This leaves only one rational conclusion:

5.2.

THE STAR/PHOTON/EARTH VELOCITIES RELATIONSHIP

$$(-u) = \frac{-c + w}{1 - cw/\lambda^2} \qquad \text{IS INDETERMINATE.}$$

Its numerator and denominator must *both* be zero.[5] Without making *any* assumption regarding the light wave's emission velocity w, TWO consequences result from statement (5.2): w MUST EQUAL c <u>AND</u> c MUST EQUAL λ.

5.3.

AS FAR AS CAN BE ASCERTAINED FROM THE CURRENT LIMITS OF MEASUREMENT PRECISION, THE SPEED OF LIGHT IS AN INSTANCE OF THE LIMIT SPEED.

FROM NOW ON, EXCEPT FOR THE NEXT CHAPTER, WE TAKE IT FOR GRANTED THAT $\lambda = c$.

5.4.

EVERY LIMIT SPEED INSTANCE EXHIBITS THE SAME SPEED IN THE REFERENCE FRAME
OF EVERY OBSERVER—AS WELL AS IN THE REFERENCE FRAME OF ITS EMITTING SOURCE.

5.5.

OUR COSMIC CONSTANT IS NUMERICALLY IDENTIFIED: $\Omega \equiv \dfrac{1}{\lambda^2} = \dfrac{1}{c^2} \equiv \dfrac{1}{89875517873681764} \dfrac{m^2}{s^2}$.

5.2 The 'second postulate' is redundant

5.6.

OBSERVED LIGHT VELOCITY CONSTANCY AND THE TRIPLET EQUATIONS DERIVED ON THE BASIS
OF SPATIAL ISOTROPY FROM THE FIXED CHRONOSITY/VELOCITY RATIO, MAKES THE SECOND
POSTULATE REDUNDANT. IT ALSO VALIDATES THE LARMOR-LORENTZ EQUATIONS, THE
RELATIVISTIC VELOCITY RELATIONSHIPS AND THE ORIGINAL SPATIAL ISOTROPY HYPOTHESIS.

Light is thus AN INSTANCE of the limit speed—just like now already several
times detected gravitational waves. Having avoided the second postulate—
insisting up front ('a priori') that the speed of light is the limit speed, a further
conclusion emerges: CONSTANCY OF OBSERVED LIGHT WAVE SPEEDS IR-
RESPECTIVE OF SOURCE. Henri Poincaré's statements on space and time
as well as our triplet velocities relationships, are raised to the status of *validated principles*. A *confirmed* cosmic boundary speed thus fits very neatly into
the scheme of things as a *consequence* of our Universe's ubiquitous chronosity
property, and not simply by virtue of some kind of providential limit speed
imposition.

Even though we have identified an instance of this speed—that of light
waves, in the next chapter we examine a way to actually measure the boundary speed as a function of the speed of light (an electromagnetic wave), should—
as is of course most unlikely—there be some tiny (currently undetectable) difference between them. This approach underlines the fact that special relativity theory not only does not need the second postulate as a *preassumption*. It
would be a valid theory even the two speed values *were to actually differ*. In
such a case however, electromagnetic theory itself would have to be revised.

Figure 5.4: Classical physics and relativity physics velocity triad surfaces. Diagram presented in the author's 2003 EJP paper.

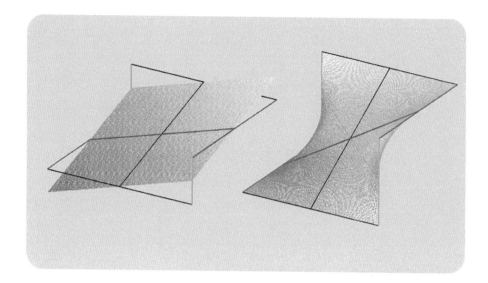

5.3   The 'contagious' limit speed

The left side flat $v|w|u$ surface of Figure 5.4 represents the Newtonian classical physics case where the limit speed would be infinite and the cyclic velocities would sum to zero i.e. $v + w + u = 0$. The right side surface models relativistic velocity composition as in equation (4.4): $v + w + u + vwu/c^2 = 0$. The six corners represent cases where all three v, w, u are unit limit speed (positive or negative). At the centre point all three are zero. Replacing w by limit speed c in (4.6) yields forward velocity $(-u) = \frac{v+c}{1+vc/c^2} = \frac{c(v+c)}{c+v} = c$ i.e. relativity velocity composition means that ADDING THE LIMIT SPEED TO ANY ARBITRARY SPEED (OR VICE-VERSA) ALWAYS PRODUCES THE LIMIT SPEED AS THE FINAL RESULT. Along the diagram's six edges two speeds are limit speed and the third may have any value between positive and negative limit speed. Each 'diagonal' reflects one of the three speeds being zero.

Figure 5.5 shows the relativity surface with velocities beyond the boundary speed. We show in the later section Cosmic boundary speed limitation how Nature would require an infinite amount of energy for any nonzero mass object to attain boundary speed $\lambda = c$ in any inertial frame of reference.

5.4   *A reference frames quartet

As also shown in the 2003 EJP paper, a further interesting formula can be derived from the triad cyclic velocities summation equation (4.4) by incorporating a fourth (orange) reference frame whose cyclic velocities relative to our green and red reference frames are y and $-z$ respectively, as schematised in Figure 5.6.

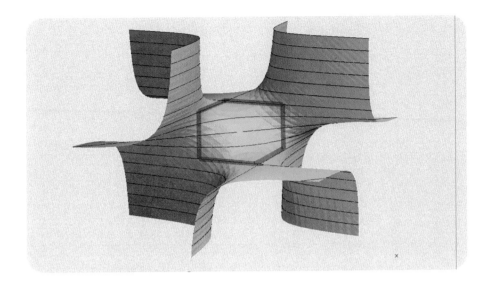

Figure 5.5: Relativistic velocity triad surface for speeds above the limit speed (were such to be possible).

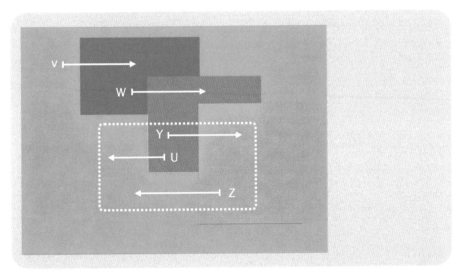

Figure 5.6: A reference frames quartet

Applying the triad equation to the red, green and orange reference frames triplet gives $-u + y + z - uyz/c^2 = 0$ i.e. $u = (y + z)/(1 + yz/c^2)$. Substituting in $(4.4)^6$ gives us

5.7.

[6] $v + w + \frac{y+z}{1+yz/c^2}$
$+ vw\frac{y+z}{1+yz/c^2}/c^2 = 0$ i.e.
$v + \frac{vyz}{c^2} + w + \frac{wyz}{c^2} + y + z + \left(\frac{vwy+vwz}{c^2}\right) = 0$ etc.

THE QUADRUPLET CYCLIC VELOCITIES RATIO

$$\Omega = \frac{1}{c^2} = \frac{v + w + y + z}{-(vwy + wyz + yzv + zvw)}.$$

6
*Measuring the Cosmic Limit Speed

AN ANTICIPATED EXPERIMENT

Zentralblatt MATH Database 1931 – 2006 **1046.83001**   © **2006 European Mathematical Society,**

Coleman, Brian   FIZ Karlsruhe & Springer-Verlag

A dual first-postulate basis for special relativity.

Eur. J. Phys. 24, No.3, 301-313 (2003). [ISSN 0143-0807] http://www.iop.org/Journals/ejp

Summary: An overlooked straightforward application of velocity reciprocity to a triplet of inertial frames in collinear motion identifies the ratio of their cyclic relative velocities' sum to the negative product as a cosmic invariant – whose inverse square root corresponds to a universal limit speed.

A logical indeterminacy of the ratio equation establishes the repeatedly observed unchanged speed of stellar light as one instance of this universal limit speed. This formally renders the second postulate redundant. The ratio equation furthermore enables the limit speed to be quantified – in principle – independently of a limit speed signal. Assuming negligible gravitational fields, two deep-space vehicles in non-collinear motion could measure with only a single clock the limit speed against the speed of light – without requiring these speeds to be identical.

Moreover, the cosmic invariant (from dynamics, equal to the mass-to-energy ratio) emerges explicitly as a function of signal response time ratios between three collinear vehicles, multiplied by the inverse square of the velocity of whatever arbitrary signal might be used.

Keywords : universal limit speed Classification : *83A05 Special relativity 83C10 Equations of motion

Figure 6.1: Equations of motion citation.

https://zbmath.org/?t=&s=0&q=py%3A2003+ai%3Acoleman.brian

The above abstract of a 2003 physics paper appeared (unexpectedly) in 2006 in the *European Mathematical Society's* reference database, classifying as 'equations of motion' the paper's formulae for both *logically identifying* as well as *measuring* (at least in theory) the normally *postulated* cosmic limit speed. This had been earlier speculated upon by two American physicists:[1,2]

> "...there appears a universal speed, the same in all inertial reference frames], whose value must be found by experiment. ...One may regard [the second postulate] as a statement about the nature of light rather than an independent postulate."
>
> *Edmund Purcell 1985*

[1] David Mermin. Relativity Without Light. *American Journal of Physics*, 52:119–124, 1984

[2] Edmund Purcell. *Electricity and Magnetism*, volume 2. McGraw-Hill, 1985

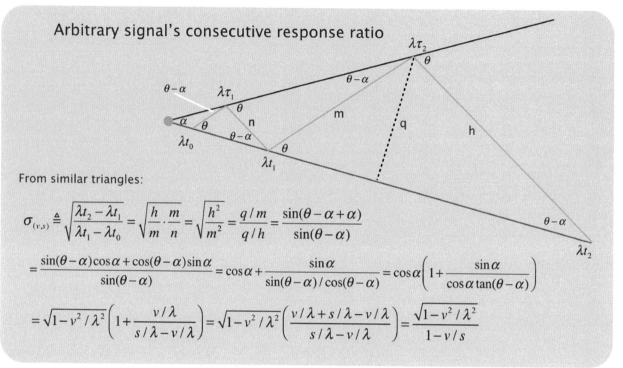

Figure 6.2: Signal response times ratio ($\Rightarrow$ Figure 4.2 and equation (4.7), with $-u = s$ and using the identity: $\sin(x + y) = \sin x \cos y + \sin x \cos y$).

[3] The stations' respective when-lines are omitted in this case since they are not needed. Also, in this scenario we consider both stations *as point objects*.

[4] This results from every triangle such as the leftmost one having its angles adding up to two right angles.

[5] Equation (6.1) was derived by the present author in 2003 using *recursive equations* instead of the simpler geometric way of Figure 6.2. $\sigma_{(v,s)}$ means here σ as a function of v and s.

6.1 *The arbitrary active signal return interval ratio*

Figure 6.2's dual frames chart shows the earlier Figure 4.2's world-lines of two nonaccelerating spacestations,[3] the blue station passing the red station at event O at relative scaled velocity v/λ. It also shows the green world-line of a 'nonobtrusive' signal being continually transmitted between them at some arbitrary but identical scaled *emission* speed s/λ, where s need not equal scaled limit speed λ. From symmetry and similar triangles, $h/m = m/n$. Also the signal's world-lines will each be at the same fixed angle θ to the emitting spacestation's where-line and at angle $\theta - \alpha$ to the approached where-line.[4]

Replacing $-u$ by s in angles formula (4.7) ($\cos\alpha\tan(\theta - \alpha) = -(\frac{u}{\lambda} + \frac{v}{\lambda})$), we recall that $\frac{v}{\lambda} = \sin\alpha$ and $\cos\alpha = \sqrt{1 - \frac{v^2}{\lambda^2}}$. The red station's *consecutive response interval ratio* $(t_2 - t_1)/(t_1 - t_0)$ is then obtainable in terms of relative velocity v/λ and signal velocity s:[5]

6.1.

ARBITRARY SIGNAL SPEED CONSECUTIVE RESPONSE RATIO S~~QUARED~~

$$p \triangleq \frac{1 - v^2/\lambda^2}{(1 - v/s)^2} = \sigma^2_{(v,s)}.$$

A crucial equation

Now we establish velocity in terms of the signal return interval ratio. Equation (6.1) rearranges as a standard quadratic[6] in v: $p + v^2 p/s^2 - 2vp/s = 1 - v^2/\lambda^2$ i.e. $(1/\lambda^2 + p/s^2)v^2 - 2vp/s + (p-1) = 0$.

$$v = \frac{p/s \mp \sqrt{p^2/s^2 - (1/\lambda^2 + p/s^2)(p-1)}}{1/\lambda^2 + p/s^2} = \frac{p/s \mp \sqrt{1/\lambda^2 + p/s^2 - p/\lambda^2}}{1/\lambda^2 + p/s^2} \cdot \frac{s^2}{s^2}.$$

[6] The standard quadratic equation $ax^2 + bx + c = 0$ solves as $x = (-\frac{b}{2} \mp \sqrt{b^2/4 - ac})/a$.

6.2.

VELOCITY SIGNAL RESPONSE FUNCTION $\left(p = \sigma^2_{(v,s)}\right)$

$$v = \frac{p - \sqrt{p - (p-1)(s/\lambda)^2}}{p + (s/\lambda)^2} \cdot s.$$

[7]Generalized velocity/signal response (6.2) allows us to establish the limit speed λ as a function of three such signal response factors—*without* the speed s of the signal used having to be equal to limit speed λ.

[7] Note: We drop *the square root plus sign case* which would involve impractical spacestation relative velocities close to the limit speed.

6.2 Ω as a conglomerate of tandem response time ratios

Let us imagine three spacestations moving relatively in a straight line. Green station G moves at unknown velocity w relative to blue station B which moves at velocity v with respect to red station R moving at cyclic velocity u relative to G. R's clock measures signal intervals returned from B to establish the velocity v-dependent consecutive response ratio p. Likewise B's clock measures signal intervals returned from G to establish w-dependent consecutive response ratio q. The $-u$-dependent ratio can be established by signals between R and G initiated by station R, saving the need for a station G clock. Clocks need neither be synchronized nor identical, since only time interval <u>ratios</u> of each clock are involved.

Denoting the respective values of $\sigma_{(w,c)}$ and $\sigma_{(-u,c)}$ as q and r, and using velocity/signal response function (6.2) for the unknown values of v, w and $-u$:

$$\frac{v}{c} = \frac{p - \sqrt{p - (p-1)\left(\frac{c}{\lambda}\right)^2}}{p + \left(\frac{c}{\lambda}\right)^2}; \quad \frac{w}{c} = \frac{q - \sqrt{q - (q-1)\left(\frac{c}{\lambda}\right)^2}}{q + \left(\frac{c}{\lambda}\right)^2}; \quad \frac{-u}{c} = \frac{r - \sqrt{r - (r-1)\left(\frac{c}{\lambda}\right)^2}}{r + \left(\frac{c}{\lambda}\right)^2}. \tag{6.3}$$

Figure 6.3: Triplet signal exchanges

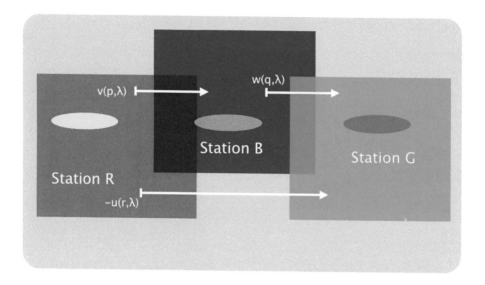

These three equations together however have *four* unknowns. Each further collinear vehicle would provide a new time response value but also introduce a new unknown velocity—an apparently hopeless 'Catch 22' situation. The dilemma is resolved however simply by adopting triad velocities ratio (4.5)

$$\Omega = \frac{1}{\lambda^2} = \frac{v + w + u}{-vwu}$$

once again for the triplet of vehicles as a whole—a great surprise.[8] The unknown velocities are replaced by the expressions containing the measured p, q and r values, the known signal speed c and the unknown i.e. λ. This yields an equation with only *one* unknown $\frac{c}{\lambda}$:

[8] In *hindsight* of course, just a 'simple' step.

6.4.

THE LIMIT SPEED RATIO'S IMPLICIT SIGNAL RESPONSE RATIOS FORMULA

$$\Omega = \frac{c^2}{\lambda^2} = \frac{\frac{p-\sqrt{p-(p-1)c^2/\lambda^2}}{p+c^2/\lambda^2} + \frac{q-\sqrt{q-(q-1)c^2/\lambda^2}}{q+c^2/\lambda^2} - \frac{r-\sqrt{r-(r-1)c^2/\lambda^2}}{r+c^2/\lambda^2}}{\frac{p-\sqrt{p-(p-1)c^2/\lambda^2}}{p+c^2/\lambda^2} \cdot \frac{q-\sqrt{q-(q-1)c^2/\lambda^2}}{q+c^2/\lambda^2} \cdot \frac{r-\sqrt{r-(r-1)c^2/\lambda^2}}{r+c^2/\lambda^2}}.$$

The above equation *implicitly* relates λ and c. A further unexpected development was that instead of a computer algorithm being needed to converge on a solution, the powerful MAPLE symbolic algebra tool[9] was capable of yielding the *explicit* solution of (6.4):

[9] Maplesoft, Waterloo Maple Inc. Ontario, Canada.

6.5.

The Limit Speed ratio's EXPLICIT signal response ratios formula

$$\Omega = \frac{c^2}{\lambda^2} = \frac{[pq(r+1) - 2(p+q)r]pq(r-1) + [(p-q)r]^2(r+1)/(r-1)}{\left\{[(p-q)r]^2 + pq(r-1)[pq(r-1) - 2(p+q-2)r]\right\}} +$$

$$\frac{4\sqrt{pqr}[pq(r+1) - (p+q)r][[pq(r-1)]^2 - [(p-q)r]^2] - 2[[pq(r-1)]^2 - [(p-q)r]^2]^2/(r-1)}{\left\{[(p-q)r]^2 + pq(r-1)[pq(r-1) - 2(p+q-2)r]\right\}^2}.$$

Verifying the explicit limit speed formula

λ can thus be measured against c even[10] if they are numerically not the same—a limit speed signal is not needed. Any non-intrusive signal with an emitter-constant speed (if a suitable signal other than an electromagnetic wave could be found) would 'do the job' in principle. If c *exactly* equals λ then (6.4) and (6.5) reduce to $r = pq$. Values where $r = pq$ would establish signal velocity c as limit speed λ. Formula (6.5) has been verified—also using MAPLE. Selecting arbitrary numerical values for c, λ, v and u, the resulting w was calculated using forward velocity equation (4.6). The corresponding p, q and r values were then computed using return interval ratio equation (6.1). Initially substitution in equation (6.5) for p, q and r did not produce a value anywhere near the preselected c/λ ratio. Maple's default computation precision setting of 10 places after the decimal point was then changed to 30 places. This yielded a result correct to more that 20 decimal point places *for all preordained values of c/λ equal to or below unity.*

[10] Their two values being different is at least *an interesting theoretical possibility compatible with and allowed by the theory of special relativity.* Such however would require a revision of the theory of electromagnetism !

The question of a difference between λ and c

Had the much reported 2011 CERN experiment near Geneva claiming neutrinos had travelled 'faster than light' been confirmed (rather than proving to be in error), then the 2003 equation (6.5) might well have proven useful. The many media statements that such an observation would invalidate the theory of relativity however, were inappropriate. Special relativity's validity as a theory of pure spacetime does not depend on whether or not electromagnetic waves propagate at the limit speed. In all probability nevertheless, 'the speed of light' c *is* an instance of the universal limit speed λ.

6.3   Ignatowski's tragic fate and legacy

6.6.

$$\text{IGNATOWSKI CONSTANT } \Omega = \frac{1}{\lambda^2} = \frac{\psi}{v} = \frac{-vwu}{v+w+u} = \frac{-(vwy+wyz+yzv+zvw)}{v+w+y+z} = F(p,q,r) = \frac{1-(t'/t)^2}{(T/t)^2}.$$

[11] B.C. An elementary first-postulate measurement of the cosmic limit speed. *European Journal of Physics*, 25:L31–L32, 2004

[12] Aleksander Solzhenitsyn. *The Gulag Archipelago*, volume 2 p.296. Westview Press/Harper & Row NY, 1973

Figure 6.4: Vladimir Ignatowski, 1875-1942. Photo kindly supplied by *Sergei Yakovlenko*, General Physics Institute, Moscow.

[11]An additional curious theoretical experiment for measuring the limit speed was described in the authors's 2004 EJP paper: $\lambda/c = (T/t)/\sqrt{1-(t'/t)^2}$.

In a landmark of 20th century history literature, *Aleksander Solzhenitsyn—* himself a physicist (although perhaps unfamiliar with Ignatowski's relativity thesis)—chronicles one of the strangest tragedies in scientific history which befell this almost forgotten yet truly important pioneer of spacetime theory.[12]

"Corresponding Member of the [Soviet] Academy of Sciences Ignatovsky was arrested in Leningrad in 1941 and accused of having been recruited by the German intelligence service when he was working for Zeiss [in Germany] in 1908 ! And he was supposed to have had a very strange assignment too: not to engage in espionage in the coming war (which was of course the center of interest of that generation of the intelligence services) but only in the next one! And therefore he had loyally served the Tsar in World War I, and then the Soviet government also, and had put into operation the only optical factory in the country (GOMZ), and had been elected to the Academy of Sciences, and then at the beginning of World War II he had been caught, rendered harmless, and shot !"

THE GULAG ARCHIPELAGO,   Aleksander Solzhenitsyn

In 1955, two years after Stalin's death, Vladimir Ignatowski was officially rehabilitated by the Government of the Soviet Union. The Georgian-born Russian scientist's 1910 paper *Das Relativitätsprinzip* on single postulate special relativity led to many other similar papers over subsequent decades which were generally ignored. Ignatowski's constant Ω—the cosmic limit speed's inverse square—has turned out to be not only simple to establish and understand, it points to 'a natural path' for an optimal exposition of special relativity.

7

*Doppler relationships

"I am more than ever convinced that the wonderful 'ornamentation' of colour in double stars and other celestial objects, will one day prove to be more than a feast for the eyes. It will serve in the perhaps distant future to determine the trajectories of heavenly bodies whose boundless distances still allow only purely optical means of measurement." Christian Doppler   1842

7.1   The relativity Doppler factor

Replacing λ and s in arbitrary signal speed response factor (6.1) with *unit scaled* limit speed yields *the limit speed signal forward interval ratio*:

7.1.

LIMIT SCALED SPEED SIGNAL RELATIVITY DOPPLER FACTOR

$$\sigma_v = \sqrt{\frac{(1-v)(1+v)}{(1-v)^2}} = \sqrt{\frac{1+v}{1-v}}.$$

Figure 7.1: Christian Doppler, Austrian physicist 1803 - 1853

Using forward velocity equation (4.6) *cyclically* we obtain

$$\frac{(1+v)}{(1-v)}\frac{(1+w)}{(1-w)} = \frac{1-\frac{w+u}{1+wu}}{1+\frac{w+u}{1+wu}} \cdot \frac{1-\frac{u+v}{1+uv}}{1+\frac{u+v}{1+uv}} = \frac{1+wu-w-u}{1+wu+w+u} \cdot \frac{1+uv-u-v}{1+uv+u+v} = \frac{(1-w)(1-u)}{(1+w)(1+u)}\frac{(1-u)(1-v)}{(1+u)(1+v)}$$

i.e. $$\frac{(1+v)^2}{(1-v)^2}\frac{(1+w)^2}{(1-w)^2}\frac{(1+u)^2}{(1-u)^2} = 1.$$

This equation directly rearranges as:

7.2.

THE CYCLIC TRIPLE RELATIVITY DOPPLER FACTORS PRODUCT

$$\sigma_v \cdot \sigma_w \cdot \sigma_u = \sqrt{\frac{(1+v)}{(1-v)}} \cdot \sqrt{\frac{(1+w)}{(1-w)}} \cdot \sqrt{\frac{(1+u)}{(1-u)}} = 1.$$

Since from (7.1) $\sigma_{-u} = 1/\sigma_u$, we may also write:

7.3.

THE FORWARD TRIPLE RELATIVITY DOPPLER FACTORS PRODUCT

$$\sigma_v \cdot \sigma_w = \sqrt{\frac{(1+v)}{(1-v)}} \cdot \sqrt{\frac{(1+w)}{(1-w)}} = \sqrt{\frac{(1-u)}{(1+u)}} = \sigma_{-u}.$$

The Doppler inter-frames signal interval ratio

Figure 7.2 represents the earlier signals response times chart Figure 6.2 *for limit speed signal world-lines* which are at ± 45 degrees to the horizontal. At each 'reflection point' the two limit speed world-lines therefore form a right angle. Signal angles with the stations' world-lines are now $\pi/4 + \alpha/2$ on emission and $\pi/4 - \alpha/2$ on reception. Also shown is a separate signal world-line emitted at *an arbitrary* red-time $t_0 + \Delta t$ which arrives at the blue station at $\tau_1 + \Delta\tau$ and is parallel to the other emission world-lines. From the geometry the signal world-line connecting events at τ_1 and t_1 equals in length both $(t_1 - t_0)\sin(\frac{\pi}{4} + \frac{\alpha}{2})$ as well as $(\tau_2 - \tau_1)\cos(\frac{\pi}{4} + \frac{\alpha}{2})$. Hence from similar triangles[1]

[1] and noting that $\sin\frac{\pi}{4} = \cos\frac{\pi}{4}$ and $\cos^2\frac{\alpha}{2} + \sin^2\frac{\alpha}{2} = 1$.

$$\frac{\Delta\tau}{\Delta t} = \frac{\tau_2 - \tau_1}{t_1 - t_0} = \frac{\sin(\frac{\pi}{4} + \frac{\alpha}{2})}{\cos(\frac{\pi}{4} + \frac{\alpha}{2})} = \sqrt{\frac{(\cos\frac{\alpha}{2} + \sin\frac{\alpha}{2})^2}{(\cos\frac{\alpha}{2} - \sin\frac{\alpha}{2})^2}} = \sqrt{\frac{1 + 2\sin\frac{\alpha}{2}\cos\frac{\alpha}{2}}{1 - 2\sin\frac{\alpha}{2}\cos\frac{\alpha}{2}}} = \sqrt{\frac{1 + \sin\alpha}{1 - \sin\alpha}} = \sqrt{\frac{1 + v}{1 - v}}.$$

7.4.

THE LIMIT SPEED SIGNAL RELATIVITY DOPPLER FACTOR EQUALS A RECEIVING STATION'S
TIME INTERVALS DIVIDED BY ITS PREVIOUS EMITTING STATION'S TIME INTERVALS.

$$\frac{\Delta\tau}{\Delta t} = \sqrt{\frac{1 + v}{1 - v}} = \sigma_v.$$

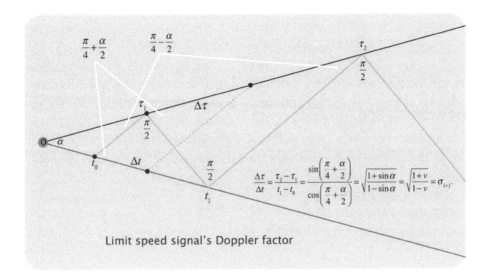

Figure 7.2: Limit speed signal response ratio

Limit speed signal's Doppler factor

7.2 Cosmology—Evidence of an expanding Universe

Why sound waves of a passing train's whistle change in pitch was first explained in 1842 by Austrian physicist *Christian Doppler*.[2] Consecutive wave crests from an approaching train's whistle arrive more rapidly at listeners' ears than from a stationary or receding train—the *experienced* sound wavelengths are longer and their frequency differs from that perceived by the train driver.

Radio waves, which include light waves, 'propagate' in every observer's inertial frame at limit speed c. This allows us to give equation (7.4) *a direct physical meaning* if we imagine that our signal comprises not radar 'pulses' but *continuous light signals* periodically 'marked' at equal wave crest intervals. Consecutive wave crest arrival intervals relate in accordance with formula (7.4).

A 'perceived' light wave frequency is inversely proportional to the experienced time interval between arriving wave crests—the emitting *source* frame interval between wave crests multiplied by the relativity Doppler factor. Characteristic light wave spectra from receding stars are thus reduced in frequency i.e. 'red-shifted' towards the lower end of the light spectrum. Rearranging (7.4) gives for a light signal's receding source speed:

7.5.

STANDARD DOPPLER VELOCITY FORMULA $\qquad \dfrac{v}{c} = \dfrac{\sigma_v^2 - 1}{\sigma_v^2 + 1}.$

[2] Peter Schuster. *Moving the Stars - Christian Doppler, His Life, His Works and Principle and the World After.* Living Edition Austria, 2005

Figure 7.3: Vesto Slipher
U.S. physicist, 1875 - 1969

In 1917 *Vesto Slipher* and in 1929 *Edwin Hubble* observed that characteristic light spectra of distant galaxies were indeed frequency-shifted. This allowed their forward signal interval ratio values to be assessed and hence from equation (7.5) their velocities. It was noticed that the fainter (and hence the further away) a galaxy was, the faster it receded. This led to the conclusion that our Universe is expanding from a 'Big Bang' event which occurred about 14 thousand million years ago. Doppler-like equations have thus enabled us to obtain formulae not only for (theoretically) measuring the limit speed, but also to discover that our Universe is 'expanding'.

Later in the Spacetime's and Geometry's missing 'HEMIX' chapter we will further 'geometrise' relationship (7.3). In book *Parts V, VI* and *VII* we deal with more complex radar scenarios.

III

FORCE, MASS AND ENERGY

Overleaf: *Nuclear bomb explosion.*

[3] B.C. Special relativity dynamics without a priori momentum conservation. *European Journal of Physics*, 26:647–650, 2005

Prelude to a 2005 physics journal publication

Considerable initial puzzlement and scepticism expressed by a *European Journal of Physics* reviewer regarding a subsequently published[3] relativity dynamics paper's 'novelty of approach', prompted a detailed elaboration:

> "Many thanks for your considerable efforts in reviewing my paper. Its raison d'être came to me very much as a surprise, so it is perhaps no wonder that the few standard results, as you call them, appear puzzling in the minimal context and form presented. ...In my opinion a major reason why (seemingly) the literature has missed the particular route of the paper is past dominance of 'relativistic mass' - a misnomer of mistaken didactic advantage. It's undeniable importance as a [misnamed] concept diverted attention and contributed to physicists missing the fact that the well known ['apocalyptic'] identities are usable as a basis, rather than being simply an interesting result or 'confirmation'. I would also argue that derivations of the relativistic dynamics equations in competent recent texts such as *Rindler* (2001), *Kogut* (2000), *T.A. Moore* (*A Traveller's Guide to Spacetime* -1995), and in classics by *Shadowitz, Smith* and *French*, as well as the paper references [1], [2], [3], [4] and (newly added) [7] (*McComb's Dynamics and Relativity* Oxford U.P. 1999), are without exception comparatively long, cumbersome and elaborate.[4,5,6,7,8,9,10]

> All employ conservation of momentum *a priori*. The common 4-vector approach (or at least use of two spatial dimensions) is in my opinion didactically problematic in that it obscures the simple one-dimensional physics at the heart of the matter. Often recourse is made to photons, unnecessarily dragging in electromagnetism. *Smith* [5] even rashly asserts the equations cannot be derived but 'must be guessed' and presents them *ad hoc*. Scrutiny of *European Journal of Physics* papers such as the recent [10] and [11], not to mention a host of papers in the *American Journal of Physics*, I feel underlines this."

[4] Wolfgang Rindler. *Relativity, Special, General and Cosmological.* Oxford Universtiy Press, 2001, 2006

[5] John B. Kogut. *Introduction to Relativity: For Physicists and Astronomers.* Harcourt, 2001

[6] T.A. Moore. *A Traveler's Guide to Spacetime: An Introduction to the Special Theory of Relativity.* McGraw-Hill, 1995

[7] Albert Shadowitz. *Special Relativity.* Dover, 1988

[8] James H Smith. *Introduction to Special Relativity.* Dover, 1965, 1996

[9] A.P. French. *Special Relativity.* Chapman and Hall, 1968

[10] W.D. McComb. *Dynamics and Relativity.* Oxford U.P., 1999

The *European Journal of Physics* reviewer graciously concluded:

> "I read carefully the author's comments as well as the new version. I must admit that my comments regarding the previous version were too strong. ...I do not think I can add much more to what is written in the authors' reply, I agree with his remarks. Therefore I recommend it for publication in European Journal of Physics."

[11] B.C. A five-fold equivalence in special relativity one-dimensional dynamics. *European Journal of Physics*, 27:983–984, 2006

The final two chapters of PART III deal with the approach of that paper and a 2006 sequel EJP paper.[11] First however, the ways a rocket's three differently perceived acceleration parameters interrelate need to be established.

8

Three acceleration perspectives

"Presentations of the spacetime theory by physicists are concerned primarily with physical issues and fail to make the epistemological problems explicit. On the contrary, they are often epistemologically vague, in order to make the physical theory appear as plausible as possible."

Hans Reichenbach   *The Philosophy of Space & Time*   1928

8.1 *An accelerating rocket scenario*

Rocket launch

[1]Let us imagine a single dimension scenario where two blue spacestations A and B, both stationary in an nonaccelerating (inertial) frame $\hat{\underline{C}}$, are moving in a forwards direction at scaled fixed velocity[2] $\hat{v}/c = \sin\hat{\phi}$ towards two red stations M and N which are both stationary in a likewise nonaccelerating 'home' frame $\underline{H}$. As schematically illustrated in figure 8.1, a yellow rocket R is launched from the 'mother' red station M towards red station N and away from blue stations A and B approaching in the distance from behind. We denote this as event MR.

Rocket rendezvous

The rocket's own-acceleration α, *which need not necessarily be constant*[3] (a restriction we consider later), is such that it reaches station N just as its ever increasing home frame scaled velocity v/c momentarily reaches $\hat{v}/c$ and—likewise coincidentally—just as blue station A also passes red station N. Rocket R is thereby *momentarily* stationary with blue station A in reference frame $\hat{\underline{C}}$. Simultaneous in frame $\hat{\underline{C}}$ to this rendezvous event NRA, blue station B happens to be passing red station M—event MB.

[1] Hans Reichenbach. *The Philosophy of Space and Time (Philosophie der Raum-Zeit-Lehre).* De Gruyter Berlin, 1928

[2] We refer to $\hat{v}$ and $\hat{\phi}$ as 'v-hat', 'phi-hat' etc.

[3] It should of course be 'smooth'. Passengers in the rocket would feel quite 'at home' if α were about ten meters per second squared as on Earth.

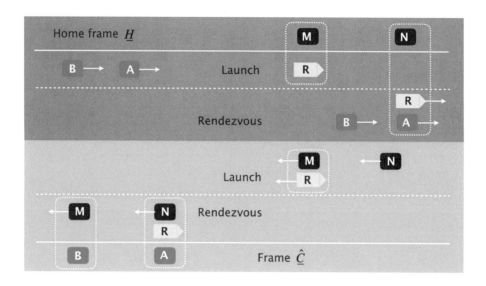

The scenario is portrayed in figure 8.2's dual reference frames chart containing red 'home' frame[4] $\underline{H}$'s reference $x|t$ axes at respective identical angles $\hat{\phi}$ to blue frame $\hat{\underline{C}}$'s $\hat{X}|\hat{T}$ axes. Event N_{LH} marks the chart's position of station N simultaneous to rocket launch from M in home frame $\underline{H}$. As M and N share the rocket's inertial home frame $\underline{H}$, their two red world-lines are parallel, mother station M's world-line being along home frame $\underline{H}$'s time axis t. Stations A and B's[5] blue world-lines are parallel to frame $\hat{\underline{C}}$'s time axis $\hat{T}$.

Having been momentarily relatively stationary with station A, the forwards accelerating rocket R then moves *away* from station A whose straight world-line will of course have been *tangent* to the accelerating rocket's curved world-line at event NRA, as illustrated. Station B's passing by of mother station M—event MB—is simultaneous in frame $\hat{\underline{C}}$ to event NRA. In frame $\underline{H}$ however, event NRA is simultaneous to the *separate* event M_{RAH} on station M's world-line.

A 'comoving' reference frame's parameters

[6]Though accelerating, the rocket itself may be assigned instantaneous ever-changing nonaccelerating i.e. inertial reference frames $\underline{C}$, each with its own particular scaled velocity $v/c = \sin\phi$ relative to the home frame. Such frames are called COMOVING INERTIAL FRAMES.

At arrival event NRA the rocket has a 'retrospective' travelled distance $\hat{X}_{RA}$ in frame $\hat{\underline{C}}$ which corresponds of course to the distance *in that frame* between stationary spacestations A and B and relates as[7]

$$\text{RETROSPECTIVE DISTANCE} \qquad \hat{X}_{RA} = \frac{x_{RA}}{\hat{\gamma}} = x_{RA}\cos\hat{\phi} \qquad (8.1)$$

[4] In general we denote reference frames by <u>underlined</u> upper case letters.

[5] Stations A and B's respective chart positions at launch are A_{LH} and B_{LH}.

[6] Frame $\underline{C}$ denotes an *arbitrary* comoving frame, whereas frame $\hat{\underline{C}}$ refers to the *specific* reference frame of stations A and B.

[7] Recalling inverse Lorentz transformation (4.2)-i
$\Delta x = (\Delta\chi + \Delta\tau.v)\gamma$,
with zero $\Delta\tau$ i.e. simultaneous in frame $\hat{\underline{C}}$.

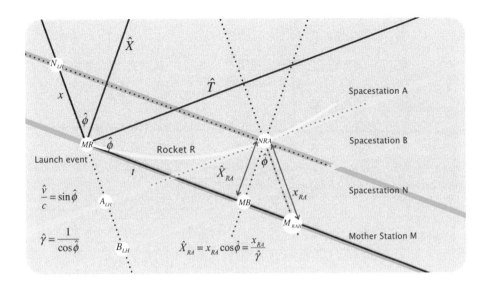

[8]where x_{RA} is the unchanging distance in home frame $\underline{H}$ between spacestations M and N. Epitomising the misnamed 'contraction' phenomenon, perceived home frame distances such as x_{RA} between events NRA and $M_{R}AH$ simultaneous in home frame $\underline{H}$, would, from the rocket's point of view in frame $\hat{\underline{C}}$, *appear* to 'be contracted' although in frame $\underline{H}$ such distances are *not* contracted. Home frame observers, of course, would perceive that spacestations A and B assessed N and M's separation *nonsimultaneously*.

[8] Where-line segment x_{RA} being parallel to frame $\underline{H}$'s x axis.

8.2   The primary acceleration relationships

'Retroperspective' comoving frames' acceleration

We now consider the rocket being momentarily stationary to station A and proceeding to a new frame $\underline{C}'$, a <u>miniscule</u> rocket *own-time increment* $\Delta\tau$ later. As schematically shown in figure 8.3, relative to rocket R in its new co-moving frame $\underline{C}'$, station A's *backwards* incremental velocity is simply $-\Delta u \approx -\alpha\Delta\tau$.[9] Mother station M's backwards velocity in station A's frame $\hat{\underline{C}}$ equals $-\hat{v}$. In the rocket's new frame $\underline{C}'$, M's *retrospective* velocity will therefore be $-(\hat{v} + \Delta v)$. Because of relativistic velocity relationship (4.6), $\Delta u \approx \alpha\Delta\tau$ is not the same as Δv i.e. $(\hat{v} + \Delta v) \neq \hat{v} + \alpha\Delta\tau$. Instead

[9] Even though own-acceleration α may actually *vary*, it may be assumed to be unchanging as $\Delta\tau \to 0$.

$$(\hat{v} + \Delta v) \approx \frac{\hat{v} + \alpha\Delta\tau}{1 + \hat{v} \cdot \alpha\Delta\tau/c^2}. \tag{8.2}$$

As $\Delta\tau \to 0$, frame $\underline{C}'$ becomes ever closer to frame $\hat{\underline{C}}$. Hence ($\Rightarrow$ figure 8.3):[10]

[10] Now dispensing with the ^ accent.

$$\frac{dv}{d\tau} = \alpha(1 - v^2/c^2). \tag{8.3}$$

Figure 8.3: Retrospective acceleration frames triplet

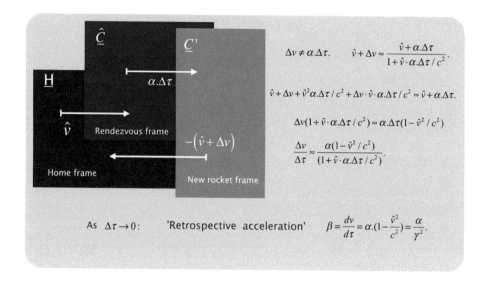

$$SUCCESSIVE\ COMOVING\ FRAMES\ RETROSPECTIVE\ ACCELERATION \quad \beta = \frac{dv}{d\tau} = \alpha\left(1 - \frac{v^2}{c^2}\right) = \frac{\alpha}{\gamma^2}.$$

(8.4)

[11] Greek *beta*. β will have a positive
value, just like a and α.

[11]Notably, whereas velocity v is quantitatively reciprocal for frame $\underline{H}$ and any comoving frame $\underline{C}$, acceleration values α for the rocket in its own comoving frame and β for successive comoving frames as perceived by the rocket, *are not reciprocal*.

The home frame acceleration value

To establish how a rocket passenger would observe passing *home frame* clock Δt interval times progressing relative to the rocket clock's own-time $\Delta\tau$ differences, we turn to *inverse Lorentz transformation* (4.2)-ii: $\Delta t = (\Delta\tau + \Delta\chi.v/c^2)\gamma$. Putting $\Delta\chi = 0$ representing the rocket as *a point object* in a comoving frame $\underline{C}$, we obtain as the Δt and $\Delta\tau$ intervals tend to zero:

$$TIME\ DILATION\ FACTOR \qquad \left.\frac{dt}{d\tau}\right|_{\Delta\chi=0} = \gamma.$$

(8.5)

This enables us to establish how *home frame* acceleration a relates to the retrospective acceleration β of a rocket observer's perceived successive comoving frames. Combining equations (8.4) and (8.5), we may write home frame velocity's perceived change rated by home time i.e.:

[12] *Roman a.*

HOME FRAME PERCEIVED FORWARD ACCELERATION:[12],[13]

[13] v could be expressed as function
of either t alone or τ alone, just as
t may be expressed as a function
of τ alone. By the chain rule of
calculus therefore:
$\frac{dv}{dt} = \frac{dv}{d\tau}\frac{d\tau}{dt}$.

$$a \triangleq \frac{d^2x}{dt^2} = \frac{dv}{dt} = \frac{dv}{d\tau \cdot \left.\frac{dt}{d\tau}\right|_{\Delta\chi=0}} = \frac{dv}{d\tau \cdot \gamma} = \frac{\beta}{\gamma} = \frac{\alpha}{\gamma^3}.$$

(8.6)

We have thus arrived at the important equations expressing how acceleration is judged from *three* different viewpoints:

1. The rocket itself perceived from a momentary comoving frame (α).

2. Successive momentary comoving frames' velocity rate of increase *perceived*[14] by a rocket's passenger as 'retrospective acceleration' ($\beta = dv/d\tau = \alpha/\gamma^2$).

   [14] Individual comoving frames do not *themselves* actually accelerate.

3. The rocket as perceived by any home frame observer ($a = dv/dt = \alpha/\gamma^3$).

8.7.

THE PRIMARY RELATIVISTIC ACCELERATION RELATIONSHIPS

$$a \triangleq \frac{dv}{dt}\bigg|_{\Delta\chi=0} = \frac{\alpha}{\gamma^3} \quad and \quad \beta \triangleq \frac{dv}{d\tau} = \frac{\alpha}{\gamma^2} = \alpha\left(1 - \frac{v^2}{c^2}\right).$$

8.3 The 'apocalyptic' dynamics identities

Finally we examine two very special mathematical relationships involving the own-acceleration α parameter, which unravel the all important relativity dynamics equations in a clearcut manner and which seemingly have not hitherto been appreciated as to their *full* usefulness.[15] Each of the following three equations uses the simple calculus formula: $dp^n/dp = n.p^{n-1}$.

Apocalypse means 'revelation'.
Greek: ἀποχάλνψις

[15] Prior to the present author's 2005 EJP paper.

$$\frac{d\left(1/\gamma^2\right)}{dv} = \frac{d\left(1 - v^2/c^2\right)}{dv} = \frac{-2v}{c^2} \quad i.e. \quad d\left(1/\gamma^2\right) = \frac{-2v}{c^2}dv \quad ;$$

$$\frac{d(1/\gamma^2)}{d(1/\gamma)} = \frac{d(1/\gamma)^2}{d(1/\gamma)} = \frac{2}{\gamma} \quad i.e. \quad d(1/\gamma) = \frac{\gamma}{2}d(1/\gamma^2) = -\frac{v}{c^2}\gamma dv \quad ;$$

$$\frac{d\gamma}{d\left(1/\gamma\right)} = \frac{d(1/\gamma)^{-1}}{d\left(1/\gamma\right)} = -\left(\frac{1}{\gamma}\right)^{-2} = -\gamma^2 \quad i.e. \quad d\gamma = -\gamma^2 d(1/\gamma) = \frac{v}{c^2}\gamma^3 dv = \frac{\gamma^3}{c^2}\frac{dx}{dt}dv.$$

Hence using equation (8.7)-i ($\frac{dv}{dt} = \frac{\alpha}{\gamma^3}$):

$$\frac{d\gamma}{dx} = \gamma^3\frac{dx}{c^2dt}\cdot\frac{dv}{dx} = \gamma^3\frac{dv}{c^2dt} = \gamma^3\frac{a}{c^2} = \frac{\alpha}{c^2}.$$

Again using (8.7)-i ($\frac{dv}{dt} = \frac{\alpha}{\gamma^3}$), the chain rule[16] and Leibnitz' rule[17] for a product's derivative yields (since $\frac{dx}{dt} = v$):

$$\frac{d(v\gamma)}{dt} = \frac{dx}{dt}\frac{d(v\gamma)}{dx} = \frac{v^2 d\gamma}{dx} + \frac{v\gamma dv}{dx}\cdot\frac{dt}{dt} = \frac{v^2\alpha}{c^2} + \frac{v\gamma}{v}\frac{dv}{dt} = \frac{v^2\alpha}{c^2} + \frac{\alpha}{\gamma^2} = \alpha\left(\frac{v^2}{c^2} + 1 - \frac{v^2}{c^2}\right) = \alpha.$$

8.8.

THE 'APOCALYPTIC' DYNAMICS IDENTITIES: $\quad \alpha = \dfrac{d(v\gamma)}{dt} = c^2\dfrac{d\gamma}{dx}.$

Own-acceleration α thus equals a nonaccelerating home frame observer's own-time-rated perception of the changing rocket's $v\gamma$ product i.e. $d(v\gamma)/dt$, as well as the same observer's own-distance-rated perception of the changing rocket's γ value i.e. $d\gamma/dx$—scaled by c^2.

These highly useful relationships will be applied in the next chapter which starts by addressing serious confusions widespread in relativity literature regarding anachronous but still extant conceptions of momentum and force.

9
Diversifying momentum and force

UPGRADING NEWTON'S 'LAWS'

> " ..after leaving the arm of the thrower, the projectile would be moved by an impetus given to it by the thrower and would continue to be moved as long as the impetus remained stronger than the resistance, and would be of infinite duration were it not diminished and corrupted by a contrary force resisting it or by something inclining it to a contrary motion."

Jean Buridan's 14th century formulation of Newton's 1st law of motion

TIME, ACCORDING TO THE ROMAN CHURCH'S FOURTH LATERAN COUNCIL IN 1215, HAD A BEGINNING. Inspired by this theological aspect, French philosopher *Jean Buridan*[1] in the 14th century challenged Aristotelian dynamics by asserting that at the onset of time celestial bodies were divinely endowed with 'IMPETUS' and their motions permanently conserved 'in regions without friction'. That moving bodies are *not* continually pushed by external influence, had in fact already been propounded in the 6th century by Alexandrian philosopher *Johannes Philoponos*.

Buridan's impetus, the product of an object's so-called 'mass' and its velocity as perceived by a relatively moving observer, was also well understood both by Galileo and Descartes.[2,3] *Isaac Newton*, in his 1687 *Principia* treatise on celestial mechanics, called this 'MOMENTUM' and epitomised it in a 'first law of motion': *Every body persists in its state of being at rest or of moving uniformly straight forward, except insofar as it is compelled to change its state by force impressed.*

Note: To avoid having to take gravitational influences into account, we restrict our considerations to small objects of minimal mass which have negligible gravity pull on one another.

Figure 9.1: Jean Buridan, French philosopher 1295-1356

[1] Occam's pupil at the Paris Sorbonne University—and its later rector.

[2] Many historical details are provided in a formidable work by:

[3] James Cushing. *Philosophical Concepts in Physics*. Cambridge University Press, 1998

©BCS IRELAND 2017 ISBN 978-1-9998410-1-0
Brian Coleman SPACETIME FUNDAMENTALS INTELLIGIBLY (RE)LEARNT

9.1 Classical momentum and classical force

9.1.

$$\text{CLASSICAL MOMENTUM} \qquad \mathfrak{P} \triangleq mv = m\frac{dx}{dt}.$$

[4]Newton's 'second law of motion', *force equals mass by acceleration* DEFINES *an arbitrary cause*—force in terms of *its quantitative effect*—a change in an object's velocity i.e. its momentum. Incidentally, this important statement attains the status of a principle[5] *only* in conjunction with his epochal gravitation law. Although 'obvious', this fact is actually rarely clarified in physics literature.

9.2.

$$\text{CLASSICAL FORCE} \qquad \mathfrak{F} \triangleq \frac{d\mathfrak{P}}{dt} \triangleq m\frac{dv}{dt} = ma.$$

9.2 Dropping the 'relativistic mass' oxymoron

Apart from his ballistics insights, the Paris mediæval philosopher is best known for his *Buridan's ass parody*: a donkey standing between two bales of hay and, unable to make up its mind which to choose, starves to death. The relativity bale much of the literature has turned to is called the 'relativistic mass' approach. Adopting the above classical concepts of momentum and force, this path introduces what is actually a fatally confusing idea called *varying* 'relativistic mass'—"*a historical artefact still causing pandemic confusion in special relativity dynamics*"[6,7] and enshrined in the expedient but misleading aphorism "*mass increases with velocity*". Notwithstanding its iconic status in the entrenched $E = Mc^2$ formula, Einstein himself highlighted the inappropriateness of the 'relativistic mass' concept in a 1948 letter to Lincoln Barnett:

> "It is not good to talk of the mass $M = m/\sqrt{1 - v^2/c^2}$ of a moving body, since no clear definition can be given for M. One should use only the rest mass [m]."

To this one might add a rhetorical question similar to the one posed in the *Meaninglessness of the present tense in relativity* section on page 34:

> Is there a 'preferred' observer among relatively moving observers, who decides how a relatively moving mass itself is 'increased' ?

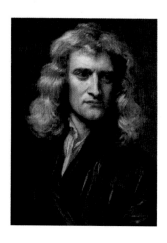

Figure 9.2: Isaac Newton, English scientist 1643-1727

[4] We use 𝕲𝔬𝔱𝔥𝔦𝔠 font to denote 'classical' momentum and force parameters.

[5] A straightforward combining of a cause—such as *gravity*, with an effect—*acceleration*.

[6] Lev Okun. *Energy and Mass in Relativity Theory*. World Scientific, 2009

[7] Gary Oas. On the Use of Relativistic Mass in Various Published Works, 2008

To resolve the matter we turn to a different bale of hay by retaining the classical puristic concept of an object's *unchanging* own-mass m as perceived in its own current reference frame but, on the other hand, *diversifying* Buridan's elementary concepts of momentum and force.

9.3   *Momentum diversified—spatial and temporal*

Mindful of relativistic movement's velocity/chronosity nature, we divide momentum into two categories—SPATIAL and TEMPORAL.

9.3.

$$\text{SPATIAL MOMENTUM} \quad p \triangleq m\frac{dx}{d\tau}\bigg|_{\Delta\chi=0} = m\frac{dx}{dt}\cdot\frac{dt}{d\tau}\bigg|_{\Delta\chi=0} = mv\gamma.$$

Spatial momentum $m.dx/d\tau = mv\gamma$ is thus *defined* as being proportional to an arbitrary observer-perceived distance change (Δx)[8] rated not by observer-own-time (Δt), but by particle (object) own-time $(\Delta\tau)$. Dimensionally the same as classical momentum $\mathfrak{P} \triangleq mv = m.dx/dt$, it differs from it by the velocity-dependent time dilation factor $\frac{dt}{d\tau}\big|_{\Delta\chi=0} = \gamma$ (page 64's equation (8.5)).

9.4.

$$\text{TEMPORAL MOMENTUM} \quad q \triangleq m\frac{dt}{d\tau}\bigg|_{\Delta\chi=0} = m\gamma.$$

Temporal momentum we define as own-mass m multiplied by a 't-direction' '*speed of time*' $dt/d\tau$—a natural spatio-temporal 'complement' of spatial momentum $m.dx/d\tau$. Object own-time τ is the rating time in this case also. Notably, our temporal momentum $m\gamma$ is *equivalent* to none other than what we have just denigrated as an oxymoron—'*relativistic mass*'—in itself a very important concept which however has drastically needed relabelling.

9.4   *Force diversified—object-frame and observer-frame*

We denote as[9] $\Phi = m\alpha$ the object's *own-acceleration* times its mass i.e. *the force manifest in its 'own' co-moving reference frame $\underline{C}$*. If a nonaccelerating arbitrary reference frame $\underline{A}$ and the object's comoving frame $\underline{C}$ were identical (v then being zero and γ one), applied relativistic force Φ and classical force $\mathfrak{F} = ma$ would be the same. So we focus on the application of force *from the perspective of an observer in the comoving frame of the object itself*. The object's own-momentum then is zero but, if subject to an applied force, its *rate of change of momentum*[10] will be nonzero.

[9] Greek upper case *Phi*.

[10] For an accelerating rocket forces Φ and $\mathfrak{F}$ *differ* (as do t and τ), except at its launching.

9.5.

$$\text{OBJECT-FRAME FORCE}\quad \Phi \triangleq m \cdot \alpha = m \cdot \frac{d^2\chi}{d\tau^2}\bigg|_{\Delta x = 0} = m \cdot \frac{dv}{d\tau}\bigg|_{\Delta x = 0}.$$

'Also Spuke Zerothruster'

[11,12]We now consider such a scenario from the 'zero thrust' (nonaccelerating) observer reference frame viewpoint. The system includes ubiquitous observers in the arbitrary reference frame $\underline{A}$, a single particle ('point object') having a fixed own-mass m and initially moving at velocity v in frame $\underline{A}$, and something abstract we call the 'observers' agent'. [13]Acting in some way the details of which we need *not* be concerned about, our arbitrary observer's agent brings to bear in frame $\underline{A}$ a force F on mass m as it proceeds along a miniscule distance Δx in that frame.

Taking account that *energy* has the dimensions of *force multiplied by distance*,[14] we may say that the agent thereby 'imparts' what we <u>define</u> as a KINETIC ENERGY INCREMENT $\Delta K \triangleq F \cdot \Delta x$ to the particle. Since *its application is maintained over observer-rated distance* Δx, we arrive, as $\Delta x \to 0$, at the DEFINITION:

9.6.

$$\text{OBSERVER-FRAME FORCE}\quad F \triangleq \frac{dK}{dx}.$$

Newton's 3rd law 'upgraded'

As stated by Newton (after whom the unit of force is named):[15]

'To every action there is always opposed an equal reaction: the mutual actions of two bodies upon each other are always equal, and directed to contrary parts.'

This fundamental principle's role in relativity is generally misunderstood and mistreated in the literature—as in (page 31)[16]: *"In general,* ACTIO=REACTIO *no longer holds, which makes the treatment of interacting bodies much more difficult."*, or in[17]: *"Logical as the third law is, there is a loophole in it..."*.

Ironically the matter is quite easily resolved by adopting—as an initial hypothesis $P1$—an 'upgraded' formulation of Newton's principle:

---

[11] Relativity enthusiast *James Joyce's* allusion to relativity, parodying *Friedrich Nietzsche's* classic *'Also Sprach Zarathustra'* (an ancient Persian philosopher).

[12] James Joyce. *Finnegans Wake.* Faber and Faber, 1939

[13] Mechanical force deployment may be manifest in a body's own reference frame (e.g. a rocket accelerated by fuelled exhaust propulsion) or in an 'observer' spacetime frame e.g. a ball struck by a golf club undergoing during an even brief period of 'contact' quite complex changes of force and speed because of its own ever changing ('co-moving') reference frame. We deliberately avoid discussing non-mechanical phenomena such as electromagnetic forces which are beyond the scope of the book— and not directly needed for our purposes.

[14] One *joule* of energy would be required to lift a weight of 1 kilogram using a force over a distance upwards of 1 meter.

[15] If applied to a one kilogram mass object over a period of one second, *one newton of force* increases the object's relative speed by a further one meter per second.

[16] Hans Stephani. *An Introduction to Special and General Relativity.* Cambridge U.P. Cambridge U.P., 3rd edition, 2004

[17] Bernard Schulz. *Gravity from the ground up.* Cambridge University Press, 2003

9.7.

P1: Observer-frame applied force F equals object-frame experienced force Φ.

To every action there is always an equal and opposite reaction whereby the forces of two bodies on each other, <u>as viewed respectively in</u> their <u>separate spacetime frames</u>, are always equal and oppositely directed.

Since separate *observer frame* and *observed object frame* are involved, we need merely say *reactions* i.e. *force manifestations* in the two spacetime frames ARE SYMMETRICALLY EQUAL. No 'loophole' is involved and the earlier cited 'presentism' mindset assertion on this topic: *"…ideas of momentum conservation fail [in relativity]…[the correct equations] must be guessed."*[18], is unwarranted.

The four forces of the apocalyptic identities

Finally, apocalyptic identities (8.8) relating α to v, γ and home frame parameters x and t, when applied to our hypothetical principle $P1$, permit a point object's relativistic force to be made manifest in four different ways:

1. OBJECT-FRAME EXPERIENCED FORCE $m\frac{dv}{d\tau}$,

2. OBSERVER TIME-RATED SPATIAL MOMENTUM CHANGE $m\frac{d(v\gamma)}{dt}$,

3. OBSERVER SPACE-RATED TEMPORAL MOMENTUM CHANGE $mc^2\frac{d\gamma}{dx}$,

4. OBSERVER-FRAME EXPERIENCED FORCE $\frac{dK}{dx}$.

9.8.

FOUR RELATIVISTIC FORCE FORMS

$$\left\{ \Phi \triangleq m\cdot\alpha \equiv m\frac{dv}{d\tau} \right\} \equiv \left\{ m\frac{d(v\gamma)}{dt} \triangleq \frac{dp}{dt} \right\} \equiv \left\{ mc^2\frac{d\gamma}{dx} \triangleq c^2\frac{dq}{dx} \right\} = \left\{ \frac{dK}{dx} \triangleq F \right\}.$$

All of these relationships are either *definitions* ($\triangleq$) or *identities* ($\equiv$) except for the single $=$ sign on the right side which results from our $P1$ hypothesised principle $\Phi = F$. This chain of interrelationships enables us to deduce in the next chapter a further four principles of relativity dynamics which are *mutually equivalent*.

10

The $E = m\gamma c^2$ *pentagon*

FIVE WAYS TO THE *correct* ICONIC EQUATION

"Conservation of energy... leads by virtue of little appreciated identities in a one-dimensional context to equality of particle-frame and 'equivalent' observer-frame forces (Newton's third law of motion relativistically 'upgraded'), to conservation of 'spatial momentum', to conservation of 'temporal momentum' (so-called 'relativistic mass') and to kinetic energy formula $K = mc^2(\gamma - 1)$. As easily shown, postulating any one of these five principles validates all the others." European Journal of Physics B.C. 2006

10.1 *Kinetic energy—imparted and acquired*

[1]Multiplying relativistic force equations (9.8) across by a miniscule observer frame distance Δx produces an expression for the imparted kinetic energy increment[2] referred to the the previous chapter.

[1] B.C. A five-fold equivalence in special relativity one-dimensional dynamics. *European Journal of Physics*, 27:983–984, 2006

[2] The term 'work' is commonly used to denote what we are referring to as 'imparted energy'.

10.1.

KINETIC ENERGY INCREMENT FORMULA

$$\text{as } \Delta x \to 0 : \qquad \Delta K = F \cdot \Delta x = \Phi \cdot \Delta x = m\frac{c^2 d\gamma}{dx} \cdot \Delta x.$$

This yields a second principle $P2$ for the total kinetic energy imparted to an object from its rest state in the arbitrary observer reference frame:

10.2.

P2: KINETIC ENERGY IN AN ARBITRARY INERTIAL FRAME $\underline{A}$

$$K = \int_{v=0}^{v=v} F \cdot dx = \int_{v=0}^{v=v} c^2 m \, d\gamma = mc^2\gamma - mc^2.$$

Kinetic energy imparted to a body thus equals its *gain* in *temporal momentum* $m(\gamma - 1)$ scaled by c^2, a product which has the same dimensions of energy. This constitutes a further key principle P3:

10.3.

P3: IN EVERY CLOSED SYSTEM, ENERGY IS CONSERVED

Energy accumulated over any set period of time may be quantitatively defined as the integral product of our observer-manifest force and the observer's reference frame distance along which such force was maintained. Naturally we have assumed that all the energy imparted to the particle contributes to its ongoing acceleration ($\Rightarrow$ the subsequent *Non-elastic collisions section).

Nuclear energy

A rearrangement of kinetic energy equation (10.2) prompts us to refer to a body's temporal momentum (scaled by c^2) as:

10.4.

TOTAL ENERGY IN ARBITRARY INERTIAL FRAME $\underline{A}$

$$E \triangleq qc^2 = m\gamma c^2 = \frac{mc^2}{\sqrt{1 - v^2/c^2}} = K + mc^2.$$

Any 'transmutation' of an object causing its mass to be reduced by (say) factor Δm, would be equivalent to an energy increment $\Delta m.c^2$ being 'released' in some other form such as kinetic energy. This is the basis of nuclear power generation and the principle behind the destructive power of nuclear bombs.

Cosmic boundary speed limitation

A further core insight emerges from equation (10.2). For a mass object's velocity v to approach limit speed c when factor $\gamma = 1/\sqrt{1 - v^2/c^2}$ tends towards infinity, *an infinite amount of kinetic energy would be required.*

ENERGY LIMITATION PREVENTS MASS OBJECTS FROM EVER ATTAINING THE COSMIC LIMIT SPEED IN ANY INERTIAL FRAME.

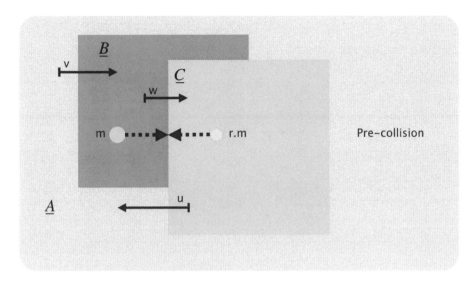

10.2   *Some thermodynamics*

Let us imagine two particles of *fixed* mass $m_1 = m$ and $m_2 = r.m$ heading for an elastic collision, as schematically illustrated in Figure 10.1. The cyclic velocities of an observer in an arbitrary observer frame $\underline{A}$ and the particle frames $\underline{B}$ and $\underline{C}$ are v, w and u respectfully (the initial inter-particle relative cyclic velocity w actually having a *negative* value from right to left—as does cyclic velocity u.). In frame $\underline{A}$ the two particles' spatial (p) and temporal (q) momenta are:

$$p_1 = mv\gamma_v, \qquad p_2 = -rmu\gamma_u, \qquad q_1 = m\gamma_v \qquad and \qquad q_2 = rm\gamma_u. \quad (10.5)$$

[3]We define an ELASTIC COLLISION as one where THE RELATIVE VELOCITY w BETWEEN THE PARTICLES MERELY CHANGES DIRECTION on collision. Post-collision particle frames are $\underline{B}'$ and $\underline{C}'$.[4] For an elastic collision:

$$W = -w \qquad and \qquad \gamma_W = \gamma_w. \quad (10.6)$$

Moreover, m_1's applied force on particle m_2 is in the opposite direction to m_2's applied force on particle m_1. Likewise m_1's experienced force due to particle m_2 is in the opposite direction to m_2's experienced force due to particle m_1.[5] Hence from frames force principle P1 (9.7), $m_1\alpha_1 = -m_2\alpha_2$. So using (9.8):

10.7.

COLLISON PARTICLES FORCE RELATIONSHIPS

$$\left\{ \Phi_1 = \frac{dp_1}{dt} \equiv \frac{c^2 dq_1}{dx} = m_1\alpha_1 \right\} = -\left\{ \Phi_2 = \frac{dp_2}{dt} \equiv \frac{c^2 dq_2}{dx} = m_2\alpha_2 \right\}.$$

We recall that arrows in our schematic diagrams indicate the velocity of the reference frame containing the arrow head—the observed reference frame, as perceived by the reference frame containing the arrow tail—the observer reference frame. (For a negative velocity actual movement is in the direction opposite to that of the arrow's.).

[3] m_2 initially has velocity $-u$ in reference frame $\underline{A}$.

[4] We denote pre-collision values in *lower case* and post-collision values in *upper case*.

[5] This actually constitutes Newton's 3rd law—considered separately for each particle *but in respective reference frames*.

Figure 10.2: Postcollision reference
frames and relative velocities

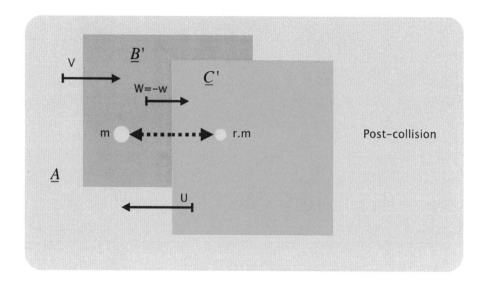

Relationships (10.7) immediately yield two further principles:

$$\frac{dp_1}{dt} = \frac{-dp_2}{dt} \ \ i.e. \ \ \int dp_1 + \int dp_2 = \int 0 \cdot dt = 0 \ \ hence \ \ (P_1 - p_1) + (P_2 - p_2) = 0.$$

10.8.

P4: ARBITRARY FRAME SPATIAL MOMENTUM SUM IS CONSERVED: $P_1 + P_2 = p_1 + p_2$.

From any observer's standpoint, spatial momentum gained by one particle
during an elastic collision, is balanced by the other particle' spatial momentum loss. Furthermore

$$\frac{dq_1}{dx} = \frac{-dq_2}{dx} \ \ i.e. \ \ \int dq_1 + \int dq_2 = \int 0 \cdot dx = 0, \ \ then \ \ Q_1 - q_1 = -(Q_2 - q_2).$$

10.9.

P5: ARBITRARY FRAME TEMPORAL MOMENTUM SUM IS CONSERVED: $Q_1 + Q_2 = q_1 + q_2$.

Likewise from any observer's standpoint, scaled temporal momentum—*energy*—
gained by one particle during an elastic collision is offset by the other particle's
temporal momentum loss.

10.3 *A five-fold equivalence

Significantly, as already pointed out in the author's 2006 EJP paper, any one
of the previous chapters principles P1, P2 and P3 could ALONE have been
adopted initially as a hypothesis from which the other two directly follow.
In other words, *principles* P1, P2 *and* P3 *are equivalent.* Clearly either P4 or
P5 could likewise be adopted as an starting hypothesis (instead of P1), and
would have led to principles P1, P2 and P3 *as consequences.*

10.10.

RELATIVITY DYNAMICS PENTAGONAL EQUIVALENCES

ALL FIVE PRINCIPLES P1 - P5—RELATIVISTIC FORCES EQUALITY, KINETIC

ENERGY FORMULA, ENERGY CONSERVATION, SPATIAL MOMENTUM

CONSERVATION AND TEMPORAL MOMENTUM CONSERVATION—

ARE *equivalent* I.E. EITHER THEY ARE ALL TRUE OR THEY ARE ALL FALSE.

10.4 *Non-elastic collisions

Our collision scenario has assumed that particle objects absorb no heat energy
during collision i.e. all imparted energy contributes to the particles' movement
changes. For such ideal 'elastic' collisions, all kinetic energy relative to an observer is reflected in the individual particles' *external* motion. On the other
hand, if two bodies are considered as a collection of individual subparticles
(e.g. *molecules*), then after an *inelastic* collision some of the energy would be
converted into heat. The resulting *internal movement energy* in nonelastic collisions still leaves the total spatial and the total temporal momenta unchanged
in every observer reference frame however. No energy is lost. The internal
heat is simply a manifestation of the particle molecules bouncing about faster.

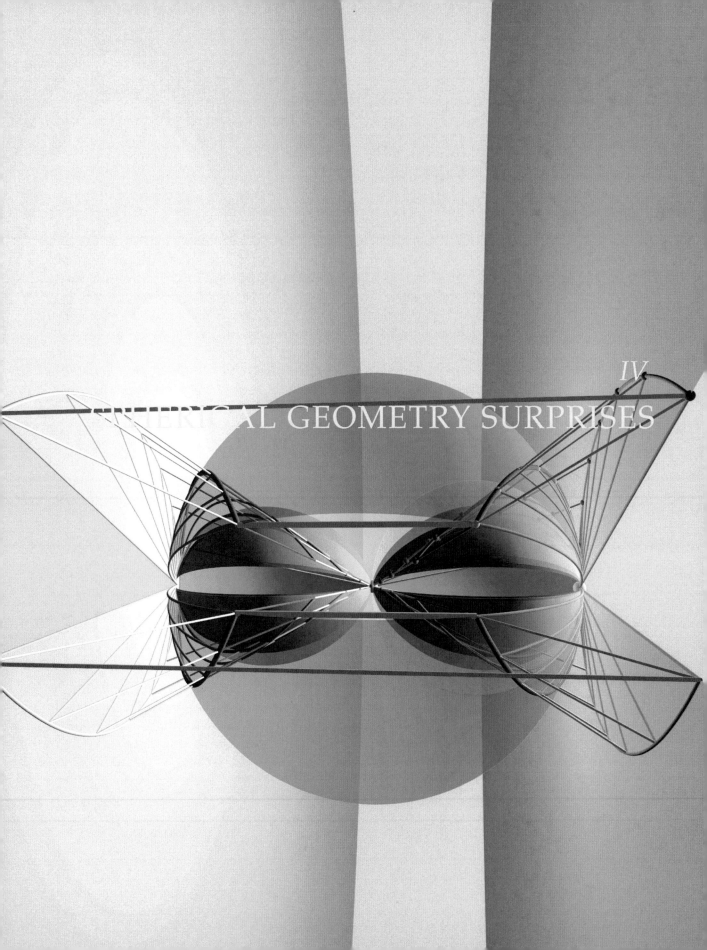

IV

SPHERICAL GEOMETRY SURPRISES

Overleaf: An 'ovoid twins' time travel framework

[6] http://www.fisica.net/relatividade/ the_non_euclidean_style_of_ minkowskian_relativity_by_ scott_walter.pdf.

[7] Arnold Sommerfeld. Über die Zusammensetzung der Geschwindigkeiten in der Relativitätstheorie (On the composition of velocities in relativity theory). *Physikalische Zeitschrift*, 10: 826–829, 1909

[8] Walter's discussion also mentions 1912/13 papers by *Emil Borel* referring to Sommerfeld's *'pseudo-spherique triangle'*.

[9] To the best of the present author's knowledge.

[10] Later in *Part VI*'s chapters 17 and 18, one or more accelerating 'increments' may have differing α values which however remain fixed for each respective increment.

[11] For a series of unforeseen reasons, this extraordinary fact has been kept *'waiting in the wings'* until this present book's publication.

Historical context on usage of spherical trigonometry in relativity has fairly recently been provided in a web essay by *Scott Walter*[6] who refers to a 1909 paper of *Arnold Sommerfeld*, a colleague of Einstein ($\Rightarrow$1911 Solvay Conference Figure 2 photo on page 4), entitled *On the composition of velocities in relativity theory*.[7] The Munich based physicist's paper described velocity relationships in three spatial dimensions but involved *imaginary* angles whose *tan* represented relative velocities rather than their *sine*.[8] By an odd series of academic oversights however, *a far more direct application of spherical triangles to relativity theory* has so far—to all appearances—been entirely absent from the literature.[9]

The unit thrust rocket chapter deals with a single accelerating object such as a rocket, whose own-thrust i.e. its self-perceived acceleration α is *constant*, with time and distance values being scaled so that α *equals one*.[10] Using The primary acceleration relationships of the previous part's opening chapter, simple calculus then yields a whole series of parameters all directly relating to the scaled velocity/chronosity *velchronos* angle which emerged in chapter 3.

The Relativity's real spherical triangles chapter then shows how A VARIANT OF THE BASIC SPHERICAL TRIANGLES COSINES LAW EPITOMISES RELATIVISTIC VELOCITY COMPOSITION—as the present author was most surprised to discover in 2004.[11] The Spacetime's and Geometry's missing 'HEMIX' chapter then introduces a unique three dimensional spiral curve which geometrically epitomises the relationship between a unit-thrust rocket's own-time τ and its scaled velocity v.

Finally a comprehensive model of a rocket's round trip time travel itinerary is then presented in the chapter A Spacetime Odyssey, where *seventeen* parameters of a rocket's return time travel journey can be portrayed together as part of a *single* geometric model. An *offshoot* of this same geometry forms the basis for the book's later final *Part VII* for an *extended* accelerating object.

11
The unit thrust rocket

"Experience entitles us to assume that Nature is the implementation of what is conceivable as the mathematically simplest. I
am convinced that purely by mathematical
means we may find those concepts and logical interrelationships which provide the key
to understanding natural phenomena."
Albert Einstein   Oxford 1933.

"Nach unserer bisherigen Erfahrung sind wir nämlich zu
dem Vertrauen berechtigt, daß die Natur die Realisierung
des mathematisch denkbar Einfachsten ist.   Durch rein
mathematischen Konstruktion vermögen wir nach meiner
Überzeugung, diejenigen Begriffe und diejenigen geset-
zlichen Verknüpfungen zwischen ihnen zu finden, die den
Schlüssel für das Verstehen der Naturerscheinungen liefern."
Herbert Spencer Lecture

[1]If an 'object' such as a rocket maintains *constant* own-acceleration α, in addition to primary relativistic acceleration equations (8.7) a remarkable series
of further direct interrelationships between acceleration parameters emerges.
Moreover, and without loss of generality, the resulting equations can be considerably streamlined by scaling times by α/c and lengths by α/c^2. This reduces all parameters[2] to 'dimensionless' form, and BOTH LIMIT SPEED c
AND THE FIXED OWN-ACCELERATION FACTOR α BECOME *one*. Numerical solutions for any particular acceleration value can then of course be subsequently quantitatively analysed by 'unscaling' time and length values.

FROM NOW ON WE SCALE TIME FOR UNIT LIMIT SPEED AND—IN MOST
CASES—LENGTH[3] FOR UNIT OWN-ACCELERATION.

[1] The briefer term *fixed thrust*
is meant to denote *fixed own-
acceleration* where rocket passengers and the rocket itself
experience unchanging acceleration. A real rocket would need to
continually lessen its actual *engine*
thrust to allow for ever decreasing
fuel mass.
[2] Velocities, which have dimensions of length divided by time,
are then 'scaled' by the factor
$(\alpha/c^2)/(\alpha/c) = 1/c$.

[3] Except in chapters 17 and
18 which deal with non-unit
own-acceleration values.

11.1   Unit own-accleration interrelationships

The velchronos angle differential

To determine how increasing velocity $\frac{dx}{dt} = v = \sin\phi$ (ϕ being the *velchronos* angle and x and t home frame values) relates to rocket own-time[4] τ for unit rocket thrust, we turn to retro-acceleration relationship (8.7)-iii:

[4] which happens to be equivalent to the parameter traditionally known in the literature as 'rapidity'.

$$\beta = \left.\frac{dv}{d\tau}\right|_{\Delta x=0} = 1/\gamma^2 = 1 - v^2 = 1 - \sin^2\phi = \cos^2\phi. \qquad (11.1)$$

[5] using the chain rule.

Since[5] $\cos^2\phi = \frac{dv}{d\tau} = \frac{d\sin\phi}{d\tau} = \cos\phi.\frac{d\phi}{d\tau}$, we immediately obtain a significant uniform acceleration relationship:

11.2.

UNIT ACCELERATION VELCHRONOS ANGLE'S RATE OF CHANGE EQUALS ITS COSINE:

$$\frac{d\phi}{d\tau} = \cos\phi = \frac{1}{\gamma}.$$

Alternately, $\frac{d\tau}{d\phi} = 1/\cos\phi = \gamma$—*the gamma factor equals the velchronos angle rate of change of rocket own-time.*

Velocity as a function of rocket own-time

The reader may be unfamiliar with *the hyperbolic functions* $\sinh\tau = \frac{e^\tau - e^{-\tau}}{2}$, $\cosh\tau = \frac{e^\tau + e^{-\tau}}{2}$ and $\tanh\tau = \frac{e^\tau - e^{-\tau}}{e^\tau + e^{-\tau}} = \frac{\sinh\tau}{\cosh\tau}$. Since $d\frac{\sinh\tau}{d\tau} = d\frac{(e^\tau - e^{-\tau})/2}{d\tau} = \frac{e^\tau + e^{-\tau}}{2} = \cosh\tau$ and $d\frac{\cosh\tau}{d\tau} = d\frac{(e^\tau + e^{-\tau})/2}{d\tau} = \frac{e^\tau - e^{-\tau}}{2} = \sinh\tau$, from *the Leibnitz formula* for differentiating a ratio[6], (11.1)'s relationship $\frac{dv}{d\tau} = 1 - v^2$ solves as:

[6] $\left(\frac{p}{q}\right)' = (qp' - pq')/q^2$ so
$d\frac{\sinh\tau}{\cosh\tau}/d\tau =$
$\frac{\cosh\tau.\cosh\tau - \sin\tau.\sinh\tau}{\cosh^2\tau} =$
$1 - \sinh^2\tau/\cosh^2\tau.$

11.3.

UNIT THRUST ROCKET VELOCITY $\sin\phi = v = \frac{(e^\tau - e^{-\tau})}{(e^\tau + e^{-\tau})} = \tanh\tau.$

[7] Christoph Gudermann. *Theorie der Potential- oder Cyklisch-Hyperbolsichen Funktionen.* Crelle's Journal der Mathematik 6, 7, 8, 9, 1833

[7]This is the unit thrust rocket own-time τ's link to the rocket's momentary *velocity-chronosity angle* ϕ parameter, where velocity $v = \sin\phi$. This relationship is known as the GUDERMANN FUNCTION.

11.4.

THE UNIFORM ACCELERATION VELCHRONOS ANGLE IS
'THE GUDERMANNIAN' OF ROCKET OWN-TIME:

$$\phi = gd(\tau) = arcsin(\tanh \tau).$$

Unit thrust home time and distances

We now turn to the inverse Larmor-Lorentz transformation's derived home frame time dilation formula (8.5) for a *point* object: $\left.\frac{dt}{d\tau}\right|_{\Delta\chi=0} = \gamma.$ [8] Also, using the identity $\cosh^2 \tau - \sinh^2 \tau \equiv 1$ and equation (11.3):

[8] $\cosh^2 \tau - \sinh^2 \tau = (e^\tau + e^{-\tau})^2/4 - (e^\tau - e^{-\tau})^2/4 = 4e^\tau.e^{-\tau}/4 = 1.$

$$\frac{1}{\cos\phi} = \frac{1}{\sqrt{1-v^2}} = \gamma = \frac{1}{\sqrt{1-\tanh^2 \tau}} = \frac{\cosh \tau}{\sqrt{\cosh^2 \tau - \sinh^2 \tau}} = \cosh \tau.$$

$$(11.5)$$

Accordingly we may write for the rocket ($\Delta\chi = 0$):

$$t = \int_0^\tau \gamma.d\tau = \int_0^\tau \cosh \tau.d\tau = \sinh \tau = \tanh \tau.\cosh \tau = v\gamma = \frac{\sin\phi}{\cos\phi} = \tan\phi.$$

$$(11.6)$$

Hence $\tanh \tau = v = \left.\frac{dx}{dt}\right|_{\Delta\chi=0} = \left.\frac{dx}{d\tau}\Big/\frac{dt}{d\tau}\right|_{\Delta\chi=0} = \left.\frac{dx}{d\tau}\right|_{\Delta\chi=0}\Big/\gamma = \left.\frac{dx}{d\tau}\right|_{\Delta\chi=0}\Big/\cosh \tau$

i.e. $$\frac{dx}{d\tau} = \tanh \tau \cosh \tau = \sinh \tau.$$

Therefore $$x = \int_0^\tau \sinh \tau d\tau = \cosh \tau - 1 = \gamma - 1 = \frac{1}{\cos\phi} - 1. \quad (11.7)$$

Also, from (11.5)–(11.6): $1 + t^2 = 1 + \sinh^2 \tau = \cosh^2 \tau = \gamma^2$ i.e.

$$\gamma = \sqrt{1+t^2}. \quad\quad (11.8)$$

Moreover, recalling relationship (8.1), for the rocket's *momentarily* perceived 'retro-distance' $\hat{X}_{RA} = \frac{x_{RA}}{\hat{\gamma}}$, from (11.2):[9]

[9] As $\tau \to \infty$, $\sin\phi \to 1$ and $\cos\phi \to 0$.

11.9.

PERCEIVED RETRO-DISTANCE χ EQUALS VELCHRONOS ANGLE'S VERSED SINE.

$$\chi = \frac{x}{\gamma} = 1 - \frac{1}{\gamma} = 1 - \cos\phi.$$

Therefore even as rocket velocity $v = \sin\phi$ approaches unit limit speed and $\cos\phi$ tends towards zero, A ROCKET'S <u>PERCEIVED</u> RETROSPECTIVE DISTANCE NEVER EVEN REACHES THE VALUE ONE, which corresponds to the *unscaled* value $\frac{c^2}{\alpha}$.

Unit thrust home frame world-lines

[10] Recalling that length scale factor is α/c^2.

[10]Finally, of major significance, (11.6)-iii and (11.7)-ii yield:

11.10.

THE UNIT THRUST HOME FRAME WORLD-LINE EQUATION: $(x+1)^2 - t^2 = 1.$

We also may recall from the Momentum diversified—spatial and temporal section's equations (9.3) and (9.4), that *spatial and temporal momenta equal $mv\gamma$ and $m\gamma$* respectively. Significantly apocalyptic force identities (8.8) for *scaled constant unit acceleration* reduce to one:

$$\frac{d(v\gamma)}{dt} = \frac{d\sinh\tau}{dt} = \frac{dt}{dt} = 1 \quad \text{and} \quad \frac{d\gamma}{dx} = \frac{d(x+1)}{dx} = 1.$$

11.2 A unit thrust courier's multi-spacestation deliveries

The single 'home' reference frame chart

[11] Figure 11.1's chart is a simpler variant of *Hermann Minkowski's* famous 1907 spacetime chart which includes *inwards inclined* axes representing a second reference frame. The latters' distance and time scalings however *differ* from those of the perpendicular home reference frame axes. This book does not use such *asymmetrical* dual reference frame charts. Notably the rocket's x and t values are both *zero* at launch. This is often not the case in textbook Minkowski chart representations which has sometimes resulted in confusion.
[12] This is in contrast to the symmetrical dual frames angle's <u>sine</u> which reflects inter-frame scaled velocity.

[11]Figure 11.1 shows a SINGLE REFERENCE FRAME $x|t$ CHART containing a unit thrust 'courier' rocket's home frame hyperbolic world-line. Also shown are straight world-lines of nonaccelerating spacestations consecutively approaching the rocket from behind, the faster relatively moving spacestations being initially further distant than the slower relatively moving ones. Each spacestation momentarily catches up with the courier rocket in turn, just as the latter's speed relative to the particular spacestation happens to be *momentarily* zero as if to receive a 'bumpless' delivery. Both vehicles then have the same instantaneous home frame scaled velocity $v_i = dx/dt = \tan\theta_i$ [12]as indicated by the corresponding spacestation's straight world-line being at that instant *tangent* to the rocket's world-line hyperbola and at respective angle θ_i to the home frame's horizontal time axis.

The rocket then pulls away in the forwards direction from the supplied spacestation which is subsequently overtaken by stations coming from behind. The increasing home frame delivery time intervals as shown correspond to equal set rocket clock intervals $\Delta\tau$, in accordance with equation (11.6)-iii: $t = \sinh\tau$.

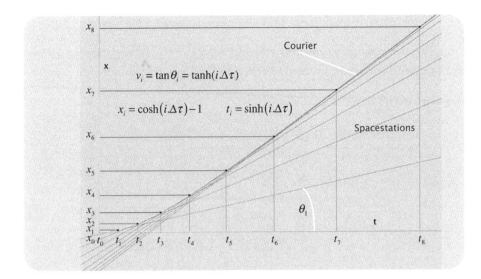

Figure 11.1: Home frame hyperbolic world-line of an accelerating 'courier' rocket and non-accelerating spacestations' straight line tangential world-lines.

Figure 11.2: Multistation deliveries' cascaded dual frames charts with rocket curved world-lines and nonaccelerating spacestation straight line world-line tangents

Staggered dual frame charts

The individual home/spacestations dual reference frames charts—each one resembling that of Figure 8.2—are shown 'staggered' at rocket own-time $\Delta\tau$ intervals in Figure 11.2, where each station's world-line (grey) is parallel to its respective frame's T_i axis (blue) which itself is at a respective velchronos angle ϕ_i angle with the corresponding home frame t_i axis (red) i.e. home frame velocity $v_i = \sin\phi_i$—equation (11.3)-i.

...and from equation 8.6 home frame acceleration relates to an object's own acceleration as $a = \alpha/\gamma^3$...

11.3   *The unit acceleration rocket's equations summarized*

Recalling that times are scaled by α/c and lengths by α/c^2, a unit thrust rocket's parameters can be summarized as follows:

11.11.

UNIT OWN-ACCELERATION VELCHRONOS ANGLE FORMULAE

(*i*) HOME TIME | SPATIAL MOMENTUM $t = \sinh\tau = v\gamma = \tan\phi$,

(*ii*) VELOCITY $v = \tanh\tau = \dfrac{t}{\sqrt{1+t^2}} = \sin\phi$,

(*iii*) DILATION | TEMPORAL MOMENTUM $\gamma \triangleq \dfrac{1}{\sqrt{1-v^2}} = \sqrt{1+t^2} = x+1 = \cosh\tau = \dfrac{1}{\cos\phi}$,

(*iv*) HOME DISTANCE | KINETIC ENERGY $x = \sqrt{1+t^2} - 1 = \cosh\tau - 1 = \gamma - 1 = \dfrac{1}{\cos\phi} - 1$,

(*v*) RETRODISTANCE $\chi = \dfrac{x}{\gamma} = 1 - \dfrac{1}{\gamma} = 1 - \dfrac{1}{\cosh\tau} = 1 - \cos\phi$ ('versed sine'),

(*vi*) HOME ACCELERATION $a = \dfrac{1}{\gamma^3} = \cos^3\phi$,

(*vii*) RETROACCELERATION $\beta = \dfrac{1}{\gamma^2} = \cos^2\phi$,

(*viii*) VELCHRONOS ANGLE CHANGE RATE $\dfrac{d\phi}{d\tau} = \dfrac{1}{\gamma} = \cos\phi$,

(*ix*) ROCKET OWN-TIME $\tau = \tanh^{-1}(\sin\phi)$,

(*x*) VELCHRONOS ANGLE $\phi = gd(\tau) = \arcsin(\tanh\tau)$—THE GUDERMANNIAN FUNCTION,

(*xi*) UNIT THRUST 'APOCALYPTIC IDENTITIES' $\dfrac{d(v\gamma)}{dt} = \dfrac{d\gamma}{dx} = 1$ ($\Rightarrow$ *Equation* (8.8)) and

(*xii*) HOME FRAME HYPERBOLA $(x+1)^2 - t^2 = \cosh^2\tau - \sinh^2\tau \equiv 1$.

The relationships between τ, t, x, χ, v and γ of a point object under unit thrust, are well known in relativity literature. Yet the rocket own-time τ parameter is still anachronistically referred to in textbooks as *'rapidity'*, notwithstanding its simple obvious physical identity. Moreover the velchonos angle ϕ's multifarious role—as will be later made especially evident in chapter 14 A Spacetime Odyssey, seems not to be generally properly appreciated.

12
Relativity's <u>real</u> spherical triangles

In every spherical triangle constructed of great circle arcs, the ratio of the versed sine [one minus the cosine] of any angle [$\hat{\phi}$] to the difference between the versed sine of the side subtending it [ϕ] and the versed sine of the difference of the arcs including it [$\beta - \alpha$], equals the ratio of the square of the whole right sine [1] to the rectangular product of the sines of the arcs around it [$\sin\alpha.\sin\beta$].
REGIOMONTANUS (JOHANNES MÜLLER) 1464

$$\frac{(1-\cos\phi) - (1-\cos(\beta-\alpha))}{(1-\cos\hat{\phi})} = \frac{\sin\alpha\sin\beta}{1}.$$

In omni triangulo sphaerali ex arcubus circulorum magnorum constante, proportio sinus versi anguli cuiuslibet ad differentiam duorum sinuum versorum, quorum unus est lateris cum angulum subtendentis, alius vero differentiae duorum arcuum ipsi angulo circumiacentium est tamquam proportio quadrati sinus recti totius ad id, quod sub sinibus arcuum dicto angulo circupositorum rectangulum.
REGIOMONTANUS   MCDLXIV
De Triangulis Omnimodis - Liber V–II.

Circles on a sphere's surface sharing its centre are called *'great circles'*. Two 'meridian' great circles through a 'north' pole and a laterally crossing third great circle enclose a *spherical triangle* such as *HMN* in Figure 12.2. For a sphere of *unit length radius*, the triangle's surface arc lengths equal their respective *centre angles* α, β, ϕ at the sphere's centre (in *radians*) but *in general* differ from their respectively opposite *surface angles* $\hat{\alpha}, \hat{\beta}$ and $\hat{\phi}$. How they all relate is described by the well known *spherical triangle sines and cosines laws*.

By the turn of the first Millennium a Persian astronomer, who also proved the identity $\sin(a + b) = \sin a\cos b + \sin b\cos a$, had derived the sines law explicitly. This mathematician then introduced two indirect equations for the direction from any location of known (co)latitude and relative longitude to the holy city of Mecca—the QIBLA, as well as its actual distance. These were implicitly equivalent to the cosines law which however did not appear in explicit form until over four centuries later. How spherical triangle sines and cosines laws are used in global navigation is described at the end of this chapter.

Figure 12.1: Abu'l-Wafa Buzjani, 940-998. Persian mathematician after whom a moon crater is named, was born in Torbate Jam, Iran.

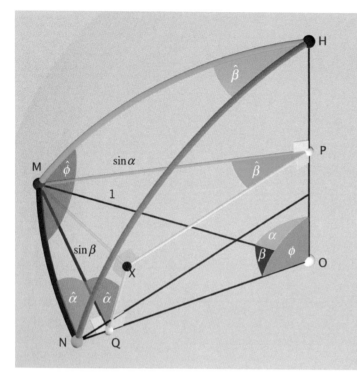

M's shortest distance MX onto plane HON equals the perpendicular $MP = \sin\alpha$ from M to OH, multiplied by the sine of plane MOH's 'door' angle $\hat\beta$ to plane HON. MX also equals the perpendicular $MQ = \sin\beta$ from M to line ON multiplied by the sine of plane MON's 'door' angle $\hat\alpha$ to plane HON:

$$MX = \sin\alpha\sin\hat\beta = \sin\beta\sin\hat\alpha.$$

Similarly: $\sin\alpha\sin\hat\phi = \sin\phi\sin\hat\alpha.$

Hence: $\dfrac{\sin\alpha}{\sin\hat\alpha} = \dfrac{\sin\beta}{\sin\hat\beta} = \dfrac{\sin\phi}{\sin\hat\phi}.$

Spherical triangle sine law proof

Figure 12.2: Spherical triangle sine law proof.

    Right angles are shown in yellow.

12.1   The spherical triangle sines and cosines laws

A simple proof of Abu'l-Wafa's sines law (12.1) is presented in Figure 12.2.

12.1.

SPHERICAL TRIANGLE SINES LAW $\dfrac{\sin\alpha}{\sin\hat\alpha} = \dfrac{\sin\beta}{\sin\hat\beta} = \dfrac{\sin\phi}{\sin\hat\phi}.$

[1] Regiomontanus / Müller Johannes. *De Triangulis Omnimodis - On Triangles of All Kinds.* Published in Nuremberg, 1464/1533

The cosines law proven *explicitly* in 1464, was formulated by [1]German astronomer and mathematician *Regiomontanus* as:

$$\frac{(1 - \cos\phi) - (1 - \cos(\alpha - \beta))}{(1 - \cos\hat\phi)} = \frac{\sin\alpha\sin\beta}{1}. \tag{12.2}$$

[2] Since $\cos(\alpha - \beta) = \cos\alpha\cos\beta + \sin\alpha\sin\beta$, equation (12.2) becomes $1 - \cos\phi - 1 + \cos\alpha\cos\beta + \sin\alpha\sin\beta = \sin\beta\sin\alpha.(1 - \cos\hat\phi)$ which becomes equation (12.3).

[2]This equation invokes the *versed sine* already encountered in the Time travel—the simple twin paradox section 3.5. Its equivalent 'modern' form is proven in Figure 12.3. Spherical triangle sines law (12.1) (directly) and cosines law (12.3) (indirectly) have been used in navigation for over a millennium.

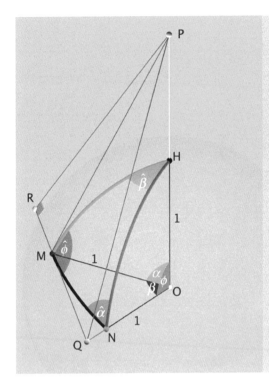

Tangent MP to arc MH meets unit radius OH extended to P. Tangent QR to arc MN meets unit radius ON extended to Q, and is perpendicular to RP. Using Pythagoras' theorem (generalised), PQ equates in triangles POQ and PRQ as:

$$PQ^2 = OP^2 + OQ^2 - 2OP.OQ\cos\phi = \frac{1}{\cos^2\alpha} + \frac{1}{\cos^2\beta} - \frac{2\cos\phi}{\cos\alpha\cos\beta}.$$

$$and \quad PQ^2 = (MQ + MP\cos(\pi - \hat{\phi}))^2 + (MP\sin(\pi - \hat{\phi}))^2$$
$$= MP^2 + MQ^2 - 2MP.MQ\cos\hat{\phi} = \tan^2\alpha + \tan^2\beta - 2\tan\alpha\tan\beta\cos\hat{\phi}.$$

Equating, multiplying by $\cos^2\alpha\cos^2\beta$ *and tidying* :

$$(1 - \sin^2\alpha)\cos^2\beta + (1 - \sin^2\beta)\cos^2\alpha$$
$$= 2\cos\alpha\cos\beta(\cos\phi - \sin\alpha\sin\beta\cos\hat{\phi}).$$

Dividing by $2\cos\alpha\cos\beta\cos\phi$: $\dfrac{\cos\alpha\cos\beta}{\cos\phi} = 1 - \sin\alpha\sin\beta\dfrac{\cos\hat{\phi}}{\cos\phi}$

i.e. $\cos\phi = \cos\alpha\cos\beta + \sin\alpha\sin\beta\cos\hat{\phi}$.

'Modern' proof of the spherical triangle cosine law

Figure 12.3: Spherical triangle cosines law proof

12.3.

SPHERICAL TRIANGLE COSINES LAW

$$\frac{\cos\alpha\cos\beta}{\cos\phi} = 1 - \sin\alpha\sin\beta\left(\frac{\cos\hat{\phi}}{\cos\phi}\right) \qquad i.e.$$

$$\cos\phi = \sin\alpha\sin\beta\cos\hat{\phi} + \cos\alpha\cos\beta$$

Regiomontanus (Johannes Müller von Königsberg).
(Geb. 6. Juni 1436, gest. 6. Juli 1476.)

Figure 12.4: Regiomontanus, German astronomer (Johannes Müller) 1436-1476. Born in Königsberg near Nuremberg.

12.2   Unit sines law ratio spherical triangles

We now consider spherical triangles *where the sine of each surface angle equals that of its opposite centre angle*. A simple case in Figure 12.5 (left) is where $\alpha = \hat{\alpha}$ and $\phi = \hat{\phi}$ are *initially* right angles, and equator arc MN equals centre angle β with pole H's surface angle $\hat{\beta}$ being any *acute* angle.[3] We wish to raise the triangle's β arc upwards from its initial equator position towards the pole point without changing β (and thereby still subtending the same angle β at the centre). This is possible only by *'tilting'* the β arc i.e. increasing angle $\hat{\phi}$ and decreasing angle $\hat{\alpha}$ or vice-versa, as in Figure 12.5 (right side).

[3] i.e. less than a right angle.

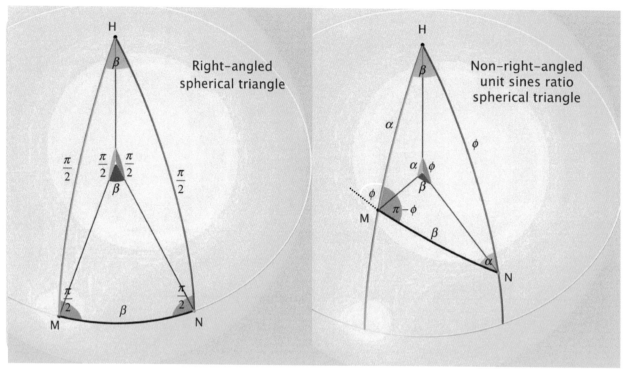

Figure 12.5: Unit sines ratio
spherical triangles

[4] Arc MN, equal to the same
equator segment in length, must be
slanted *sideways*—unless α were *a
right angle*.

[5] $\sin(\pi - \phi) = \sin \pi \cos \phi -
\cos \pi \sin \phi = \sin \phi.$

[6] $\cos(\pi - \phi) = \cos \pi \cos \phi +
\sin \pi \sin \phi = - \cos \phi.$

Hence NO EXCLUSIVELY ACUTE SPHERICAL TRIANGLE CAN HAVE UNIT
SINE RATIO ANGLES. On the other hand, if surface angle $\hat{\phi}$ is *obtuse* (greater
than a right angle) and equal to *the supplement* of acute centre angle ϕ *which
need not be a right angle* i.e. $\hat{\phi} = \pi - \phi$, then, as in Figure 12.6, arc MN will form
an obtuse angle with meridianal arc HM[4] and *a very surprising set of conditions
emerges*. Sine ratio $\sin \hat{\phi} / \sin \phi = \sin(\pi - \phi) / \sin \phi$ [5]remains *plus one*, acute
angle $\alpha = \hat{\alpha}$ and lateral arc segment β equals the likewise acute longitudinal
'door' angle $\hat{\beta}$. This yields what we call A RELATIVITY SPHERICAL TRIAN-
GLE. [6]Ratio $\cos \hat{\phi} / \cos \phi = \cos(\pi - \phi) / \cos \phi$ is now ($\Rightarrow$Figure 12.6) *minus one*
and cosines law (12.3)-i centre angles α, β, ϕ relate as:

$$\frac{\cos \alpha \cos \beta}{\cos \phi} = 1 - \sin \alpha \sin \beta \left(\frac{-\cos \phi}{\cos \phi} \right) = 1 + \sin \alpha \sin \beta. \tag{12.4}$$

The triple gammas velocity formulae

Using gamma factor (3.3) and velocity equation (4.6) ($-u(1 + vw) = v + w$):

$$\frac{\gamma_u^2}{\gamma_w^2 \gamma_v^2} = \frac{(1 - w^2)(1 - v^2)}{1 - u^2} = \frac{1 + (vw)^2 - v^2 + 2vw - 2vw - w^2}{1 - u^2} = \frac{(1 + vw)^2 - (v + w)^2}{1 - u^2} = \frac{(1 + vw)^2 (1 - u^2)}{1 - u^2}.$$

This provides us with an alternative relativistic velocity composition equation:[7]

[7] Since we have chosen v, w and u as *cyclic* velocities, they may be interchanged freely in equation (12.5).

12.5.

THE TRIPLE GAMMAS RELATIONSHIP $\quad \dfrac{\gamma_u}{\gamma_w \gamma_v} = 1 + vw.$

12.3 *Spherical triangles' hitherto missed relativity connection*

[8]Assuming spherical triangle *centre* angles α, β, ϕ are all acute, we substitute $\sin\alpha = v$, $1/\cos\alpha = \gamma_v$, $\sin\beta = w$, $1/\cos\beta = \gamma_w$, $\sin\phi = -u$ and $1/\cos\phi = \gamma_u$ in (12.5). This gives us *unit sines ratio spherical triangles' cosines law* (12.4).

[8] Symbol $\Longleftrightarrow$ means that the equations are *equivalent* i.e. each one implies the other.

12.6.

EVERY UNIT SINES LAW RATIO SPHERICAL TRIANGLE'S CENTRE ANGLES

RELATE AS A TRIPLET OF REFERENCE FRAME SCALED CYCLIC VELOCITIES :

$$\frac{\cos\alpha \cos\beta}{\cos\phi} = 1 + \sin\alpha \sin\beta \qquad\Longleftrightarrow\qquad \frac{\gamma_u}{\gamma_v \gamma_w} = 1 + vw.$$

$$\Updownarrow \qquad\qquad\qquad\qquad \Updownarrow$$

$$\sin\phi = \frac{\sin\alpha + \sin\beta}{1 + \sin\alpha \sin\beta} \qquad\Longleftrightarrow\qquad (-u) = \frac{v + w}{1 + vw}.$$

$$\Updownarrow \qquad\qquad\qquad\qquad \Updownarrow$$

$$\sin\alpha + \sin\beta + (-\sin\phi) + \sin\alpha \sin\beta(-\sin\phi) = 0 \Longleftrightarrow v + w + u + vwu = 0.$$

SPHERICAL GEOMETRY DIRECTLY PORTRAYS SPECIAL RELATIVITY VELOCITY COMPOSITION—AN EXTRAORDINARY HITHERTO UNAPPRECIATED CONNECTION.

The unit sines law ratio condition where $\beta = \hat{\beta}$ may be worded as:

12.7.

THE UNIT RADIUS RELATIVITY SPHERICAL TRIANGLE'S LONGITUDINAL CRITERION: THE CENTRE-SUBTENDED 'LATERAL' ARC LENGTH EQUALS THE OPPOSITE (TOP) SPHERICAL TRIANGLE ANGLE, WHICH IS ALSO ITS LONGITUDINAL DIFFERENCE.

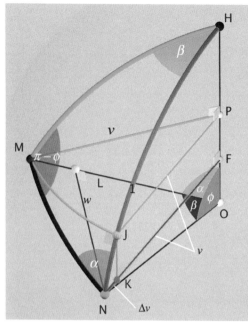

$$\frac{\cos\alpha\cos\beta}{\cos\phi}=1+\sin\alpha\sin\beta \qquad\qquad \frac{\gamma_u}{\gamma_v\gamma_w}=\left(1+\frac{vw}{c^2}\right).$$

Squaring: $(1-\sin^2\alpha)(1-\sin^2\beta)=(1+\sin\alpha\sin\beta)^2(1-\sin^2\phi)$

i.e. $1-\sin^2\alpha-\sin^2\beta+\sin^2\alpha\sin^2\beta$
$$=1+2\sin\alpha\sin\beta+\sin^2\alpha\sin^2\beta-\sin^2\phi(1+\sin\alpha\sin\beta)^2$$

Hence $\sin^2\phi(1+\sin\alpha\sin\beta)^2=\sin^2\alpha+\sin^2\beta+2\sin\alpha\sin\beta$

Therefore $\sin\phi=\dfrac{\sin\alpha+\sin\beta}{1+\sin\alpha\sin\beta}.$ $-u=v+\Delta v=\dfrac{v+w}{1+vw}.$

Relativity velocity composition visualised

Figure 12.6: Velocity addition visualized

Direct portrayals of relativity velocity composition

Figure 12.6's spherical triangle arcs represent *in radians*, angles whose sines respectively equal *scaled* forward velocities v, w and $-u$ in accordance with page 41's section Relativistic velocities of a triplet of reference frames. The triplet reference frame velocities equal the perpendiculars (red, green and blue) from vertices M and N, onto radii OH and OM. Velocity increment Δv is represented by segment NK of the perpendicular to the vertical axis.

12.4   *Relativity spherical triangle volume and area relationships

[9] An observer viewing the tetrahedron's lesser lateral faces as positive ('inside'), would view the greater lateral face HON as negative ('outside').

The area of a triangle with two unit sides equals half its enclosed angle's *sine* e.g $HON = \sin(\phi)/2$ (recalling that $-u = \sin\phi$ is positive). [9]Also the volume of a *tetrahedron* equals a third of any of its four faces' area (e.g. HON) multiplied by the perpendicular from the opposite vertex. Using sines law Figure 12.2's perpendicular equation $MX = \sin\alpha\sin\beta$, we obtain $6V = \sin\alpha\sin\beta\sin\phi = \sin\alpha + \sin\beta - \sin\phi$. Hence from (4.4):

12.8.

A RELATIVITY TETRAHEDRON'S VOLUME EQUALS ONE SIXTH OF THE SUM OF ITS PIVOTED 'SIGNED' AREAS AS WELL AS THEIR PRODUCT.

$6V = \sin\alpha\sin\beta\sin\phi = \sin\alpha + \sin\beta - \sin\phi = v + w + u = vw(-u).$

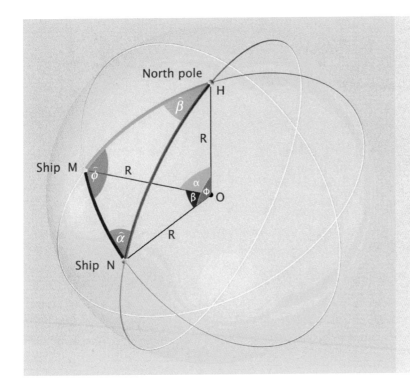

$$\frac{\cos\alpha\cos\phi}{\cos\beta} = 1 - \sin\alpha\sin\phi\frac{\cos\hat\beta}{\cos\beta}$$

Surface distance

$$R\beta = R\arccos\left(\cos\alpha\cos\phi + \sin\alpha\sin\phi\cos\hat\beta\right)$$

Meridianal inclination

$$\hat\alpha = R\arcsin(\sin\alpha\sin\hat\beta / \sin\beta)$$

Cosine law application in marine navigation

Figure 12.7: Determining surface distance between ships

Applying the 17th century *Herriot/Girard* theorem[10] relating the area A of a (unit radius) spherical triangle to the sum of its surface angles, we may write for a relativity spherical triangle's angles:

$$A = \hat\alpha + \hat\beta + \hat\phi - \pi = \alpha + \beta + (\pi - \phi) - \pi.$$

[10] Published in 1626 by *Albert Girard*, this theorem was discovered in 1603 by *Thomas Herriot*, the English astronomer who introduced the potato to Europe.

12.9.

A RELATIVITY SPHERICAL TRIANGLE'S AREA EQUALS THE SUM OF ITS TWO LESSER CENTRE ANGLES MINUS ITS 'COMPOSITE VELOCITY' CENTRE ANGLE: $A = \alpha + \beta - \phi$.

A notable example is a right angled (limit speed) spherical triangle's 'hemilune' area $A = \alpha + \beta - \phi = \pi/2 + \beta - \pi/2 = \beta$. Any velocity of velchron angle β added to a limit velocity of velchron angle $\alpha = \pi/2$, results in the same limit velocity $\phi = \pi/2$.

12.5   *Spherical cosines and sines laws in global navigation*

The cosines law's use in navigation is shown in Figure 12.7 (using equations (12.3) with angles β and ϕ *interchanged*).

12.10.

SPHERICAL TRIANGLE COSINES LAW

$$\frac{\cos\alpha\cos\phi}{\cos\beta} = 1 - \sin\alpha\sin\phi\left(\frac{\cos\hat{\beta}}{\cos\beta}\right) \quad \text{i.e.} \quad \cos\beta = \sin\alpha\sin\phi\cos\hat{\beta} + \cos\alpha\cos\phi.$$

[11] *colatitude* being the angle from the sphere's north pole, as opposed to from the equator—latitude.

Surface distance MN equals Earth's radius times β for known colatitudes α and ϕ, and known longitudinal *difference* angle $\hat{\beta}$:[11]

$$\text{ARC LENGTH MN} = R\beta = R\arccos(\cos\alpha\cos\phi + \sin\alpha\sin\phi\cos\hat{\beta}). \quad (12.11)$$

Viewed from location N, M's *meridianal direction angle* $\hat{\alpha}$ is then also obtainable (having calculated angle β) using sines law (12.1):

$$\text{ARC MN MERIDIANAL INCLINATION } \hat{\alpha} = \arcsin\left(\sin\alpha\sin\hat{\beta}/\sin\beta\right).$$
$$(12.12)$$

Equations (12.11) and (12.12) thus enable two ships' relative distance and their respective directions to be established if their longitude and (co)latitude values are known.

13

Spacetime's and (Geometry's ?) missing 'HEMIX'

'It seems very pretty,' she said when she had finished it, 'but it's rather hard to understand!' (You see she didn't like to confess, ever to herself, that she couldn't make it out at all.) 'Somehow it seems to fill my head with ideas—only I don't exactly know what they are! However, somebody killed something: that's clear, at any rate—' 'But oh!' thought Alice, suddenly jumping up, 'if I don't make haste I shall have to go back through the Looking-Glass, before I've seen what the rest of the house is like!'
THROUGH THE LOOKING GLASS AND WHAT ALICE FOUND THERE   Lewis Carrol 1871

13.1   Cascaded relativity tetrahedra

[1] Two world-lines representing a pair of nonacclerating spacestations relatively moving along a straight line were portrayed in the dual reference frame chart of chapter 7's Figure 7.2. An interesting geometric offshoot of the relativity spherical triangle represents *a triplet* of such spacestations. The 'RELATIVITY TETRAHEDRON' of Figure 13.2 is formed by the connecting lines between the triangles' vertices as well as to the hemisphere's centre, where velchron angles α, β and ϕ are subtended by the respective radial sides which constitute *spacestation world-lines* of three lateral face dual frames charts. It is assumed that as the three spacestations' clocks coincidentally passed a reference point, their respective own-time clocks were synchronised.

Also shown are emitted and reflected radar signal trajectories on each lateral face chart. Notably, by virtue of the Doppler factors relationship (7.3) illustrated in Figure 7.2, the emission radar trajectory across the α chart continues through the β chart and meets up with the ϕ chart emission trajectory. The same applies to the reflection trajectory back across the β chart which continues back across the α chart to meet up with the ϕ chart reflection trajectory.

Figure 13.1: Alice chatting about physics and epistemology

[1] Lewis Carrol (Charles Lutwidge Dodson). *Through the Looking-Glass, and What Alice Found There.* Macmillan London, 1871

Figure 13.2: A relativity tetrahedron's radar trajectories

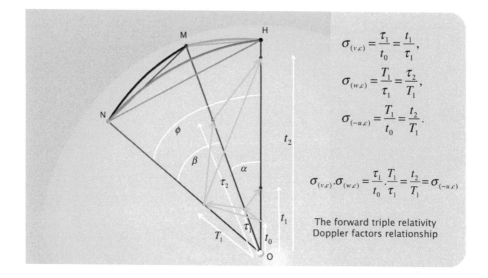

$$\sigma_{(v,c)} = \frac{\tau_1}{t_0} = \frac{t_1}{\tau_1},$$

$$\sigma_{(w,c)} = \frac{T_1}{\tau_1} = \frac{\tau_2}{T_1},$$

$$\sigma_{(-u,c)} = \frac{T_1}{t_0} = \frac{t_2}{T_1}.$$

$$\sigma_{(v,c)} \cdot \sigma_{(w,c)} = \frac{\tau_1}{t_0} \cdot \frac{T_1}{\tau_1} = \frac{t_2}{T_1} = \sigma_{(-u,c)}$$

The forward triple relativity Doppler factors relationship

Figure 13.3: Cascaded relativity triangles/tetrahedra—and their relativity polyhedron

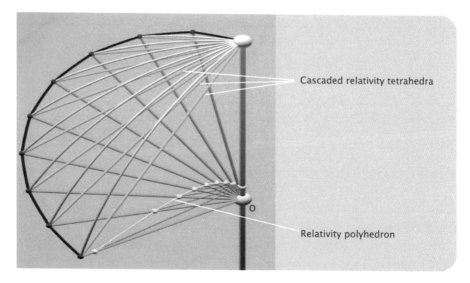

Cascaded relativity tetrahedra

Relativity polyhedron

Figure 13.3 shows 'cascaded' relativity tetrahedra representing consecutive reference frame velocity triplets of spacestations at differing home frame velocities. Here also it is assumed that the spacestations coincidentally passed a home frame reference point together as their clocks were synchronised. In accordance with equation (12.7), the angle between the vertical axis home frame world-line and each spacestation's world-line—the corresponding spherical triangle's arc length—constitutes the respective velchronos angle.

*A relativity Doppler polyhedron

Trajectories of a radar signal emitted from a home frame reference point (subsequent to the spacestations coincidentally passing one another), cross each

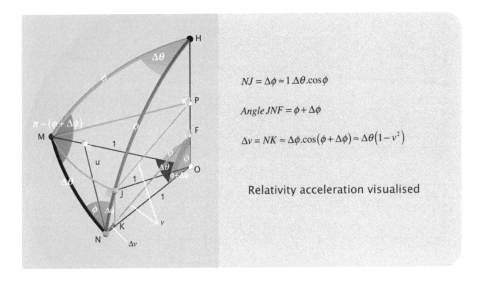

$$NJ = \Delta\phi \approx 1.\Delta\theta.\cos\phi$$

$$Angle\ JNF = \phi + \Delta\phi$$

$$\Delta v = NK \approx \Delta\phi.\cos(\phi + \Delta\phi) \approx \Delta\theta(1 - v^2)$$

Relativity acceleration visualised

dual frames chart face and likewise meet up as described previously. As illustrated, each consecutive pair of inertial spacestations moves at *the same* differential relative velocity. Even if these velocities were to differ however, the geometry would be just as valid and respective radar trajectories would likewise meet together. Particularly notable, at each spherical triangle vertex j, adjacent surface angles are α_j and $\pi - \phi_{j+1} = \pi - \alpha_{j+2}$. Therefore since $\alpha_{j+2} > \alpha_j$ the lateral two arcs join *discontinuously*—except in the limit case of *cascaded differential relativity spherical triangles* we describe next. Likewise notable is the 'RELATIVITY POLYHEDRON' comprising a series of cascaded tetrahedra whose top planar triangle surfaces are formed by respective photon world-lines joined to the radar emission event point on the home frame vertical world-line.

13.2   The differential relativity spherical triangle

The previous chapter's Figure 12.6 centre angles α, β and ϕ we now relabel in Figure 13.4 as a unit thrust rocket's *initial*, *differential* and *final* velchron angles ϕ, $\Delta\theta$ and $\phi + \Delta\phi$ respectively over a miniscule rocket own-time period $\Delta\tau$. Of special interest are *differential spherical triangles* and *incremental tetrahedra* as $\Delta\tau$ and accordingly angles $\Delta\theta$ and $\Delta\phi$ all together tend towards zero.

[2]The rocket's differential velocity Δv is obtained by rotating point M about axis OH through 'door' angle $\Delta\theta$ to point J on arc HJN, and dropping a perpendicular onto point K on perpendicular NKF which equals velocity $v + \Delta v$. From the geometry,[3] the incremental velocity Δv—segment NK—reflects SPHERICAL TRIANGLE ACCELERATION COMPOSITION:

$$\Delta v \approx 1.\Delta\theta \cos\phi \cos(\phi + \Delta\phi) \approx 1.\Delta\theta \cos^2\phi \approx \Delta\theta(1 - v^2). \qquad (13.1)$$

[2] A tangent to arc HJN at vertex N is perpendicular to radius NO. Also line NKF is perpendicular to HO. Hence angles JNK and HON both equal $\phi + \Delta\phi$.

[3] $NJ = MN \cos\phi$,
   $NK = NJ \cos(\phi + \Delta\phi)$ etc.

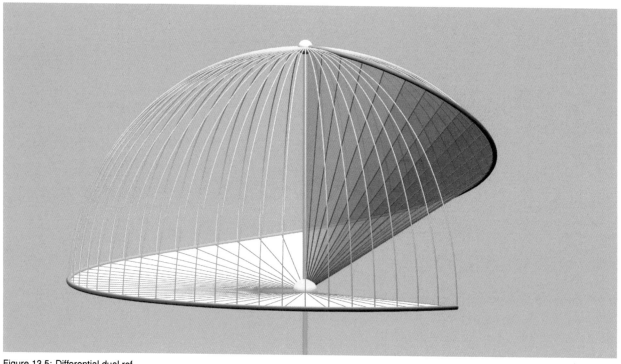

Figure 13.5: Differential dual reference frame charts, velchronos angle arcs and 'tetrahedral serpentine' history-line.

[4] Or just by differentiating velocity equation (11.3) ((11.11)-ii):
$$\frac{dv}{d\tau} = \frac{d\tanh\tau}{d\tau} = \frac{d(\sinh\tau/\cosh\tau)}{d\tau} = \frac{\cosh\tau\cosh\tau - \sinh\tau\sinh\tau}{\cosh^2\tau} = \frac{1}{\cosh^2\tau} = \frac{1}{\gamma^2}.$$

In the limit $\frac{dv}{d\theta} = \cos^2\phi = 1 - v^2 = \frac{1}{\gamma^2}$. This has the same form as The unit thrust rocket chapter's retro-acceleration equation (11.11)-vii established in chapter 8 for arbitrary thrust α:[4]

$$\text{RETRO-ACCELERATION} \qquad \beta = \frac{dv}{d\tau} = \frac{1}{\gamma^2}. \qquad (13.2)$$

13.3.

IN THE LIMIT AS $\Delta\theta$, $\Delta\theta$ AND $\Delta\phi$ TEND TOWARDS ZERO, SPHERICAL TRIANGLES' LATERAL ARC INCREMENT $d\theta$ EXACTLY REPRESENTS A UNIT THRUST ROCKET'S OWN-TIME DIFFERENTIAL $d\tau$.

13.3   *The hemix: a 'transcendental* OWN-HISTORY-LINE'

As angle increments become ever smaller, the number of cascaded reference frames becomes infinite and differential rocket's own-time arc segments share a smooth continuous spherical curve—as in Figure 13.5. Just as where-line and when-line segments of a dual *inertial* reference frames chart reflect time and distance intervals, arc segments of this curve correspond to an individual rocket's clock time intervals over continually changing comoving reference frames. From the unit radius sines laws criterion (12.7), the rocket's accumulated own-clock time $\tau = \int_0^\tau d\tau$ equals the curve's path length as well as its 'swept longitude' i.e. its vertical axis-pivoted 'door' angle. We label this unique curve, which plays a key role in many of the book's remaining chapters,

'THE HEMIX OWN-HISTORY-LINE' and assign it A SPECIAL [5]SYMBOL: $\mathfrak{H}$.

[5] $\mathfrak{H}$'s font is called 'Euclid Fraktur'.

In addition to expressing our unit radius spherical curve parameters in *spherical coordinates* $_{Sph}[1, \theta, \phi]$ where θ is *longitude* and ϕ *colatitude*, we now need to also think in terms of *cylindrical coordinates* $_{Cyl}[r, \theta, z]$ and of course *cartesian coordinates* $[x, y, z]$ (without suffix). The hemix's cylindrical radius coordinate r is also its colatitude's sine i.e. from (11.11)-ii the rocket's momentary velocity $r = \sin\phi = v = \tanh\tau$. Its cylindrical elevation z equals its colatitude's cosine i.e. $z = \cos\phi = 1/\gamma = 1/\cosh\tau$.

13.4.

PROPERTIES OF THE HEMISPHERICAL HEMIX $\mathfrak{H}$

ROCKET OWN-TIME τ EQUALS CURVE PATH LENGTH AND TRAVERSED LONGITUDE θ.

MERIDIANAL INCLINATION EQUALS COLATITUDE ϕ WHERE $\sin\phi = v$.

COLATITUDE ϕ'S RATE OF CHANGE EQUALS ITS COSINE: $\dfrac{d\phi}{d\tau} = \cos\phi = \dfrac{1}{\gamma}$.

The second property results from the curve always meeting a vertical meridian at angle ϕ; the third property corresponds to unit-thrust relationship (11.11)-viii.

Hemix vector coordinates

Later in PARTS VI and *VII* we will require the hemix's *vector coordinates*. Since a unit radius sphere is involved, these are expressed most simply in spherical longitude and colatitude coordinates $\theta = \tau$ and ϕ respectively:

13.5.

HEMIX VECTOR COORDINATES

$$\mathfrak{H} = {}_{Sph}[1, \tau, \phi] = {}_{Cyl}[v, \tau, \frac{1}{\gamma}] = {}_{Cyl}[\tanh\tau, \tau, \frac{1}{\cosh\tau}] = [\tanh\tau\cos\tau, \tanh\tau\sin\tau, \frac{1}{\cosh\tau}].$$

Figure 13.6: Loxodromes of Pedro Nuñes 1502-1578.

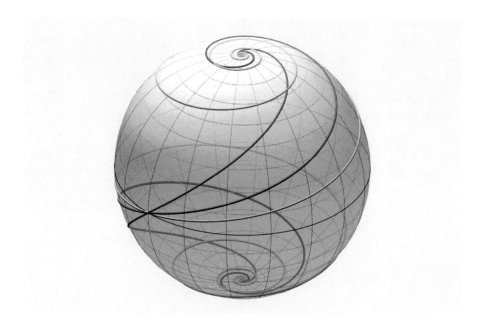

[6] B.C. Bell's twin rockets non-inertial length enigma resolved by real geometry. *Results in Physics*, 7:2575–2581, July 2017

[7] Robert C. Yates. *A Handbook on Curves and their Properties.* J. W. Edwards - Ann Arbor, 1947

[8] T. S. Davies. On the equations of loci traced upon the surface of the sphere, as expressed by spherical co-ordinates. *Transactions of the Royal Society of Edinburgh*, XII: 259–362, 379–428, 1834

[9] http://www.mathcurve.com

Our hemispherical curve has several further equivalent properties which, together with other details of mathematical interest, are described in the author's 2017 paper [6].

Surprisingly, in the literature on curves (known to the present author) such as *Yates* 1947 *Handbook on Curves*[7] or *Davies'* prolonged two-part 1834 treatise[8] on spherical curves, no colatitude-dependent meridianal slope curve is mentioned. The same applies (currently) to the interesting French ENCY-CLOPÉDIE DES FORMES MATHEMATIQUE REMARQUABLES.[9]

13.4 *The hemix's 16th century sibling:* THE LOXODROME

A related spherical curve, discovered in 1537 by Portuguese mathematician *Pedro Nuñes*, is defined by its meridianal inclination not being variable, as with our hemix, but *constant*. The Portuguese used the loxodrome *'rhumb line'* to navigate the oceans—whereby ships remain on a fixed oceanic path just by proceeding at specific fixed angle to the direction of the north pole.

In the next chapter we will use the hemix to portray the relativistic intricacies of an acceleration rocket. Applying this geometry later to an *extended* accelerating medium leads to the solution of the (hitherto) enigmatic *'Bell's string paradox'*.

14

A Spacetime Odyssey

'Ever since St. Augustine [354 - 430], people have wrestled with [time], and there are all sorts of things it isn't. It isn't a flow of something, because what does it flow past? We use time to measure flow. How could we use time to measure time? We are stuck in it, each of us time travels into the future, one year, every year. …It might be that you can build a time machine to go into the future, but not into the past.'
CARL SAGAN author of CONTACT   1986

Each time somebody participates in a casual round trip he or she 'ages' slightly less than stay-at-home persons, although such time 'dilation' ('stretching') is not noticed by the traveller. Stay-at-home people on the other hand, would record the traveller's *own-clock as having ticked more slowly* whereas the latter would observe stay-at-home people as having become relatively older.

In the final section of chapter 3, Mirages of 'length' and time, we considered a spacestation passenger hopping over into the leading compartment of another passing spacestation, and later hopping back again into a tail compartment of his original spacestation. His or her time would be 'dilated' by a factor equal to the versed sine $(1 - \cos \alpha)$ of the spacestations' velchronos angle α. In this chapter we look at a more realistic and less hazardous time travel scenario, a round trip in an accelerating rocket which we can *geometrically portray* in considerable detail with the help of the previous chapter's hemix curve.

©BCS IRELAND 2017 ISBN 978-1-9998410-1-0
Brian Coleman SPACETIME FUNDAMENTALS INTELLIGIBLY (RE)LEARNT

14.1   Time travel ovoidal projections

A coherent ovoids framework

Fixed thrust relationships (11.11) listed on page 86 mostly involve powers of the factor $\cos\phi = 1/\gamma$. With this in mind, we set up a geometric framework of five 'OVOID'[1] surfaces centered about a vertical axis. [2]With ρ_n being the *spherical radius* distance of a point on each ovoid from origin reference point $O = [0,0,0]$, and ϕ as the colatitude velchronos angle, these ovoids are defined by the equation $\rho_n = \cos^n\phi = \gamma^{-n}$ for *ovality factors* $n = -1, 0, 1, 2$ and 3.

[3]As shown in Figure 14.3 (with cutouts for clarity), these are

- unit height 'gamma' plane $z = 1$ i.e. $\rho_{-1} = 1/\cos\phi = \gamma$,

- unit radius hemisphere $\rho_0 = \cos^0\phi = 1$,

- unit diameter 'contraction' sphere $\rho_1 = \cos\phi = \gamma^{-1}$,

- retro-acceleration ovoid $\rho_2 = \cos^2\phi = \gamma^{-2}$ and

- home acceleration ovoid $\rho_3 = \cos^3\phi = \gamma^{-3}$.

Hemix 'distance ray' stereographic projections

Analogous to the well known *Mercator* mapping of our spherical world globe (https://en.wikipedia.org/wiki/List_of_map_projections), we now incorporate our previous chapter's hemix on the unit radius hemisphere and, using a ρ 'DISTANCE RAY' pivoted at the origin O, project this curve onto the other four surface ovoids. Expressed in *cylindrical* coordinates,[4] the hemix curve $\mathfrak{H}$ is $_{Cyl}[v, \tau, 1/\gamma]$ ($\Rightarrow$equations (13.5)), the gamma surface curve G is $_{Cyl}[v\gamma, \tau, 1] = _{Cyl}[t, \tau, 1]$ and the 'contraction' surface curve F is $_{Cyl}[v/\gamma, \tau, 1/\gamma^2]$, all of course having rocket own-time τ as shared longitude and velchron angle ϕ as shared spherical colatitude coordinates.

Seventeen time travel relativistic parameters

For any arbitarary point j on the hemix, the respective projected points on the other surfaces are a, b, f and g. Line jq is a perpendicular onto the vertical axis. As portrayed in Figure 14.3, the following *seventeen* parameters are directly represented in the geometric structure, mostly as functions of the velchronos angle ϕ:

[1] In maths textbooks the term 'ovoid' is used slightly differently.

[2] Greek *rho*.

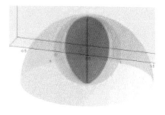

Figure 14.1: Astronomy Ireland 2005 lecture web graphic.

[3] A 'skeleton glimpse' of this hitherto unpublished geometry (deduced in 2004), appeared in a 2005 web announcement of a Dublin lecture on time travel presented by the present author: http://www.inarchive.com/page/2011-08-14/http://www.astronomy.ie/lecture0507.html .

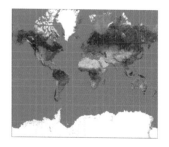

Figure 14.2: Mercator projection. Image uploaded Sept. 2015 to Wikipedia by *Daniel R. Strebe*.

[4] Cylindrical coordinates $[r, \theta, z]$ represent *cylindrical radius*, *longitude angle* and *elevation* respectively.

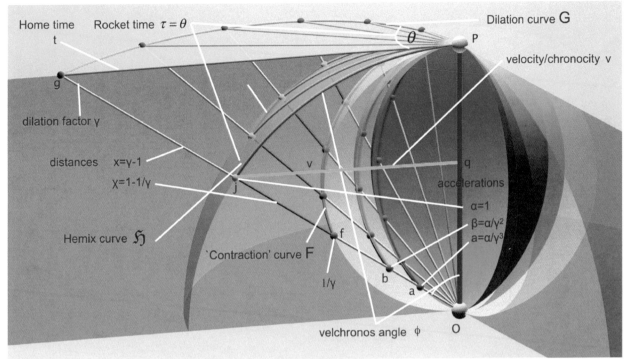

Figure 14.3: Rocket acceleration parameters

[5] Temporal momentum, spatial momentum, total energy and kinetic energy are described in section Momentum diversified—spatial and temporal on page 69, section Kinetic energy—imparted and acquired on page 73, and section Nuclear energy on page 74.

5

- Og: 'Dilation' | temporal momentum | total energy $\gamma = \frac{1}{\cos\phi}$.

- Oj: unit limit speed | unit acceleration | unit mass.

- Of: 'pseudo contraction' factor $\frac{1}{\gamma} = \cos\phi$.

- fj: retro-distance $\chi = 1 - \frac{1}{\gamma} = 1 - \cos\phi$ (versed sine).

- jg: home distance | kinetic energy $x = \gamma - 1 = \frac{1}{\cos\phi} - 1$.

- Ob: retro-acceleration $\beta = \frac{1}{\gamma^2} = \cos^2\phi$.

- Oa: home accleration $a = \frac{1}{\gamma^3} = \cos^3\phi$.

- jq: velocity $v = \sin\phi$.

- Pg: home time | spatial momentum $t = v\gamma = \tan\phi$.

- Hemix arc length Pj: rocket own-time $\tau = gd^{-1}(\phi)$.

- Meridian arc length Pj: velchronos angle ϕ.

- Angle POj: velchronos (velocity/chronocity) angle $\phi = gd(\tau)$.

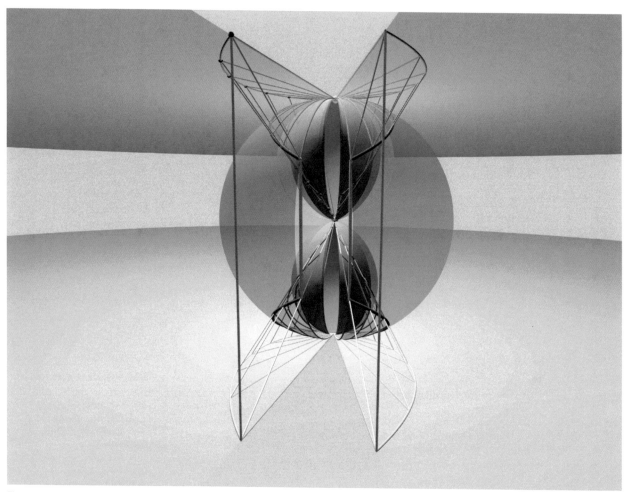

Figure 14.4: A time travel return trip

For a fixed unit own-thrust rocket, its relativistic parameters—scaled velocity/chronosity, dilation and contraction factors, forward and retro accelerations, home and rocket times and distances, spatial and temporal momenta and kinetic and total energies—are elementary functions of velchronos angle ϕ. Accordingly it seems reasonable to argue that this velocity/chronosity VELCHRONOS ANGLE of our symmetrical dual reference frames chart should be the preferred parameter of movement in relativity, rather than 'velocity'.

14.2 *An outgoing and return spacetime itinerary*

Let us consider a unit thrust rocket's 'time travel' return journey. Just as *one quarter* of its fuel is spent and the rocket attains a certain speed, it is caused to 'flip over' so as to reverse thrust. This results in it gradually deaccelerating until it becomes *momentarily* stationary with respect to its launch home frame

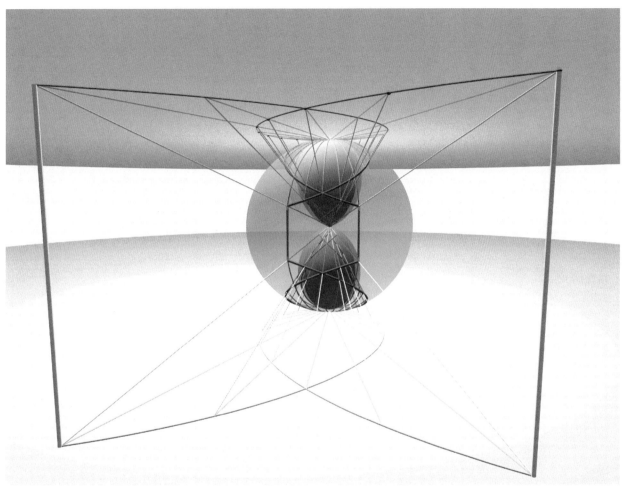

Figure 14.5: A *longer* time travel return trip

location. The rocket immediately then continues to accelerate backwards to-wards the home base until *three quarters* of its fuel is spent. Again it is flipped over—as its reaches its maximum reverse direction speed—and slows down until it arrives at zero relative speed at it original launch location—with all of its fuel exhausted. To portray this odyssey with our spherical geometry, we take the Figure 14.3 hemix graphics ovoidal structure as its first phase, and *horizontally* mirror it to establish an equivalent *final* reverse phase of the rocket's four phase journey. These first and fourth phases are then *vertically* mirrored to produce the second and third phase geometric model parts.

The resulting models in Figures 14.4 and 14.5 each contain an upper and lower 'dilation' plane, two 'contraction' unit diameter spheres and a complete unit radius sphere. The top left hemix starting at the upper pole, stretches to the rocket's maximum forward speed point. Connected by the left verti-cal *'thrust reversal instantaneous tunnel'*, the second bottom left hemix reflects the rocket slowing down until it arrives a point of furthest distance, at zero relative speed. The third phase is that of the bottom right hemix whose end point is also connected through a right vertical *return* thrust reversal tunnel to the upper right hemix which smoothly returns back to the original outward journey point at the top pole.

Each of the hemices is dotted at regular interim periods showing the current velchronos angle arc from the respective pole. The retro- and home distances, as well as the gamma and pseudo-contraction factors, are reflected in the respective 'distance ray' intervals. The rocket time and home time intervals are likewise the same as in the previous Figure 14.3—the respective accumulated hemix path lengths and dilation plane home time radials. Thus this geometric model comprehensively portrays the parameters of a time travel return journey as experienced under constant rocket thrust.

A further surprise is this geometry's crucial role in laying bare the solution to the hitherto unsolved question of *'non-inertial relativistic length'*—the topic of the final book *Part VII* ROLLER-COASTING SPACETIME—an issue which has been intriguing physicists since 1959.

V

AN OCCAM STEEPLECHASE

Overleaf: Orion constellation
Courtesy of NASA

[6] Exceptions being   .

F Sears and R Brehme. *Introduction to Special Relativity*. Addison Wesley, 1968; and Dragan Redžic. Relativistic Length Agony Continued. *Serb. Astron. J.*, 188:55 – 65, 2014

At this point in the book we begin to consider *more than one* accelerating point object. The next chapter 'Time dispersal' and 'retro-separation' focuses on a sparsely hitherto dealt with topic.[6] A pair of rockets launched together when spatially apart, accelerate at a constant unit-thrust rate for a certain period and then suddenly together *cease* to accelerate. This scenario, which somewhat resembles the finale of a steeplechase when horses stop trying to run faster as they arrive at the finishing post, utilises the symmetrical dual frames chart of the Three acceleration perspectives chapter's Figure 8.2.

Two significant parameters are involved: the accelerating rocket duo's ever diverging *own-time clock dissimultaneities* in their ever changing comoving interial frame, and the front rocket's pre-shutdown 'retrospective' separation from rear rocket which is always (except at launch and after the rear rocket's shutdown) *relatively nonstationary* in each such inertial comoving frame. We introduce in this context a possibly hitherto unfamiliar concept: *the 'resynchronisation time gap frame'*.

The Two curious radar intervals chapter portrays home frame chart worldlines which are identical parallel hyperbolae in accordance with page 86's equation (11.11)-xii. One emerging direct insight—wrongly assumed as needing *general relativity*—is that a rocket *permanently* accelerating faster than 1g never sees an event over a light year away (its 'asymptotic horizon'). More surprising no doubt to many is that, as inter-rocket radar trajectories are simple upwards and downwards diagonal lines in accordance with unit scaled limit speed, it becomes immediately apparent that, *in terms of rocket clock intervals*, the radar periods VARY. Oddly, even though these intervals are also easily derived analytically, they are not evident in relativity textbooks[7,8]—an extraordinary ambivalence commented upon somewhat satirically in chapter 16's Evidence unwittingly 'withheld' section.

[7] As already referred to in the book's *Prologue*, most physicists seem still to believe that the limit speed principle also applies for identical fixed acceleration rockets, and that such intervals must be *constant*—as wrongly assumed even for example in:

[8] D A Desloge and R J Philpott. Uniformly accelerated reference frames in special relativity. *American Journal of Physics*, 55: 252–261, 1987

An important *Gedankenexperiment* (thought experiment) is then discussed: A photon's unit thrust medium-timed crossing rates. A radar-emitted 'photon' crosses a continuously co-accelerating medium between the rockets, whose individual increments are imagined as having clocks readable by a photon's third party agent as the photon passes them by. Further aspects of this scenario are treated in the book's final main *Part VII*—ROLLER-COASTING SPACETIME.

15

'Time dispersal' and 'retro-separation'

"The best method...is to become acquainted with the real scope and modes of application of conceptions which, in the popular language of superficial exposition—and even in the unguarded and playful paradox of their authors, intended only for the instructed eye, often look bizarre enough. But ...much advantage will accrue if men of science become their own epistemologists, and show to the world by critical exposition in non-technical terms of the results and methods of their constructive work, that more than mere instinct is involved in it: the community has indeed a right to expect as much as this."

Joseph Larmor—prefacing Poincaré's *Science and Hypothesis* 1902

15.1 Two rockets' rendez-vous with two spacestations

As perceived by ubiquitous home frame observers[1], two simultaneously launched unit own-thrust rockets remain the same home frame fixed distance L apart as long as they continue to accelerate identically. This chapter exlores the *behind the scenes 'interphenomena'* which occur when the two rockets simultaneously *cease* accelerating as they together reach an arbitrary 'shutdown speed' $\breve{v} = \tanh \breve{\tau}$ in that frame (the overhead *breve* denoting *shutdown*).

[1] By this we mean observers stationary in home frame $\underline{H}$ who are *imagined* to conveniently be coincidentally present at any desired arbitrary position.

We imagine that just as rear rocket r and front rocket f shut off their motors, by coincidence they meet and dock at two nonaccelerating spacestations R and F each of which had been approaching them all along from behind at the same home frame $\breve{v}$ speed. This is illustrated in Figure 15.1, where the stations' straight world-lines are tangential to the rockets' initially hyperbolic world-lines and then overlap the subsequently inertial rockets' straight world-line sections.

©BCS IRELAND 2017 ISBN 978-1-9998410-1-0
Brian Coleman SPACETIME FUNDAMENTALS INTELLIGIBLY (RE)LEARNT

Figure 15.1: Home frame hyperbolic world-lines of uniformly accelerating rockets docking at two spacestations

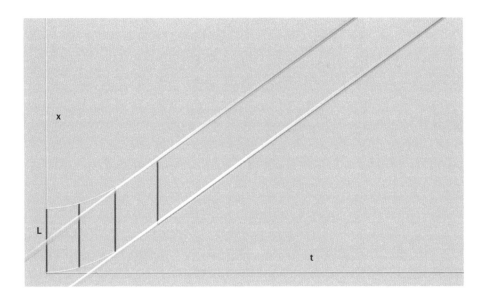

Home/spacestation frames' world-lines

[2] Events we denote by double characters e.g. fF means rocket f's arrival at spacestation F.

[2]Now let us look at this scenario in Figure 15.2's *symmetrical dual reference frame chart* which resembles that of earlier Figure 8.2, with launch home frame $\underline{H}$'s red reference $x|t$ axes and shutdown frame $\underline{\check{C}}$'s blue reference $X|T$ axes. Rear rocket launch event $r0$ (the chart's 'reference origin') and front rocket launch event $f0$ are simultaneous in frame $\underline{H}$. Parallel to the chart's T-axis are straight world-lines (transparent white) of spacestations R and F which are each at related shutdown speed $\check{v}$ relative to the home frame and thus stationary in frame $\underline{\check{C}}$.

Both rockets accelerate through continually varying intermediate comoving frames, as represented by the chart's *curved* yellow world-lines.[3] From equations (11.11)-v,iii, ever-changing comoving frame $\underline{C}$ variables $\chi|\tau$ (where $\chi = 1 - 1/\sqrt{1 + t^2}$ and $\tau = \sinh^{-1} t$), are of course not directly represented in the chart—in contrast to home frame $\underline{H}$ variables $x|t$ and shutdown frame $\underline{\check{C}}$ variables $X|T$. Incidentally, it is worth noting that the *acceleration phase* congruent[4] curved world-line segments connecting events $r0$ and rR and events $f0$ and fF respectively, are horizontally *symmetrical*. These curves are 'mappings' of the rockets' home frame *asymmetric* hyperbolae of Figure 15.1—geometric transformations of the dual reference frame chart's *symmetric* world-lines.

[3] The acceleration phase world-lines' vertical (Z) and horizontal (Y) coordinates *implicit* (but not shown) in Figure 15.2, relate to $\underline{H}$ coordinates $x|t$ and $\underline{\check{C}}$ coordinates $X|T$ as:

$$Y = t \cos \tfrac{\phi}{2} - x \sin \tfrac{\phi}{2}$$
$$= X \sin \tfrac{\phi}{2} + T \cos \tfrac{\phi}{2} \text{ and}$$
$$Z = x \cos \tfrac{\phi}{2} - t \sin \tfrac{\phi}{2}$$
$$= T \sin \tfrac{\phi}{2} + X \cos \tfrac{\phi}{2},$$

where the inter-axes shutdown velocity angle $\check{\phi} = \arcsin \check{v}$.

[4] equal in shape and size but not necessarily in *position*.

[5] Were the rockets to have continued accelerating, then after arrival each would have proceeded in a *forwards* direction away from its spacestation.

In shutdown frame $\underline{\check{C}}$, at launch rear rocket r is ahead of nonaccelerating spacestation R and moves *backwards* towards it as its negative relative speed in $\underline{\check{C}}$ tends towards zero. Just as its motor is shut down, r 'backs onto' R (event rR) and remains 'docked'—their two world-lines *overlap from then on.*[5] Likewise front rocket f 'backs onto' (event fF) the other inertial spacestation F also moving at home-frame related speed $\check{v}$, and also remains docked.

15.2   Shutdown time and distance 'dispersals'

[6]On shutdown, home frame observers could record identical home times for the two arrivals i.e. $t_{fF} = t_{rR} = \breve{t} = \sinh \breve{\tau}$ (equation (11.11)-i), and note that the rockets remain *during and after acceleration* a constant home frame distance $x_{fF} - x_{rR} = L$ apart. CRUCIALLY however, in shutdown frame $\breve{C}$ the rocket arrivals are *time-dispersed*.[7] Recalling equations (11.11), from the Larmor-Lorentz transformations (4.1)-i,ii, frame $\breve{C}$'s $X|T$ parameters relate to frame $\underline{H}$'s $x|t$ as:[8]

$$\breve{\Sigma} \triangleq (X_{fF} - X_{rR}) = \left[(x_{fF} - x_{rR}) - (t_{fF} - t_{rR})\breve{v}\right]\breve{\gamma} = L\breve{\gamma}.$$

$$\breve{\Theta} \triangleq -(T_{fF} - T_{rR}) = -\left[(t_{fF} - t_{rR}) - (x_{fF} - x_{rR})\breve{v}\right]\breve{\gamma} = L\breve{v}\breve{\gamma}.$$

15.1.

SHUTDOWN FRAME ULTIMATE DISTANCE DISPERSAL

$$\breve{\Sigma} \triangleq L\breve{\gamma} = L \cosh \breve{\tau} = L/\cos \breve{\phi}.$$

15.2.

SHUTDOWN FRAME ROCKET ARRIVALS' TIME DISPERSAL

$$\breve{\Theta} \triangleq L\breve{v}\breve{\gamma} = L \tanh \breve{\tau} \cosh \breve{\tau} = L \sinh \breve{\tau} = L\breve{t} = L \tan \breve{\phi}.$$

Figure 15.2's 'DISPERSALS TRIANGLE' ($rR - fF - fS$) represents the rockets' launch separation L, *initial* shutdown time dispersal $\breve{\Theta} = L\breve{v}\breve{\gamma} = L \tan \breve{\phi}$ and *ultimate* synchronisation spatial separation $\breve{\Sigma} = L\breve{\gamma} = L/\cos \breve{\phi}$. We call event fS the front rocket's 'RE-SYNCHRONIZATION' event. At event fS, spacestation F's docked front rocket's own-time will be $\tau_{fS} = \tau_{fF} + \breve{\Theta} = \breve{\tau} + L \sinh \breve{\tau}$. These dispersal equations make an interesting comparison with the later chapter 17's 'rigor mortis' dispersal equations (17.12) and (17.13). Significantly, the dispersal time to dispersal distance ratio equals scaled velocity v which approaches *one* as home frame time t becomes ever larger.

A finishing post time gap

In frame $\breve{C}$, front rocket's launch—event $f0$, is seen to occur earlier than rear rocket's launch event $r0$ which occurs at the same shutdown frame time as rocket f's event fa i.e. as the front rocket is already well on its way (backwards) towards its destination spacestation F.[9] Likewise as judged in frame $\breve{C}$, simultaneous to f's arrival at spacestation F—event fF, rear rocket r at event rG is still a distance from spacestation R equal to $\mathfrak{X} \triangleq rG - RG$. We call $\mathfrak{X}$ THE REAR ROCKET'S TIME DISPERSED SOLO GAP DISTANCE.

[6] We refer to rocket clocks *themselves* as τ_r and τ_f, and to their event values as e.g. τ_{rR} and τ_{fF}.

[7] The two spacestation inertial clocks T_F and T_R may be presumed to have been already mutually synchronised. Their absolute clock readings are irrelevant, only their *difference* is significant.

[8] $\triangleq$ means *'is defined as'*. Θ is Greek upper case *Theta* and Σ Greek upper case *Sigma*.

[9] The front rocket's whereline through event $f0$ intersects the T axis at an earlier T-time than that of event $r0$—the rear rocket's launch.

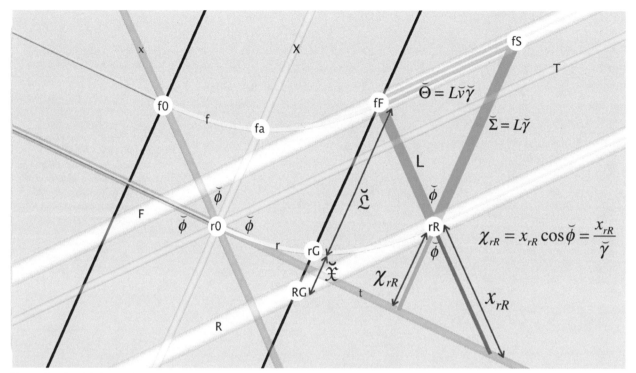

Figure 15.2: *Loedel chart with rocket and spacestation world-lines and shutdown frame space and time 'dispersals' triangle*

[10] in shutdown frame $\underaccent{\smile}{C}$ in a negative X axis direction.

Although still accelerating *forwards* in home frame $\underline{H}$, in shutdown frame $\underaccent{\smile}{C}$ rear rocket r continues to *move backwards*[10] towards spacestation R at ever *decreasing* speed, until a further time period corresponding to dispersal time extent $\breve{\Theta} = fS - fF = L\tan\breve{\phi} = L\sinh\breve{\tau}$ has elapsed and the frame $\underaccent{\smile}{C}$ dispersed solo gap distance $\mathfrak{X}$ has been covered. 'Ultimately', both rockets then coexist simultaneously at rest in the spacestations' shared reference frame $\underaccent{\smile}{C}$, permanently separated by distance dispersal value $L\breve{\gamma}$.

Simultaneous to event fS in frame $\underaccent{\smile}{C}$, spacestation R has the same clock reading $T_{rR} = T_{fS}$ as that of spacestation F, but R's just then docked rear rocket's clock time $\tau_{rR} = \breve{\tau}$ is BEHIND F's earlier docked front rocket's clock time τ_{fS} by $\breve{\Theta} = \tau_{fS} - \breve{\tau} = L\sinh\breve{\tau}$. Thus, even though in home frame $\underline{H}$ the rockets continue to share home time t, show identical clock own-times τ and remain separated by the unchanged launch separation L, the two docking spacestations stationary in the shutdown frame and a distance $L\breve{\gamma}$ apart therein would simultaneously register *different readings* of the rocket clocks. This prompts the question:

Is there some 'standpoint' which explains the rear rocket's apparent 'time loss' ?

Shutdown 'time gap re-synchronization' frame

For any preset shutdown time $\check{\tau}$ exceeding $\check{\Theta} = L \sinh \check{\tau}$ and simultaneous in frame $\check{C}$ as front rocket f arrives at spacestation F (event fF), rear rocket r's *primary* clock reaches at event rG an own-time $\check{\Phi}$ which,[11] added to the final shutdown *dispersal time* $\check{\Theta}$, will equal the rear rocket's final shutdown own-time i.e. $\check{\Phi} \triangleq \check{\tau} - \check{\Theta}$. Recalling equation (11.11)-ii, at rocket velocity $\hat{v} \triangleq \tanh \check{\Phi} = \tanh(\check{\tau} - \check{\Theta})$, there will therefore be a *specific* inertial comoving frame we call the 'REAR ROCKET'S TIME GAP FRAME' $\hat{G}$.

[11] $\check{\Phi}$ is Greek upper case *Phi*.

15.3.

THE RE-SYNCHRONIZATION ONSET TIME $\check{\Phi} \triangleq \check{\tau} - \check{\Theta} = \check{\tau} - L. \sinh \check{\tau}.$

15.4.

A UNIQUE PARALLEL 'TIME GAP' INERTIAL FRAME HOSTS A BACKGROUND SOLO REAR ROCKET ACCELERATION RE-SYNCHRONISATION PHASE (PROVIDED $L < \check{\tau} / \sinh \check{\tau}$).

The 'event horizon' case

From equation (15.3), the re-synchronisation onset time is $\check{\Phi} = \check{\tau} - L. \sinh \check{\tau}$. For any specific nonzero shutdown time, $\check{\tau}$ is less than $\sinh \check{\tau}$.[12] So for the re-synchronisation onset time to be nonzero, L must be less than one and also less than $\check{\tau} / \sinh \check{\tau}$. Therefore, subsequent to launchings, no background frame can host the re-synchronization of the rear rocket where launch separation L is not less than $\check{\tau} / \sinh \check{\tau}$.

[12] Taking into account $\sinh \check{\tau}$'s *Taylor expansion*.

As explained in Unit thrust rockets' asymptotic horizon section on page 118, events spatially apart in any inertial frame by more than scaled length L equal to *one*, are beyond the limit of our mathematical relationships.[13] In such post-launch cases re-synchronizations may be envisaged only by considering the separation length to be divided into multiple subsections L_i where each $L_i < \check{\tau} / \sinh \check{\tau}$. Naturally, each intermediate increment's re-synchronization resembles that of the rear rocket for a shorter medium.

[13] One intriguing *consequence* of there being a limit speed in our cosmos.

16.1   The unit own-thrust home frame 'world-surface'

Reflecting equation (11.11)-xii, Figure 16.1's *single 'home' frame chart* shows hyperbolic world-lines for unit thrust rear and front rockets r and f, and for *intermediate* unit own-thrust rockets each of which may be thought of as *an 'increment'* l ($0 \le l \le L$) *of an idealized 'co-accelerating' medium*. Their identical home frame travelled distances under acceleration—x—are represented by respective *chart position* $x + l$ values. Identified by its initial 'launch' distance l from the rear rocket, each such unit thrust rocket or increment will have an imagined own-time τ-clock zeroed at launch. ~~Replacing x by $x - l$ in~~ [2] (11.11)-xii gives us *a homogeneously accelerating medium's* home frame world-surface:[3]

[2] Chart position x represents increment l's <u>travelled</u> $x - l$ home frame distance since its launching.
[3] Each identical hyperbola represents a fixed-l increment. For the rear rocket $l = 0$, whereas for the front rocket $l = L$.

16.1.

THE UNIT OWN-THRUST MEDIUM HOME WORLD-SURFACE

$$(x \;\cancel{\;\;} + 1)^2 - t^2 = 1 \qquad (0 \le l \le L).$$

Radar pulses we conveniently call 'photons'[4] propagate in inertial frames at unit scaled limit speed $\frac{dx}{dt} = 1$.[5] In the home frame $x|t$ chart, photon world-lines therefore appear as upwards or downward *diagonal lines* starting at periodic rocket own-time intervals on our rear rocket's home frame lower world-line, and reflected back downwards from the upper front rocket world-line. Figure 16.1 also displays vertical lines spaced at fixed $\Delta\tau$ rocket own-time intervals[6] corresponding to increasingly greater Δt intervals, since from (11.11)-i, $t = \sinh \tau$. It is immediately evident from this basic diagram that *the rear inter-rocket radar intervals vary in terms of the equal own-time emission intervals*. As later commented upon on page 120's section Evidence unwittingly 'withheld', this simple conclusion appears not to have been discussed openly in relativity textbooks. We now proceed to determine these intervals *analytically*.

[4] Actual radar signals of course use *wave pulses* rather than photons—a descriptively useful 'equivalent'.
[5] ⇒The 'contagious' limit speed on page 46.

[6] at $t_1 = \sinh \Delta\tau$,
$t_2 = \sinh 2\Delta\tau$,
$t_3 = \sinh 3\Delta\tau$ etc.

16.2   Emitted photon transit times

Using 'accents' instead of cumbersome subscripts, we assign to an emitted photon the encountered rear rocket r and front rocket f own-times on emission ($\acute{\tau}$—'tau acute'), reflection ($\hat{\tau}$—'tau hat'), return/re-emission ($\grave{\tau}$—'tau grave') and re-reflection ($\check{\tau}$—'tau check'). Variables τ, t and x *without* an accent, denote values of an arbitrary *intermediate* increment ($0 < l < L$) encountered by the photon. All rocket and (imagined) increment clocks will have been zeroed at launch in the home reference frame. For a photon emitted from the rear rocket r at rocket own-time[7] $\acute{\tau} = \sinh^{-1} \acute{t}$ i.e. at home-frame time $\acute{t} = \sinh \acute{\tau}$, r will have accelerated to a home-frame position $\acute{x} = \cosh \acute{\tau} - 1$.

[7] $\sinh^{-1}$ denotes the *inverse function* of the hyperbolic sine, <u>not</u> the actual *inverse value* of the function.

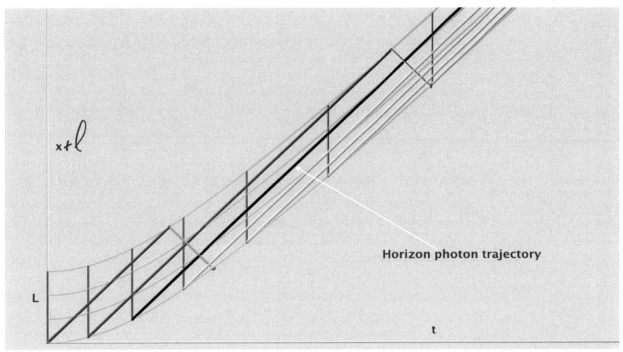

x+l

L

Horizon photon trajectory

t

Figure 16.1: Home frame world-surface of a uniformly accelerating medium, with radar trajectories and fixed velocity loci

The same photon arrives at an arbitrary unit thrust increment l at its own-time $\tau = \sinh^{-1} t$, i.e. at home-frame time $t = \sinh \tau$ when that increment has home-frame position $x + l = \cosh \tau - 1 + l$. [8]Since the photon travels at unit speed in the home frame we may write: $x + l - \acute{x} = t - \acute{t}$.

Hence $(\cosh \tau - 1 + l) - (\cosh \acute{t} - 1) = \sinh \tau - \sinh \acute{t}$ i.e.:
$\cosh \tau - \sinh \tau = \cosh \acute{t} - \sinh \acute{t} - l$. This yields:[9]

[8] Using equation (11.11)-iv, $\acute{x}$ denotes an emission event position, in this case that of the rear rocket.

[9] Noting that $\cosh \rho \pm \sinh \rho$
$= (e^{\rho} + e^{-\rho})/2$
$\pm (e^{\rho} - e^{-\rho})/2 = e^{\pm \rho}$.

16.2.

OUTGOING TRANSIT PHOTON EQUATION $e^{-\tau} = e^{-\acute{t}} - l$ i.e. $\dfrac{\partial l}{\partial \tau} = e^{-\tau}$.

Since $\acute{t}$ is the *front rocket's clock time on photon arrival*, where $l = L$, replacing l by L and τ by $\acute{t}$ in (16.2) gives us:

16.3.

OUTGOING PHOTON REFLECTION EQUATIONS $e^{\acute{t}} = 1/(e^{-\acute{t}} - L)$ i.e. $e^{-\acute{t}} = e^{-\acute{t}} + L$

16.3   Unit thrust rockets' asymptotic horizon

'The fate' of emitted photons, usually treated only in general relativity, can understood by defining a key distance parameter:

16.4.

AN ASYMPTOTIC HORIZON PHOTON'S EMISSION TIME $\bar{\tau} \triangleq \ln(1/L)$.

For a photon emitted at asymptotic horizon emission home time, $e^{-\hat{t}} = e^{-\bar{\tau}} = L$ and $e^{\hat{t}}$ in equation (16.3)-i would be infinite. The photon would asymptotically approach but never actually never reach the front rocket and also not be reflected. Our asymptotic horizon establishes, as a function of a *photon's emission time*, the forward rocket's launch separation whereby the photon would tend to surf but never actually reach the forward rocket.

Figure 16.1 shows the diagonal trajectories of photons emitted at rocket own-time intervals of $\Delta\tau = 3\pi/32$ from the rear rocket and reflected back from the front rocket. The third outgoing trajectory (in black) is that of a 'horizon photon' where $\hat{t}_2 = 2 \cdot \frac{3\pi}{32} = 0.5890$, the chosen launch separation distance is $L = e^{-\hat{t}_2} = 0.5548 \ L$. Hence only the first two photons ($\hat{t}_0 = 0$ and $\hat{t}_1 = \frac{3\pi}{32} = 0.2945$) are reflected. Neither of course is a photon emitted after that time instant reflected.

A photon emitted at launch from the rear rocket towards a front rocket a scaled unit length distant ($\hat{t} = 0$, $L = e^0 = 1$), approaches it asymptotically as $\tau \to \infty$. With an earth gravity thrust,[10] such a length would be $c^2/g \approx 9 \cdot 10^{15}$ meters—*coincidentally just under one light year*, and one unit of scaled time $c/10 \approx 3 \cdot 10^7$ would likewise be just under one year. [11]Our asymptotic horizon is equivalent to the *event horizon* familiar to *general relativity* and, as *R H Good* pointed out in 1987: "...*is a dominant landmark in the accelerated frame*".

[10] $g \approx 10m/s^2$.

[11] R H Good. Behind the event horizon. *European Journal of Physics*, 8(3):174–175, 1987

16.5.

A ROCKET <u>PERMANENTLY</u> ACCELERATING FASTER THAN $1g$ NEVER SEES AN EVENT OVER A LIGHT YEAR AWAY IN ANY OF THE ROCKET'S COMOVING FRAMES.

16.4   Returning photons

[12] i.e. $e^{\hat{t}} < 1/L$. Otherwise the photon never reaches the front rocket.

[13] $\hat{x} + L$ being the front rocket's position as the photon is reflected.

A reflected photon whose emission time $\hat{t} < \ln(1/L)$,[12] travels *backwards* to meet an arbitrary increment l at home time $t = \sinh\tau$ and home *position* $x + l = \cosh\tau - 1 + l$, over equal home-frame time and distance intervals:[13] $t - \hat{t} = (\hat{x} + L) - (x + l)$.

Substituting, $\sinh \tau - \sinh \hat{\tau} = (\cosh \hat{\tau} - 1 + L) - (\cosh \tau - 1 + l)$ i.e. $e^{\tau} - e^{\hat{\tau}} = L - l$ which gives using (16.3)-i:

16.6.

Returning photon transit equations $l = -e^{\tau} + L + 1/(e^{-\hat{\tau}} - L)$ i.e. $\dfrac{\partial l}{\partial \tau} = -e^{\tau}$.

For the rear rocket $l = 0$ and $\tau = \hat{\tau}$. Hence, again using (16.3)-i:

16.7.

RETURNED PHOTON EQUATIONS $e^{\hat{\tau}} = L + 1/(e^{-\hat{\tau}} - L) = L + e^{\hat{\tau}}$.

Since $e^{\hat{\tau}} = 1/(e^{-\hat{\tau}} - L)$, for a *returned* photon we obtain:

$$\check{\tau} - \hat{\tau} = \ln\left[L + \frac{1}{e^{-\hat{\tau}} - L}\right] - \ln\left[\frac{1}{e^{-\hat{\tau}} - L}\right] = \ln\left[\frac{L + \frac{1}{e^{-\hat{\tau}} - L}}{\frac{1}{e^{-\hat{\tau}} - L}}\right] = \ln\left[L(e^{-\hat{\tau}} - L) + 1\right]. \qquad (16.8)$$

Thus for $e^{-\hat{\tau}}$ very close to L, $\check{\tau} - \hat{\tau} \approx \ln(1) = 0$.

16.9.

FOR AN EMISSION TIME $\hat{\tau}$ NEAR HORIZON VALUE $\ln 1/L$, A PHOTON'S RETURNING

UNIT THRUST MEDIUM'S TRAVERSING TIME TENDS TOWARDS ZERO.

Re-emitted photons

Imagining the same photon reflected again i.e *re-emitted* forwards towards the front rocket, we obtain for the front rocket *re–reflection* time $\check{\tau}$, replacing $\hat{\tau}$ with $\check{\tau}$ and $\hat{\tau}$ with $\check{\tau}$ in (16.3) and using (16.7)-ii:

16.10.

RE-EMITTED REFLECTION EQUATIONS $e^{\check{\tau}} = \dfrac{1}{e^{-\check{\tau}} - L} = \dfrac{1}{1/(L + e^{\hat{\tau}}) - L}$ i.e. $e^{\check{\tau}} e^{-\hat{\tau}} = \dfrac{(L + e^{\hat{\tau}})e^{-\hat{\tau}}}{1 - L(L + e^{\hat{\tau}})}$.

16.5 Unit thrust inter-rocket radar intervals

From return equation (16.7)-i: $e^{\check{t}}e^{-\acute{t}} = \left[L + 1/(e^{-\acute{t}} - L)\right]e^{-\acute{t}}$.

16.11.

THE REAR ROCKET'S RADAR INTERVAL $\quad \check{t} - \acute{t} = \ln\left[\left(L + 1/(e^{-\acute{t}} - L)\right)e^{-\acute{t}}\right]$.

[14] Otherwise the photon is never reflected.

(16.11) applies for reflections where $e^{-\acute{t}} - L > 0$ i.e. $\acute{t} < \ln(1/L)$.[14] Computer generated Figure 16.1 shows trajectories of photons reflected back from the front rocket. Substitution of $L = 0.5548$, $\Delta\tau = 3\pi/32$, $\acute{t}_0 = 0$ and $\acute{t}_1 = 3\pi/32$ in (16.11) gives us: $\check{t}_0 - \acute{t}_0 = \frac{3\pi}{32} \cdot 3.497$ and $\check{t}_1 - \acute{t}_1 = \frac{3\pi}{32} \cdot 4.977$.

Re-emitted photon transit equation (16.10)-iii yields directly:

16.12.

THE FRONT ROCKET'S RADAR INTERVAL $\quad \check{t} - \acute{t} = \ln\left[\dfrac{Le^{-\acute{t}} + 1}{1 - L(L + e^{\acute{t}})}\right]$.

From the *Measuring the Cosmic Limit Speed chapter's *limit speed principle* (5.4) (normally known as the 'second postulate'), the cosmic limit speed—'the speed of light'—remains the same in all inertial frames but this principle does not apply in 'non-inertial' frames.

16.13.

RADAR INTERVALS BETWEEN IDENTICAL THRUST ROCKETS <u>VARY</u>.

THE 'SECOND POSTULATE' <u>DOES NOT APPLY</u> FOR ACCELERATING EXTENDED OBJECTS.

16.6 Evidence unwittingly 'withheld'

As outlined in the PROLOGUE section Equations that did not bark in the light, most physicists still erroneously maintain that radar intervals between identically accelerating rockets must be *constant*. As a result, radar periods (16.11) and (16.12), which as we have seen are easily established *solely* on the basis of the two well known standard acceleration relationships (11.11)-i and (11.11)-iv, are not apparent in contemporary relativity textbooks.

[15]It seems appropriate to parody this 'academic reticence' by recalling a famous extract from one of *Conan Doyle's* renowned crime books:

Detective: *"Is there any other point to which you would wish to draw my attention?"*
Sherlock Holmes: *"To the curious incident of the dog in the night-time."*
Detective: *"The dog did nothing in the night-time."*
Sherlock Holmes: *"That was the curious incident."*

A fallacy's domino effect

What might be called one of the most remarkable *'domino effect'* blunders in the history of relativity is exemplified in a much cited *otherwise* formidable 1987 *American Journal of Physics* paper. Referring to the rear rocket's radar interval, the paper's two authors insisted that *"the elapsed time $\tau_3 - \tau_1$ for the round trip...should be constant"* ([16] page 255, sections IV and V). This led them to likewise incorrectly infer that *"the proper [i.e. own-] distance between any two [identically accelerating] observers remains constant."* Just like the sacrosanct overgeneralised Minkowski metric, how such *perpetuum mobile* dogmas remain part of the 'relativity catechism' has been succinctly described by *Thomas Ryckman:*[17]

> "Yet as pious children of this world, to borrow an expression of Hermann Weyl's, we know that if an assertion is repeated sufficiently often while remaining unchallenged in the forum of debate, it commonly enters into currency as accepted background knowledge."

[16] D A Desloge and R J Philpott. Uniformly accelerated reference frames in special relativity. *American Journal of Physics*, 55: 252–261, 1987

[17] Thomas Ryckman. *The Reign of Relativity*. Oxford Universtity Press, 2005

16.7   A photon's unit thrust medium-timed crossing rates

Finally an important *Gedankenexperiment.*[18] We denote each increment's 'NON-INERTIAL OWN-LENGTH' FROM THE MEDIUM'S REAR END as

$$\lambda(l,\tau) = l \cdot \epsilon(\tau) \qquad (0 \le l \le L)); \qquad \epsilon(\tau) = \partial\lambda/\partial l,$$

$\epsilon(\tau)$ being the NON-INERTIAL OWN-EXPANSION FACTOR (explained later on). All increments *of virtually zero mass* are imagined to have minuscule unit thrust rockets clocks recordable by third parties as they are crossed by radar photons. Each such third party observer would note ever increasing readings of increment clocks whose comoving frame continually *changes.* Assuming the third parties could somehow ascertain the medium's non-inertial own-length $\lambda(l,\tau)$ traversed by their respective radar photons, we label each $\partial\lambda/\partial\tau$ changing value as the 'medium-timed non-inertial own-length's photon crossing rate'.[19] Equations (16.2) and (16.6) relate the own-times τ of increments l crossed by outgoing and returning photons respectively which had been emitted at any set rear rocket own-time $\acute{t}$. Accordingly:

[18] 'Thought experiment'

[19] NOT to be confused with the unit limit speed of the photon as perceived momentarily in every *inertial* comoving frame.

16.14.

FOR AN EMITTED PHOTON'S MEDIUM-TIMED CROSSING RATE : $\dfrac{\partial \lambda}{\partial \tau} = \dfrac{\partial \lambda}{\partial l} \cdot \dfrac{\partial l}{\partial \tau} = \epsilon(\tau) \cdot e^{-\tau}.$

16.15.

FOR A REFLECTED PHOTON'S MEDIUM-TIMED CROSSING RATE : $-\dfrac{\partial \lambda}{\partial \tau} = -\dfrac{\partial \lambda}{\partial l} \cdot \dfrac{\partial l}{\partial \tau} = \epsilon(\tau) \cdot e^{\tau}.$

Photon crossing rates in the limit

As $\tau \to \infty$, the medium approaches unit limit speed in the inertial home frame and an outgoing photon would tend to 'surf' an accelerating medium's increment. The third party observer would report that the photon took ever longer increment clock intervals to cross the medium i.e. $\partial \lambda / \partial \tau$ tends ultimately to approach the value zero. One might assume our homogeneously accelerating medium's 'non-inertial own-length' Λ must surely increase indefinitely since outgoing photons take ever longer to reach the front rocket and do not do so at all for photons emitted after the 'horizon emission time'.

On the other hand, photons emitted or reflected from the front rocket would take *an ever decreasing medium time intervals* to reach the rear rocket and so would tend to 'ubiquitously' backwards traverse the entire forwards moving medium *momentarily* i.e. 'cross' it at a speed *approaching infinity*. Photon's medium-timed crossing rates *are always below one and decrease towards zero* for *co-directional* photons, and *above one and increase towards infinity* for *counter-directional* photons. Any radar length measurement would thus differ, depending on whether photons are co-directional or counter-directional.

Therefore as own-time τ tends ('in unison') towards infinity, by virtue of equations (16.14) and (16.15) the unit thrust medium expansion factor must match the following two conditions:

16.16.

A UNIT THRUST MEDIUM'S EXPANSION LIMIT CONDITIONS

as $\tau \to \infty$: $\epsilon(\tau) \cdot e^{-\tau} = 0$ and $\epsilon(\tau) \cdot e^{\tau} = \infty.$

We refer again to these two important requirements in *Part VII*'s chapter The unit thrust medium own-surface.

VI

THE RELATIVITY CURATE'S EGG

The last two parts of this book deal with *an extended accelerating medium*. In the 'cherry picked' (one might say) special 'rigor mortis'/'rigid motion' acceleration case treated in the next Rigor Mortis acceleration chapter, observers stationary in each passing comoving frame would perceive the medium's differently accelerating increments as remaining at unchanged separation distances. This situation differs considerably from the later treated *homogeneously accelerating* medium scenario.

In the chapter Two real—Euclidean—metric own-surfaces, we discuss two *real metric* own-surfaces representing an extended one-spatial dimension medium's *intrinsic own-time* and *'own-length' parameters* which are independent of outside observers. The trivial nonaccelerating inertial medium case is represented by a rectangular mesh. The rigor mortis case, likewise oddly simple yet seemingly hitherto unknown is represented by a simple hand-held fan shaped own-surface which very neatly epitomises what has been commonly known as 'rigid motion' acceleration.

In addressing each of these cases we deliberately bypass the standard relativity textbook *complex variable Minkowski spacetime* approach. The 'Minkowski metric' has its uses in particle physics, but entails serious limitations not generally appreciated or acknowledged by most of the physics community who appear content to remain oblivious of this fact. This has led to widespread misunderstandings, as remonstrated in chapter 19's opening quotation of an *American Journal of Physics* 1987 paper which itself had made a concerted effort—unfortunately with only limited success—to address the core issues of accelerating i.e. 'non-inertial' frames of reference.

17
Rigor Mortis acceleration

'Special relativity is not equipped to describe observations in noninertial frames.'
(An overpessimistic view)   Leo Sartori   *Understanding Relativity* 1996

17.1   *Non-unit fixed own-thrust relationships*

[1]Although relativity literature up to now has had great difficulties with regard to analysing an accelerated extended medium, there is one special single spatial dimension case—handled very awkwardly in textbooks—where *partial* clarity has been achieved. To examine this case, we first look at a medium whose 'increments' each have fixed own-thrust α which, though fixed, *may individually differ* from increment to increment.

Time and distance equations (11.11) relate to *unit acceleration*, with times scaled by α/c and distances by α/c^2 for any preset own-acceleration value α value. To deal with *nonidentical* fixed accelerations in this chapter and in the following chapter, we retain scaled limit speed as *one* i.e. $c = 1$, but *rescale* equations (11.11)-i-iv and xiii for increments' *general* fixed own-thrust α values:

17.1.

ARBITRARY FIXED OWN-ACCELERATION RELATIONSHIPS:

$t\alpha = \sinh \tau\alpha, \ \ v = \tanh \tau\alpha, \ \ \gamma = \cosh \tau\alpha, \ \ x\alpha = \cosh \tau\alpha - 1, \ \ (x\alpha + 1)^2 - (t\alpha)^2 = 1.$

[1] Leo Sartori. *Understanding Relativity*. Univ. of California Press, 1996

17.2   A one-off single frame world-surface

[2]Paralleling chapter 16's section The unit own-thrust home frame 'world-surface', world-lines of fixed thrust rockets with acceleration distances x are represented on the home frame world surface by respective chart position $x + l$ values. As in Figure 16.1, Figure 17.1's home frame $x|t$ chart shows a fixed thrust rear rocket r's hyperbolic world-line[3] parameterised by equation (17.1)v with *unit own-acceleration* $\alpha_r = 1$ chosen for convenience. The top world-line is that of a front fixed thrust rocket f launched at initial home frame position $x = L$ and represented by the equation $((x - L)\alpha_f + 1)^2 - (t\alpha_f)^2 = 1$ for a fixed own-acceleration α_f.

An unlimited number of such rockets with individual fixed own-thrust α values and (imagined) own-time synchronized τ-clocks, are identified by their individual launch distance l ($0 \leq l \leq L$) from the rear rocket. Similar to equation (16.1), the resulting home frame world-surface is:

$$((x - l)\alpha + 1)^2 - (t\alpha)^2 = 1; \qquad 0 \leq l \leq L. \tag{17.2}$$

17.3   Corresponding fixed thrust radar intervals

As in chapter 16's section Emitted photon transit times, home frame $x|t$ chart radar trajectories are upwards or downward *diagonal lines* starting at periodic rocket own-time intervals on our rear rocket's home frame lower world-line, and reflected back downwards from the upper front rocket world-line. As before, we assign to an arbitrarily emitted light photon the respectively encountered rear rocket r and front rocket f own-times: on emission, $(\acute{\tau})$, reflection $(\hat{\tau})$, return/re-emission $(\check{\tau})$ and re-reflection $(\check{\tau})$.

From (17.1)-i and (17.1)-iv, for a photon emitted from the unit thrust rear rocket r at any arbitrary own-time $\acute{\tau} = \sinh^{-1} \acute{t}_r$ i.e. at home-frame time $\acute{t}_r = \sinh \acute{\tau}$, rocket r will have travelled under (unit) acceleration to a home-frame position $\acute{x}_r = \cosh \acute{\tau} - 1$, since $t_0 (= 0)$. The same photon arrives at the front rocket f with own-acceleration α_f at own-time $\hat{\tau} = \sinh^{-1}(\hat{t}_f \alpha_f)/\alpha_f$, i.e. at home-frame time $\hat{t}_f = \sinh(\hat{\tau}\alpha_f)/\alpha_f$ when f has home-frame position $\hat{x}_f + L = \left[\cosh(\hat{\tau}\alpha_f) - 1\right]/\alpha_f + L$.

As the photon travels at unit limit speed in the home frame, then $\hat{x}_f + L - \acute{x}_r = \hat{t}_f - \acute{t}_r$ i.e.[4]

[4] Recalling again that
$\cosh \rho \pm \sinh \rho$
$= (e^\rho + e^{-\rho})/2$
$\pm (e^\rho - e^{-\rho})/2 = e^{\pm\rho}$.

$$\left(\frac{\cosh \hat{\tau}\alpha_f - 1}{\alpha_f} + L\right) - (\cosh \acute{\tau} - 1) = \frac{\sinh \hat{\tau}\alpha_f}{\alpha_f} - \sinh \acute{\tau}.$$

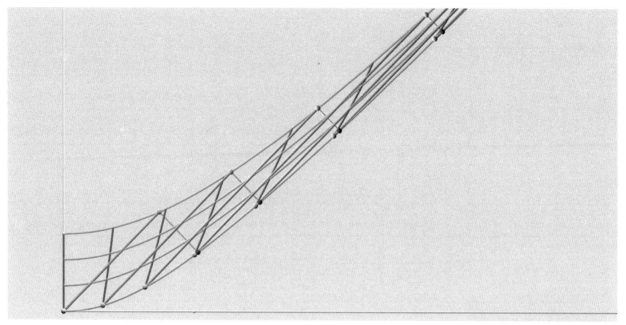

This yields a FORWARD TRANSIT EQUATION:

$$\frac{e^{-\hat{\tau}\alpha_f}}{\alpha_f} = e^{-\hat{\tau}} + \frac{1}{\alpha_f} - 1 - L. \tag{17.3}$$

The reflected photon meets unit thrust rear rocket r at home time $\grave{t}_r = \sinh\grave{\tau}$ and home frame *position* $\grave{x}_r = \cosh\grave{\tau} - 1$, over equal home-frame distance and time intervals $(\hat{x}_f + L) - \grave{x}_r = \grave{t}_r - \hat{t}_f$ i.e.

$$\left(\frac{\cosh\hat{\tau}\alpha_f - 1}{\alpha_f} + L\right) - (\cosh\grave{\tau} - 1) = \sinh\grave{\tau} - \frac{\sinh\hat{\tau}\alpha_f}{\alpha_f}.$$

This gives a RETURN TRANSIT EQUATION

$$\frac{e^{\hat{\tau}\alpha_f}}{\alpha_f} = e^{\grave{\tau}} + \frac{1}{\alpha_f} - 1 - L \qquad \text{i.e.} \qquad e^{\grave{\tau}} = \frac{e^{\hat{\tau}\alpha_f}}{\alpha_f} - \frac{1}{\alpha_f} + 1 + L. \tag{17.4}$$

Imagining this photon to itself be reflected again i.e *re-emitted* forwards towards the front rocket, we obtain for the front rocket *re-reflection* time $\check{\tau}$ (replacing $\hat{\tau}$ with $\check{\tau}$ and $\hat{\tau}$ with $\check{\tau}$ in (17.3)):

$$\frac{e^{-\check{\tau}\alpha_f}}{\alpha_f} - \frac{1}{\alpha_f} + 1 + L = e^{-\grave{\tau}}. \tag{17.5}$$

Multiplying (17.3) by (17.4)-i and (17.4)-ii by (17.5) we obtain:

17.6.

FORWARD GENERAL RADAR EQUATION $\dfrac{1}{\alpha_f^2} = \left[e^{-\hat{\tau}} + \dfrac{1}{\alpha_f} - 1 - L\right]\left[e^{\check{\tau}} + \dfrac{1}{\alpha_f} - 1 - L\right],$

17.7.

REVERSE GENERAL RADAR EQUATION $1 = \left[\dfrac{e^{\hat{\tau}\alpha_f}}{\alpha_f} - \dfrac{1}{\alpha_f} + 1 + L\right]\left[\dfrac{e^{-\check{\tau}\alpha_f}}{\alpha_f} - \dfrac{1}{\alpha_f} + 1 + L\right].$

17.4 The 'rigor mortis' scenario

[5] Max Born. Die Theorie des starren Elektrons in der Kinematik des Relativitätsprinzips (The theory of the rigid electron in the kinematics of the relativity principle). *Annalen der Physik*, 30 (1-56), 1909

Ever since the advent of modern spacetime theory over a century ago,[5] an acceleration scenario called 'RIGID MOTION' has played a notable role in relativity literature. What is meant is an extended medium whose constituent parts i.e. 'increments' accelerate at fixed but nonidentical rates in such a way that, viewed from the medium's rear end r in each current comoving inertial frame, all other increments remain be stationary in the same comoving frame. This means that as well as continually sharing respective ever changing comoving frames, distances between increments as perceived in these frames remain the same. Notably however, as will be shown presently, all increments age at different rates relative to one another. For these very reasons, quite apart from confusion evoked by the 'rigid motion' term itself,[6] the present author prefers to refer to this special case as 'RIGOR MORTIS' ACCELERATION.

[6] In differential geometry *rigid motion* has a meaning quite unrelated to relativity theory.

Rigor mortis fixed radar intervals

[7] As already intimated in 2003 using an elaborate *4-velocity vector approach* on p. 115 of:
[8] Nicholas Woodhouse. *Special Relativity*. Springer London, 2003

If we impose[7,8] THE DIFFERENTIAL OWN-ACCELERATIONS CONDITION:

$$\frac{1}{\alpha_f} = 1 + L \quad \text{i.e.} \quad \alpha_f = \frac{1}{1+L}, \tag{17.8}$$

then forward equation 17.6 becomes $e^{(\check{\tau}-\hat{\tau})} = \frac{1}{\alpha_f^2} = (1+L)^2$:

17.9.

FORWARD 'RIGOR MORTIS' RADAR INTERVAL $\check{\tau} - \hat{\tau} = 2\ln(1+L) = 2\ln(\frac{1}{\alpha_f}).$

From reverse equation (17.7) $e^{-(\check{t}-\hat{t})\alpha_f} = \alpha_f{}^2 = 1/(1+L)^2$:

17.10.

REVERSE 'RIGOR MORTIS' RADAR INTERVAL $\check{t} - \hat{t} = 2(1+L)\ln(1+L) = \dfrac{2}{\alpha_f}\ln(\dfrac{1}{\alpha_f})$.

17.11.

THE 'RIGOR MORTIS' RADAR INTERVALS RATIO $\quad \dfrac{\check{t}-\hat{t}}{\check{t}-\hat{t}} = \dfrac{1}{1+L} = \dfrac{\alpha_f}{1}$.

'RIGOR MORTIS' FORWARD AND REVERSE RADAR INTERVALS ARE CONSTANT AND THEIR RATIO EQUALS THE ROCKET ACCELERATIONS' RATIO.

Rigor mortis space and time dispersals

For any set $v = \tanh(\tau_f\alpha_f) = \tanh\tau_r$ and $\gamma = \cosh(\tau\alpha_f) = \cosh\tau_r$, (17.1)-i-iv and (17.8)-i yield the rockets' home frame *time dispersal*

$$t_f - t_r = \frac{\sinh(\tau_f\alpha_f)}{\alpha_f} - \frac{\sinh\tau_r}{1} = \gamma v\left[\frac{1}{\alpha_f} - 1\right] = \gamma vL,$$

and their home frame *distance dispersal*

$$(x_f + L) - x_r = \frac{\gamma-1}{\alpha_f} + L - \gamma + 1 = \gamma\left[\frac{1}{\alpha_f} - 1\right] - \frac{1}{\alpha_f} + L + 1 = \gamma L.$$

From the Larmor-Lorentz transformations (4.1)-ii for the corresponding co-moving frame, time dispersal turns out to be zero:[9,10]

$$\Delta\tau = \gamma\left[(t_f - t_r) - v(x_f + L - x_r)\right] = \gamma\left[\gamma vL - v\gamma L\right] = 0. \qquad (17.12)$$

From the corresponding equation (4.1)-i, the comoving frame's distance dispersal remains equal to the rockets' launch separation:

$$\gamma\left[(x_f + L - x_r) - v(t_f - t_r)\right] = \gamma\left[\gamma L - v^2\gamma L\right] = \gamma^2 L\left[1 - v^2\right] = L. \quad (17.13)$$

Recalling (17.8) and (17.1) $v = \tanh\tau\alpha$, we obtain for any arbitrary increment's own-time τ (with rear rocket thrust $\alpha_r = 1$):

17.14.

RIGOR MORTIS OWN-TIME CLOCKS RELATIONSHIP $\quad \tau\alpha = \tau_r\alpha_r = \tau_r.1$.

[9] Equations (17.12) and (17.13) were already established in 2010 as solutions to a set of mathematical equations by

[10] Jerrold Franklin. Lorentz contraction, Bell's spaceships and rigid body motion in special relativity. *Eur. J. Phys.*, 31:291–298, 2010

Figure 17.2: "True Humility"
    Punch magazine 1895 cartoon

    Bishop: "I'm afraid you've got a
bad egg, Mr Jones";
    Curate: "Oh, no, my Lord,
I assure you that parts of it are
excellent!"

17.5   The 'rigor mortis' home frame world-surface

Denoting the rear rocket as 'increment l_0', medium increments are identified by their relative launch distance l from the rear rocket l_0 $(0 \leq l \leq L)$. If each medium increment l accelerates at $\alpha = 1/(1 + l)$ with each increment's curve elevated from start at $x_{i0} = l$, then using general acceleration medium home world-surface equation (17.2) gives[11] $(x - l + 1 + l)^2 - t^2 = (1 + l)^2$ i.e.

[11] Replacing x by $x - l$ and multiplying by $1/\alpha = (1 + l)^2$

17.15.

THE HOME FRAME'S RIGOR MORTIS MEDIUM'S WORLD-SURFACE EQUATION

$$(x + 1)^2 - t^2 = (1 + l)^2.$$

Emitted and reflected radar trajectories appear as diagonal lines (scaled $c = \pm 1$). Substituting $L = 0.57$ and $a_f = 1/(1 + L) = 0.637$ in equation (17.9) and dividing by the chosen rocket own-time period $3\pi/32$ between respective emissions yields 3.063. This clearly corresponds to each of the chart's radar response intervals in terms of the rear rocket's own-time emission interval.

Figure 17.1's fixed own-time (light blue) trajectories represent co-moving frame's increments sharing identical home frame velocity, whose distributed lengths add up—*simultaneously in the particular comoving frame*—to the constant unchanging launch separation L (equation (17.13)).[12]

[12] Of course in the home frame the rockets observed at any set v value are separated by $Ł/\gamma$, but such observations are *non-simultaneous* in that frame.

Fixed velocity 'rigor mortis' world-surface loci

The fixed own-time *tilted* fixed velocity loci traced at regular rocket clock own-time intervals, simply connect each individual increment's hyperbola point corresponding to the respective shared home frame velocity. Schematically represented by *straight rectangular strips* in textbook [13]'s Figure 3.3 (p.72), such loci are actually straight lines. Thus for each rear rocket own-time $\tau = n.\Delta\tau$ (with $\Delta\tau$ fixed, $n = 0, 1, 2, 3 \ldots$), the coordinates for increment l (whereby $\alpha = 1/(1+l)$) are, using (17.1):

$$t = \sinh(\frac{\tau_n}{1+l}).(1+l) \qquad \text{and} \qquad x = \left[\cosh(\frac{\tau_n}{1+l}) - 1\right](1+l) + l. \tag{17.16}$$

> [13] Wolfgang Rindler. *Relativity, Special, General and Cosmological.* Oxford Universtiy Press, 2001, 2006

The rigor mortis accelerations condition

17.17.

IN EVERY COMOVING FRAME ALL ACCELERATING MEDIUM INCREMENTS ARE SIMULTANEOUSLY RELATIVELY STATIONARY IN 'RIGOR MORTIS' MODE, WITH SEPARATION AND INTER-ROCKET RADAR INTERVALS UNCHANGED, IF AND ONLY IF THE OWN-ACCELERATIONS CONDITION APPLIES:

$$l = \frac{1}{\alpha} - \frac{1}{\alpha_r} \quad (\text{I.E.} \quad \alpha = \frac{\alpha_r}{1 + l\alpha_r} = \frac{1}{1+l}).$$

ROCKET OWN-TIMES ARE PERCEIVED AS INVERSELY PROPORTIONAL TO THEIR RESPECTIVE MOMENTARY OWN-ACCELERATION VALUES. CONTRARY TO ENTRENCHED OPINION, THIS IS THE SOLE ACCELERATING EXTENDED MEDIUM SCENARIO WHERE THE MINKOWSKI METRIC APPLIES.

17.6   The good-in-spots bad egg

It is worth mentioning in the present context, that[14] just like chapter 16's radar equations (16.11) and (16.12), neither radar equations (17.6), (17.7), (17.9), (17.10), (17.11) nor loci equations (17.16) appear to be evident in relativity textbooks.[15] Presumably this is partly because the Minkowski metric equation, in its one spatial dimension form, *correctly but very awkwardly* establishes the validity of the rigor mortis acceleration scenario (generally termed 'rigid motion'). That metric is also applicable for accelerating point objects i.e. *particles*—its main raison d'être. Nevertheless, as we shall show in chapter 20, the Minkowski metric is generally speaking invalid for an accelerating extended medium even in special relativity—with the <u>sole</u> exception (where *extended* media are concerned) of the rigor mortis acceleration case.

> [14] Prior to the author's 2016 *Results in Physics* paper.
>
> [15] Naturally the author would appreciate being notified should this not be the case.

18

Two real—Euclidean—metric own-surfaces

'Why is philosophy so complicated? It ought to be entirely simple. Philosophy unties the knots in our thinking that we have, in a senseless way, put there. To do this it must make movements that are just as complicated as these knots are. Although the result of philosophy is simple, its method by convention cannot be if it is to succeed. The complexity of philosophy is not a complexity of its subject matter, but of our knotted understanding.'
Ludwig Wittgenstein

In attempting to resolve the question of the length an accelerating extended medium in a special relativity context, conventional physics has inappropriately adopted 'Minkowski spacetime' as a *generalised* principle. Fraught with misconstrued complexities and epitomised by a pseudo-Euclidean geometry *complex variables* 'metric' equation, this nonvisualisible path happens to be correct for *particle physics* ('point objects') and, in its one-spatial dimension form, also correctly represents (as we shall see presently) the 'rigid motion' scenario treated in the previous Rigor Mortis acceleration chapter. As will be subsequently explained in detail in this book's final *Part VII* however, contrary to what is still upheld in much of the literature for *all other extended accelerating medium scenarios* Minkowski spacetime is inapplicable.[1,2]

This chapter introduces an alternate *real* metric approach involving *real variable* metric equations and corresponding visualisable 'own-surfaces' which are individually specific to several acceleration scenarios. One such surface will later reveal the kernel solution of the long contested Bell's string paradox enigma, the uniformly ('homogeneously') accelerating extended medium case. For the moment, we focus on the simple zero acceleration case and the rigor mortis acceleration case whose own-surface turns out to have the surprisingly familiar yet curious shape of a Chinese hand-held fan.

[1] B.C. Minkowski spacetime does not apply to a homogeneously accelerating medium. *Results in Physics*, 6:31–38, January 2016

[2] B.C. Bell's twin rockets non-inertial length enigma resolved by real geometry. *Results in Physics*, 7:2575–2581, July 2017

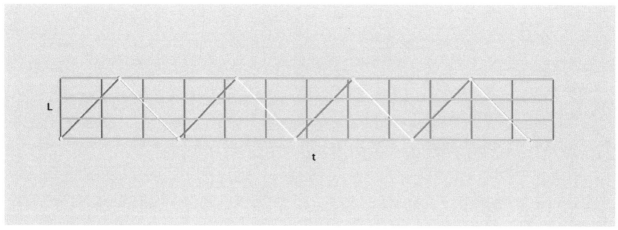

Figure 18.1: A nonaccelerating
medium's metric own-surface

18.1 *Increment curves and medium curves*

The SPACETIME OWN-SURFACE METRIC is a straightforward idea, where
single spatial dimension scenarios are concerned. We confine our deliberations
to a medium whose individual increments each independently maintain a
fixed own-thrust α which may differ however from increment to increment,
or even, as in our initial special simple case, all have zero thrust.

Our *real variables* own-surfaces will host two sets of curves—'INCREMENT
CURVES' and 'MEDIUM CURVES' embedded in a two or perhaps three dimensional real (*Euclidean*) mathematical space.[3] Increment curve path lengths
will trace 'own-clock-time' τ progressions of individual increments. These
will be crossed by the medium curves where each point's curved length λ
from the rear's increment reflects the medium point's 'own-length'[4] from the
rear end.

[3] Not to be confused with our
spacetime's spatial dimensions.

[4] A concept we discuss later in
further detail.

18.2 *The simple nonaccelerating own-surface*

The simplest possible example of an extended object's spacetime own-surface
is of course that of a *nonaccelerating* one-spatial dimensional medium such as
a long 'floating' spacestation—a rectangular lattice. As shown in Figure 18.1,
horizontal increment lines trace identical own-times τ of increments all stationary in a *single* inertial comoving frame[5] and identified by their *initial separation distance l* from the rear end. Vertical lines represent the whole medium
at regular equal own-time intervals. In this elementary case $\tau = t$, the time parameter of the medium's unchanging comoving frame, and each increment's
own-separation from the medium's rear remains unchanged i.e. $\lambda = l$.

[5] Here we again use the single
frame chart discussed under The
single 'home' reference frame chart
on page 84.

Notably, this own-surface's straight line increment and medium curves remain parallel to the unchanging home own-frame's time and space coordinates. The chart also shows *radar trajectories* emitted at regular time intervals and reflected between the front and rear ends, which are diagonal lines corresponding to scaled unit limit speed in the unchanging inertial reference frame.

18.3   The rigor mortis medium's own-surface

The PROLOGUE's section The REAL variables metric surface, outlined several mostly long drawn out approaches in the literature dealing with what we label 'rigor mortis' acceleration—an accelerating extended medium's increments remaining relatively stationary in every momentary comoving frame and sharing its momentary velocity relative to a 'home' launch frame. Since in this case increments never 'move apart' in any comoving frame, the medium always has the same fixed length in such frames.

In the previous chapter Rigor Mortis acceleration, radar equations established the definitive rigor mortis acceleration condition (17.17). Nevertheless this criterion may be determined in an even simpler way.

A shortcut to chapter 17's rigor mortis condition

[6]From the Non-unit fixed own-thrust relationships section's equation (17.1)-ii, the home frame velocity of each such medium curve's increment with a fixed own-thrust α, relates as $v = \tanh(\alpha\tau)$. Therefore, for any set velocity, increment curve lengths (own-times) $\tau = \tanh^{-1}(v)/\alpha$ are inversely proportional to their respective α values. As their separations $\Delta\lambda = \Delta l$ are fixed as v increases, *rigor mortis own-surface increment curves must remain equally spread i.e. they must be parallel.*[7] We denote this as *condition (A)*.

Figure 18.2's 'exploded' extract shows miniscule $\Delta\lambda$, $\Delta\tau$ and Δs segments where Δs is part of a forward radar trajectory. Both forward and reverse radar trajectories have unit limit speed $\frac{d\lambda}{d\tau} = 1$ in each momentary inertial frame. Accordingly, each must cross medium curves and increment curves *symmetrically i.e. the latter curves must be at right angles*[8] (B). This also means that *fixed length medium curves must be straight lines* (C). Conditions (A), (B) and (C) *alone* determine that the rigor mortis medium's own-surface must be a circular strip shaped like a hand-held fan[9] as in Figure 18.2. If rear increment own-acceleration $\alpha_r = 1$, then $\Delta\tau.\alpha = \Delta\tau_r.1$ and from the geometry

$$\frac{1+l}{1} = \frac{\Delta\tau}{\Delta\tau_r} = \frac{1}{\alpha} \quad \text{i.e.} \quad l = \frac{1}{\alpha} - \frac{1}{1}.$$

This exactly matches chapter 17's rigor mortis condition (17.17).

[6] For convenience Figure 18.2's medium length is selected as $L = 0.5555$, a value slightly less that of the earlier chapter Rigor Mortis acceleration's Figure 17.1 in order that the forward radar period (equation (17.9)—$2\ln(1 + 0.5555) = 3.\frac{3\pi}{32}$) is an integral multiple (3) of the set emission interval period.

[7] If we assume this own-surface is *planar*.

[8] Since in a miniscule planar triangle in the limit, angles add up to two right angles.

[9] Often called a 'Japanese fan', such a fan actually originated in China.

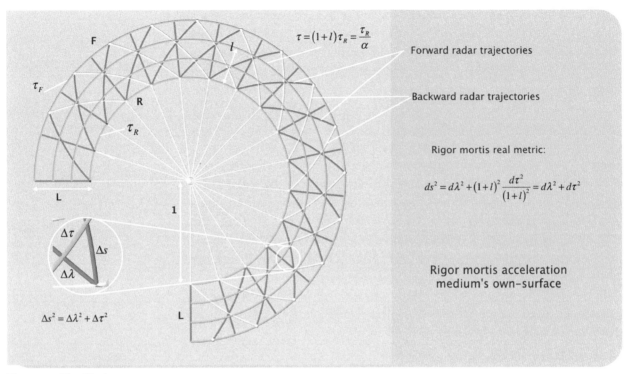

Figure 18.2: Rigor Mortis own-surface—the egg's good spots

Characteristics of the rigor mortis metric own-surface

Figure 18.2's own-surface is shown for rear rocket own-time $0 \leq \tau_r \leq 3\pi/2$. The inner increment curve corresponds to the rear increment r whose acceleration is chosen for convenience as *one* i.e. $\alpha_r = 1$. Increment curves (in green) appear as *circular arc segments of radius* $(1+l) = 1/\alpha$ which 'metrically' correspond to respective increments' *differing* elapsed own-time since launch:

$$\tau = \tau_r/\alpha = \tau_r(1+l). \tag{18.1}$$

These are crossed by straight radial medium curves spread along the surface at rear increment own-time intervals $\Delta\tau_r = 3\pi/32$. The more slowly accelerating increments nearer the front increment f require greater clock own-times τ than those nearer rear increment r to attain the same shared home frame velocity $v = \tanh \tau_r = \tanh(\tau\alpha) = \tanh(\tau/(1+l))$, and so be relatively stationary to one another in each respective comoving frame.

The own-surface fixed velocity straight line loci[10] *metrically* reflect the perceived unchanging total length of the medium in each co-moving frame $\underline{C}$. A rigor mortis medium's curve therefore always has the same total 'own-length' L, just as in the zero acceleration scenario. Each own-surface point represents *an event* on the medium characterised by an increment's medium curve *dis-*

[10] In mathematics a curve reflecting a fixed parameter is called a *locus* (plural: *loci*).

tance $\lambda(=l)$ from the rear increment, as well as by *a specific increment own-time* τ corresponding to the circular arc path length.

The rear rocket's increment curve in Figure 18.2 is portrayed as a unit radius *planar* circular arc curve (in a 3-dimensional space where $z = 0$) as: $[\cos \tau_r, \sin \tau_r, 0]$. [11]For convenience we use both *cylindrical* coordinates $r = 1 + l$, $\theta = \tau = \tau_r \alpha = \tau_r/(1+l)$, $z = 0$, and *cartesian* coordinates $x = r \cos \theta$, $y = r \sin \theta$, $z = 0$. We may therefore denote for each increment curve l where $0 \le l \le L$:

$$[\cos \tau, \sin \tau, 0]\,(1+l) = \left[\cos \frac{\tau_r}{1+l}, \sin \frac{\tau_r}{1+l}, 0\right](1+l).$$

This may be expressed as a surface $\mathfrak{R}p$:[12]

[11] *r* here denotes a *cylindrical radius* coordinate—not to be confused with the same letter's usage as *a subscript denoting a rear rocket increment.*

[12] We denote our *planar* rigor mortis surface as $\mathfrak{R}p$.

18.2.

THE RIGOR MORTIS PLANAR OWN-SURFACE

$$\mathfrak{R}_P(\tau_r, l) =_{Cyl} \left[1+l, \frac{\tau_r}{1+l}, 0\right] = \left[\cos \frac{\tau_r}{1+l}, \sin \frac{\tau_r}{1+l}, 0\right](1+l); \qquad 0 \le l \le L.$$

18.4 *The 'hemicised' rigor mortis own-surface*

Next we show how our intrinsic own-surface may be 'reshaped' so that increments' own-time τ range may be extended indefinitely. By virtue of its radial straight line medium curves, Figure 18.2's rigor mortis planar own-surface is a *'ruled surface'*.[13] It may therefore be *isometrically reshaped* without altering its intrinsic metric properties whereby distances between any two own-surface points (events)—over the surface itself—remain unchanged. One such isometric change would be the surface rolled up in the shape of a cone. If made of paper, the surface would not tear if so deformed.

[13] A ruled surface is one upon which *a series of straight lines* may be drawn—such as our radially distributed medium curves.

Figure 18.3 shows another reshaped surface. Each circular increment curve arc of Figure 18.2's *planar* own-surface is twisted—without being stretched or compressed—into the form of the spherical curve of the earlier chapter Spacetime's and Geometry's missing 'HEMIX'. This is possible because from equation (13.4)-i each hemix's path length—its respective increment's own-length τ—is proportional to its traversed 'equatorial' longitude. Each hemix increment curve representing an arbitrary fixed acceleration $\alpha < 1$ will lie on a hemisphere of radius $1/\alpha = 1 + l$.

As shown on the 'hemicised' rigor mortis own-surface, respective fixed velocity v medium curves, which are straight lines, remain likewise unchanged both in length and as well as shared longitude angle θ. Each such medium curve is rotated so that its inline radius forms a *colatitude angle* ϕ with the

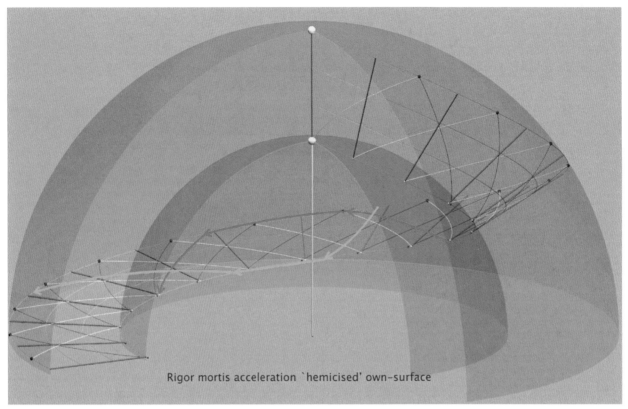

Rigor mortis acceleration `hemicised' own–surface

Figure 18.3: The 'hemicised' rigor
mortis own-surface

vertical axis, where comoving velocity $\sin\phi = v = \tanh\frac{\tau}{1+l} = \tanh\tau_r$. *Intrinsically* therefore *it is still the same own-surface*, in spite of being transformed and re-embedded in a three dimensional mathematical space.

Also shown in Figure 18.3 are the emitted and reflected radar trajectories still manifesting unchanging radar emission-return own-time periods in terms of $\Delta\tau$ intervals. Notably, this own-surface shape tends *asymptotically* to become 'equatorial' as $\tau_r = \tau/(1 + l)$ approaches infinity i.e. it may progress endlessly. We refer to another such own-metric surface again later.

18.5　*Migrants on a rigor mortis gravity train*

Let us imagine a series of 'compartment rockets' constantly accelerating differently in accordance with the rigor mortis criterion and somehow joined together with connecting chambers allowing passengers to migrate between rockets. The passengers of each compartment age relatively in accordance with their respective own-acceleration which depends on its relative distance from the rearmost rocket: $\frac{\tau}{\tau_r} = \frac{1}{\alpha} = \frac{1+l}{1}$. Their respective own-time clocks, synchronised at launch, would increasingly diverge. Notably, the physical basis behind this is their differently experienced gravity-like acceleration. Of course other than sensing such differing accelerations, passengers would not notice any difference in his or her individual biological feeling of 'getting older'.

Our 'compound spaceship' could house a colony where every member of the community would continue to remain stationary at unchanging distances relative to everybody else. Passengers could choose to move towards either the rear rocket r or the front rocket f, depending on whether they prefer to age either more slowly or more quickly compared with passengers in other rocket compartments. The dark green and cyan paths trajectories on the hemicised own-surface represent passengers choosing to age at a different rate relative to other passengers, by moving towards the more slowly accelerating front rocket whose inhabitants ages at a faster relative rate, or towards the more rapidly accelerating rear rocket whose inhabitants age more slowly.

A rigor mortis gravitational field

Notably, if instead of our rigor mortis gravity train compartments each independently producing its own specific thrust, were it possible to arrange *a gravity field* whereby gravity pull across the medium was imposed in accordance with the equation $g = \frac{1}{1+l}$, *then the same effects would be achieved*. Significant in this context also, recalling chapter 17's equation (17.14), are how rigor mortis compartment clocks relate i.e. $\tau = \tau_r.(1 + l) = \tau_r/g$.

18.6   The rigor mortis 'real metric'

In general a surface's 'differential metric' relates any two minimally apart event points—in the limit. Adopting Figure 18.2's planar surface's centre as its origin and using radial coordinates (r, θ), from equation (18.2) we obtain $r = 1 + l$ and $\theta = \tau_r = \tau/(1 + l)$. Therefore $dr = dl$ and $d\theta = d\tau/(1 + l)$ and a surface's metric interval is $ds^2 = dr^2 + r^2 d\theta^2$ i.e. $ds^2 = dl^2 + (1 + l)^2 \frac{d\tau^2}{(1+l)^2}$. Hence, since in this rigor mortis case $\lambda = l$:

18.3.

THE RIGOR MORTIS OWN-SURFACE METRIC $ds_\mathfrak{R}^2 = d\tau^2 + d\lambda^2.$

Notably, this metric applies to both planar own-surface as well as 'hemicised' own-surface. Since all distances and angles remain unchanged, both surfaces are intrinsically the same i.e. *'isometric'*.

Although a rigor mortis medium's increments after launch no longer share simultaneities in the home frame due their 'contrived' acceleration differences, the increments are simultaneously relatively stationary in each instantaneous comoving frame and medium length remains unchanged. Paradoxically however, *in each such comoving frame all increment clock own-times simultaneously differ.*

18.7 Relativity's pseudo-Euclidean Minkowski metric

If we replace the *positive* sign in our visualisable *real variables* rigor mortis own-surface metric (18.3) by a *negative* sign, we obtain the *equivalent* yet non-visualisable complex variable[14] Minkowski spacetime metric interval equation:[15]

$$ds^2_{\mathfrak{MM}} = d\tau^2 - d\lambda^2. \tag{18.4}$$

[14] Associated with the imaginary square root of *negative* values.

[15] Sometimes written as $ds^2 = d\lambda^2 - d\tau^2$.

Our real metric surface approach has resolved the rigor mortis topic at a quite elementary level which nevertheless reflects several advanced differential geometry concepts familiar to relativists used to dealing with the issue in a traditional if more obscure mathematical way. One the one hand, proponents of Minkowski spacetime may well approve of (and be surprised by) their banner metric equation actually having a real variable equivalent. On the other hand however, traditionally educated physicists may feel less comfortable with the arguments and conclusions of this book's remaining chapters.

These deal with the mathematics and physics of an extended accelerating medium which *differs* from the Minkowski metric's well established 'rigid motion' showcase. The homogeneously accelerating unit thrust medium which has been tangled over since the scenario—better known as 'BELL'S STRING PARADOX'—was first pondered upon over half a century ago.

VII

ROLLER-COASTING SPACETIME

HOW DOES A UNIFORMLY CO-ACCELERATING MEDIUM BETWEEN TWO IDENTICALLY ACCELERATING ROCKETS 'EXPAND'? This seemingly straightforward topic first achieved prominence in 1959 in the *American Journal of Physics*.[16] Roughly three decades later in that same journal,[17] another two American physicists made a serious attempt to clarify the matter but, at the same time, used the opportunity to severely castigate relativity literature's hitherto very inadequate traditional approaches to the issue.[18] The enigma of an accelerating medium's 'length' became known as[19] *Bell's string paradox* or *Bell's spaceship paradox*, after *John Bell* in 1976 uncovered highly diverse opinions among his CERN colleagues on the topic.[20] Yet the late Irish physicist's own deliberations on the matter were likewise inconclusive.

This final book part's first chapter The unit thrust medium own-surface establishes a unique 'missing link' *differential geometry criterion* solely on the basis of expected *uniformity* and *monotonic increase* over own-time of the homogeneously accelerating medium expansion itself. The resulting 'own-surface' Υ turns out to be *a unit pitch helicoidal extension* of the same hemix curve[21] epitomising a point object's unit acceleration which we have already established in chapter 13, Spacetime's and Geometry's missing 'HEMIX'. The over decades much disputed expansion factor meets chapter 16's already determined expansion limit conditions, and reveals that *Bell' accelerating string does expand but does* NOT *break if it may stretch by up the square root of two*. Four different perspectives of the 'length' of a constant homogeneous thrust medium are then contrasted. The chapter ends with a discussion of a 'non-inertial present tense'.

A Relativity Cosmographicum's real spacetime metrics chapter *extrinsically* corroborates the new metric own-surface by showing how accelerating 'medium curves' constitute the intersection of generic surfaces 'encased' in what is termed A HELICOIDAL RELATIVITY SEXTET. A unit thrust 'gravity train' scenario is then described which epitomises unit thrust conditions experienced by spatially spread passengers of an idealised train. Then the unit thrust surface's real metric is derived. This equation turns out to be *wholly irreconcilable* with Minkowski's renowned metric. Where special relativity is concerned therefore, the latter must be considered as *overgeneralised* except for point objects or the special 'one-off' rigor mortis (so-called 'rigid motion') acceleration case.

Finally the subsequent optional chapter *Radar mappings from inertial home frame onto own-surface Υ *intrinsically* validates own-surface Υ by exactly conforming to all conceivable radar trajectory 'mappings' criteria for a uniformly accelerating medium. The book concludes with an Epilogue chapter.

[16] E Dewan and M Beran. Note on stress effects due to relativistic contraction. *American Journal of Physics*, 27:517–8, 1959

[17] D A Desloge and R J Philpott. Uniformly accelerated reference frames in special relativity. *American Journal of Physics*, 55: 252–261, 1987

[18] Notwithstanding its concerted efforts and *a two year journal review period* however, the 1987 paper itself likewise failed to arrive at a feasible solution. Ironically the authors themselves had succumbed to the naive assumption that *the limit speed constancy principle* valid in inertial frames of reference, must also apply to *identically accelerating* rockets. Accordingly, they, and by implication the journal's editorial board and reviewers, took it for granted that such rockets' radar intervals must be *constant*. Extraordinarily, not only is this widely held 'intuitive' rule of thumb thoroughly wrong, it is an entirely simple matter to establish that the forward and reverse radar intervals actually *vary*, as we have already seen in chapter 16 ($\Rightarrow$A fallacy's domino effect on page 121).

[19] Honoured for his renowned contributions to quantum physics by a *Route Bell* within the Geneva CERN complex.

[20] John Bell. *Speakable and Unspeakable in Quantum Mechanics*, chapter How to teach special relativity (1976), pages 67–68. Cambridge University Press, 1987

[21] Both the hemix curve and the 'hemicoid' surface appear to be unknown—even in differential geometry textbooks.

19

The unit thrust medium own-surface

SOLVING 'BELL'S SPACESHIP PROBLEM'

'The approach is unnecessarily formal or abstract, key concepts are left undefined, a working knowledge of general relativity is assumed, no attempt is made to give a physical interpretation of the coordinates introduced, the relationship between different sets of coordinates used is not made, and no investigation of the properties of the frame is made.' Desloge & Philpott *Uniformly accelerated reference frames in special relativity* 1985/7

19.1 A further perpetuated error in relativity literature

As highlighted in chapter 15, 'Time dispersal' and 'retro-separation', a uniformly accelerating medium's spatially apart events which are simultaneous in the home frame, are *dissimultaneous* in every comoving inertial frame $\underline{C}$. It is therefore incorrect to assert (as in [1,2] and [3,4]) that a home frame 'contracted' length L relates *during actual acceleration* to a comoving inertial frame's 'expanded' length $L\gamma$, although this is still naively upheld in many relativity textbooks and papers—just like the inter-rockets' constant radar intervals myth. The $L\gamma$ term reflects not an accelerating 'length' but a *post-shutdown phase* inertial frame's *final separation distance* between the rockets. The widely held simplistic 'inverse contraction' γ expansion factor applies only when both rockets cease accelerating—*not beforehand*.

No *inertial frame length assessment* is possible for an accelerating extended medium, with the sole 'expedient' exception of the *'rigor mortis'* accelerating medium dealt with in the previous book section, which retains its definable inertial own-length in every comoving inertial frame because its respective increments accelerate *differently* in accordance with condition (17.17), so staying relatively stationary in such inertial frames.

©BCS IRELAND 2017 ISBN 978-1-9998410-1-0
Brian Coleman SPACETIME FUNDAMENTALS INTELLIGIBLY (RE)LEARNT

[1] Wolfgang Rindler. *Relativity, Special, General and Cosmological.* Oxford Universtiy Press, 2001, 2006
[2] Exercise 3.24 (incorrect): *A certain piece of elastic breaks when it is stretched to twice its unstretched length. At time $t = 0$, all points of it are accelerated longitudinally with constant proper acceleration α, from rest in the unstretched state. Prove that the elastic breaks at $t = \sqrt{3}c/\alpha$ [when $\gamma = 2$].*
[3] Jerrold Franklin. Lorentz contraction, Bell's spaceships and rigid body motion in special relativity. *Eur. J. Phys.*, 31:291–298, 2010
[4] p.294 (incorrect):
"...a cable connecting the two ships would snap when
$d' = \gamma.d = d_{max}."$

19.2   *Intrinsic own-surface criteria for a unit thrust medium*

As already explained in section 16.7 A photon's unit thrust medium-timed crossing rates, if we identify each unit thrust medium's individual increment by its original *home frame* launch position l ($0 \leq l \leq L$), we may refer to its distance along in-between increments as a 'NON-INERTIAL OWN-LENGTH' $\lambda(l,\tau) = l \cdot \epsilon(\tau)$, where $\epsilon(\tau) = \partial\lambda/\partial l$ will be the *non-inertial own-expansion factor* which we wish to establish. The *identically accelerating* whole medium's non-inertial own-length $\Lambda = L.\epsilon(\tau)$ will 'share' common own-time τ not in respective ever changing comoving *inertial frames* $\underline{C}$ due to inertial frame time dissimultaneities, but in what we label NON-INERTIAL 'PROXY' FRAMES $\underline{\Pi}$. Such frames—alien to our natural sense of space and time—have relevance *only as long as the medium uniformly accelerates*.

A uniformly accelerating medium's *'expansion'* must meet chapter 16's *limit conditions* (16.16): $\epsilon(\tau) \cdot e^{-\tau} = 0$ and $\epsilon(\tau) \cdot e^{\tau} = \infty$ as $\tau \to \infty$. This of course directly invalidates the endemically held γ-factor expansion since in the limit $\gamma.e^{-\tau} = \cosh\tau.e^{-\tau}$ becomes 0.5 rather than *zero*.[5] Moreover, the 'dispersal time' $L\gamma v$ to 'dispersal distance' $L\gamma$ ratio equals scaled velocity v which approaches limit *one* as home time $t \to \infty$. This suggests that the non-inertial own-length of a co-accelerating medium between the rockets will, prior to shutdowns, be *of the same order of magnitude as their initial launch separation* L. **Special note:** Our *idealised* medium increments are assumed to have their own individual clocks and 'minuscule' rockets so that no inter-increment pushing or pulling, which would also entail time delays, is involved. Moreover, each increment's 'mass' is assumed to be zero *in the limit* so that neither energy nor inter-increment gravitational forces need be considered.[6]

A simple question

We approach the Bell's non-inertial length problem by searching for *a unit thrust medium's real metric own-surface* which we will label Υ (Greek *Upsilon*). A precedence for this is The rigor mortis medium's own-surface introduced in the previous chapter. Should such a surface Υ exist for our homogeneously accelerating extended medium case, it will likewise not directly represent *observer-related coordinates*—as do inertial home frame[7] world-surfaces—but instead will metrically reflect *object-related parameters* i.e. the medium's progressing own-times (*'clock times'*) and expanding non-inertial own-length *as experienced along the medium itself*. So we pose a simple question apparently not addressed (in this form) even in geometry literature:

> Is there a way in which a flexible flat rectangular strip may be transformed to a smooth and regular *open* surface so that lateral lines increase in length *as well as in curvature* both uniformly and monotonically ?

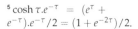

[5] $\cosh\tau.e^{-\tau} = (e^{\tau} + e^{-\tau}).e^{-\tau}/2 = (1 + e^{-2\tau})/2.$

[6] This scenario is reflected—somewhat simplistically—by its original designation as *'Bell's string paradox'*, whereby the 'string' itself is assumed to have negligible mass.

[7] i.e. as viewed by observers stationary in the home frame who view the medium passing at ever increasing speed.

[8]If it exists, such a surface Υ might host fixed-τ *medium curves* metrically corresponding to the medium's expanding 'non-inertial own-length' λ. These would be crossed by identical fixed-l *increment curves* whose path lengths trace progressing own-time τ. Expansion factor $\partial\lambda/\partial l = \epsilon(\tau)$ would need to be uniform along each medium curve since the medium expands to the same extent along its own-length. Since each fixed-l increment curve on Υ must thereby *identically* relate geometrically with neighbouring increment curves, they must be *congruent*[9] and *helicoidally* spread in accordance with some constant *inverse pitch* factor m i.e. *translated by l along a vertical axis and axially rotated by angle $l.m$.* Moreover fixed-τ curves will then be *axially concentric helices* reflecting the medium's monotonically increasing 'own-length' $\Lambda = L.\epsilon(\tau)$ as shared own-time τ progresses. Hence surface Υ must be *a helicoid* generated by a rear rocket ($l = 0$) *generator increment curve* we denote as curve Q.

A promising case here might seem to be the familiar *multi-level car parking driveway* with its helicoidally distributed radial lines and concentric helices increasing in length with *cylindrical radius r.* Such helices' *curvatures* however, increase with r only up to $r = 1/m$ (m is the helicoid's constant inverse pitch, with angles measured in radians) and thereafter *decrease* ($\Rightarrow$ APPENDIX equation (34) in the author's recent *Results in Physics* publication[10]) i.e. such a surface's inwards bending first increases and then decreases. Moreover fixed-l curves are not identical and the surface would not meet further necessary conditions discussed in subsequent chapter 21.

19.3   *The missing own-surface Υ*

As it turns out, if we not only limit cylindrical radius r of the helicoid's generator curve to within $1/m$, but also require its *longitude θ* and *spherical radius R* coordinates to be likewise monotonic with increasing own-time τ so that the generated helicoid is *free of all intermittent ($\tau < \infty$) topological inflections*, a unique *helicoid* emerges. As proven in the 2017 paper's Appendix, this special surface, which we designate as 'HEMICOID' Υ, *is the sole inflection-free real surface mathematically possible which uniformly expands laterally and is open.* Thus this unique helicoidal surface Υ can actually be evolved *with no reference to relativistic mathematics.* The key properties of surface Υ, whose helicoidal pitch $1/m$ is *one*, have been already outlined in 2012.[11]

Of primary significance, our surface Υ's generating curve Q representing the rear rocket, is none other than the basic spherical geometry curve already established in chapter 13's Spacetime's and Geometry's missing 'HEMIX' which epitomises the relationship between an accelerating rocket's scaled own-time and home frame velocity: hemix vector (13.5) $\mathfrak{H} = [\tanh\tau\cos\tau, \tanh\tau\sin\tau, \frac{1}{\cosh\tau}]$. Indeed we have already deployed curve $\mathfrak{H}$ in the previous chapter's section The 'hemicised' rigor mortis own-surface.

[8] A monotonic function may be *only constant*, *only increasing* or *only decreasing*.

[9] i.e. identical in shape and size, but not necessarily in position.

[10] B.C. Bell's twin rockets non-inertial length enigma resolved by real geometry. *Results in Physics*, 7:2575–2581, July 2017

[11] B.C. Relativity Acceleration's Cosmographicum and its Radar Photon Surfings—A Euclidean Diminishment of Minkowski Spacetime, February 2012. URL http://www.dpg-verhandlungen.de/year/2012/conference/goettingen/part/gr/session/4/contribution/4

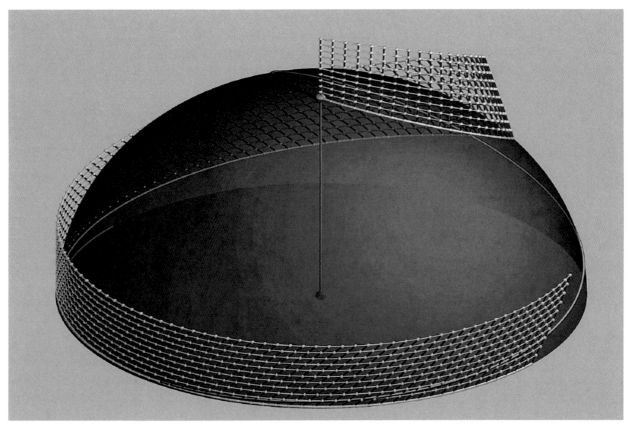

Figure 19.1: The unit thrust medium's hemicoidal metric own-surface Υ.

'Helicoidising' hemix curve $\mathfrak{H}$ gives us what we call A 'HEMICOID':

19.1.

UNIFORM ACCELERATION OWN-SURFACE

$$\Upsilon(\tau, l) = {}_{Cyl}\left[\tanh\tau, \tau + l, \frac{1}{\cosh\tau} + l\right] = \left[\tanh\tau\cos(\tau + l), \tanh\tau\sin(\tau + l), \frac{1}{\cosh\tau} + l\right].$$

[12] Very strangely, all geometry books known to the author define a *'generalised helicoid'* as having only a *linear* or *planar* generating curve and do not envisage a helicoid such as surface Υ.

[13] To the best of the present author's knowledge.

Generator nonplanar[12] hemix curve $\mathfrak{H}$ turns out to have the simplest imaginable characteristics. It is confined to a hemisphere and its path length continually reflects its traversed longitude. Significantly $\theta = \tau$ is also the parameter traditionally known as *rapidity* and $v = \tanh\tau = r = \sin\phi$ (and hence $1/\gamma = \sqrt{1 - v^2} = \cos\phi$). Further unusual characteristics of this curve are described in the author's 2017 *Results in Physics* paper. Quite astonishingly, like its also unique generator curve $\mathfrak{H}$, surface Υ appears[13] to be entirely absent not only in relativity literature but also in geometry textbooks.

[14]Similar to the world-lines and lines of home frame time simultaneity obtained by adopting fixed values for l and t in world-surface equation (16.1), equations for metric surface Υ's increment and medium curves in Figure 19.1 are likewise obtained using fixed l and τ values in equation (19.1)-ii.

[14] Since from (19.4) and (19.5) $\lambda = l.\sqrt{1 + \tanh^2 \tau}$, a fixed-$l$ value corresponds to a fixed-λ value. Also since $t = \sinh \tau$, a fixed-t value corresponds to fixed-τ value.

Own-surface Υ's helices and hemices

Figure 19.1's 'hemicoid' own-surface[15] Υ shows lateral medium helices tracing momentarily shared own-τ-time where $0 \leq \tau \leq 3\pi/2$ i.e. for rocket scaled speed range $0 \leq v \leq \tanh(3\pi/2) = 0.99983861....$ These are crossed by individual increment hemices spread uniformly in accordance with an expanding λ-value equal to the modulus of each fixed-τ medium helix's tangent vector.

[15] This actual diagram was first presented in an unsuccessful submission to the *American Journal of Physics* in 2009. ($\Rightarrow$ Epilogue chapter.)

τ-differentiating Υ, the dot product's square root confirms that increment curves are unit speed i.e. have as path length parameter own-time τ:

$$\Upsilon_\tau = \frac{\partial \Upsilon}{\partial \tau} = \left[\frac{\cos(\tau + l)}{\cosh^2 \tau} - \tanh \tau \sin(\tau + l), \frac{\sin(\tau + l)}{\cosh^2 \tau} + \tanh \tau \cos(\tau + l), \frac{-\sinh \tau}{\cosh^2 \tau} \right].$$
$$(19.2)$$

[16]

$$|\Upsilon_\tau| = \sqrt{\frac{\partial \Upsilon}{\partial \tau} \cdot \frac{\partial \Upsilon}{\partial \tau}} = \sqrt{\frac{1}{\cosh^4 \tau} + \tanh^2 \tau + \frac{\sinh^2 \tau}{\cosh^4 \tau}} = 1. \qquad (19.3)$$

[16] Cross products cancel out. $\frac{1 + \sinh^2 \cosh^2 \tau + \sinh^2 \tau}{\cosh^4 \tau}$ $= \frac{\cosh^2 \tau.(1 + \sinh^2)}{\cosh^4 \tau} = 1.$

The *lateral expansion factor* $\epsilon(\tau)$ results from l-differentiation:

$$\Upsilon_l = \frac{\partial \Upsilon}{\partial l} = \left[- \tanh \tau \sin(\tau + l), \tanh \tau \cos(\tau + l), 1 \right]. \qquad (19.4)$$

19.5.

UNIFORM ACCELERATION NON-INERTIAL EXPANSION

$$\epsilon(\tau) = \frac{\partial \lambda}{\partial l} = |\Upsilon_l| = \sqrt{\frac{\partial \Upsilon}{\partial l} \cdot \frac{\partial \Upsilon}{\partial l}} = \sqrt{1 + \tanh^2 \tau} = \sqrt{1 + v^2}.$$

[17]Crucially, surface Υ's medium curves' expansion factor $\epsilon(\tau)$ *meets the necessary unit thrust medium's expansion limit conditions* (16.16):

[17] (19.4)'s dot product $\frac{\partial \Upsilon}{\partial l} \cdot \frac{\partial \Upsilon}{\partial l} = \tanh^2 \tau \sin^2(\tau + l) + \tanh^2 \tau \cos^2(\tau + l) + 1 = \tanh^2 \tau + 1.$

$$\sqrt{1 + \tanh^2 \tau} \cdot e^{-\tau}|_{\tau \to \infty} = 0; \qquad \sqrt{1 + \tanh^2 \tau} \cdot e^\tau|_{\tau \to \infty} = \infty.$$

The subsequent two chapters present further validations of this real metric surface's relevancy to non-inertial length expansion which we now contrast with three other related length perspectives.

Figure 19.2: Various 'lengths' between uniformly accelerating rockets.

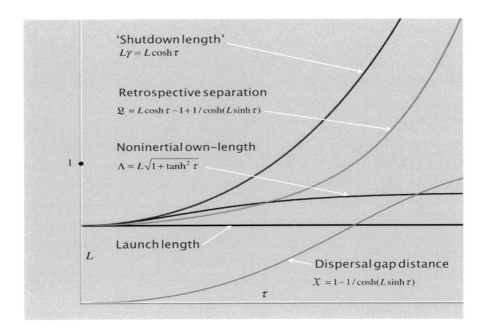

19.4 The medium's 'lengths' in four reference frames

Page 114's section Front rocket's 'retrospective' separation $\mathfrak{L}$ described how in every comoving frame $\underline{C}$ up to the instant of motor shutdown, the front rocket would view the rear rocket as always *relatively moving backwards* and consequently not sharing the same *inertial* frame $\underline{C}$. Also its clock becomes increasingly out of synchronism i.e. 'own-time dispersed' from the front rocket in each such frame. Accordingly, $\mathfrak{L}$ is a medium's (inertial frame) '*separation distance*' rather than a '*length*' and tends to become *infinite* as time increases.

Figure 19.2 shows the four unit thrust 'lengths': *launch length* L, *post-shutdown length* $L\gamma$, *retrospective separation* $\mathfrak{L}$ and *non-inertial own-length* Λ, as well as the dispersal gap distance $\mathfrak{X} = L\gamma - \mathfrak{L}$:

- L—*constant* length in inertial home frame $\underline{H}$,

- $L\breve{\gamma} = L\cosh\tau$—*ultimate* length in inertial shutdown frame $\underline{\breve{C}}$,

- $\mathfrak{L} = L\cosh\tau + \frac{1}{\cosh(L\sinh\tau)} - 1$—'*retrospective separation*' perceived in inertial time gap frame $\underline{G}$ and

- $\Lambda = L\epsilon(\tau) = L\sqrt{1 + \tanh^2\tau}$—'*non-inertial length*' associated with an accelerating 'proxy' non-inertial comoving frame $\underline{\Pi}$.

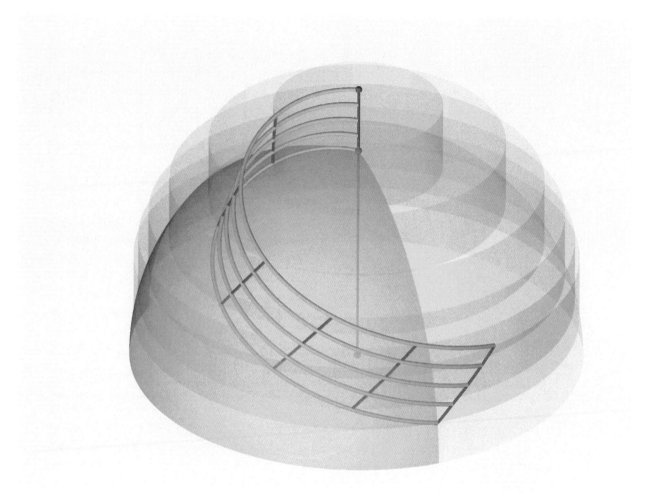

Figure 19.3: The unit thrust mediums' non-inertial 'proxy' frames.

Recalling Figure 15.2's dual home/shutdown frames spacetime chart, co-moving frames $\underline{C}$ cease changing with permanent shutdown frame $\underline{\check{C}}$. Proxy frames $\underline{\Pi}$ 'exist' only prior to the front rocket's shutdown. Inertial time gap frame $\underline{G}$, which parallels ever changing frames $\underline{C}$, has only relevance during acceleration (since the front rocket's shutdown could always be imminent).[18] Thus the 'length' of a uniformly accelerating medium *differs* depending on which of the frames $\underline{H}$, $\underline{\Pi}$, $\underline{C}/\underline{G}$ or $\underline{\check{C}}$ it is perceived <u>from</u>. The above diverse 'lengths' contrast with the relatively simple 'rigor mortis' case where own-length Λ and retrospective length $\mathcal{L}$ both remain equal to unchanging comoving frames length L i.e. $\Lambda = \mathcal{L} = L$ and dispersal gap distance $\mathfrak{X}$ is always zero.

[18] In inertial time gap frame $\underline{G}$, the front rocket shuts down *before* the rear rocket does.

19.5 *Non-inertial 'present tenses'*

Like the rigor mortis case, the unit thrust medium after launch does not 'collectively relate' to a home frame's present tense because of *absence of shared simultaneities between shared velocity spatially apart increments therein*. A rigor mortis medium's differently accelerating constituent increments however do share a *'comoving inertial frame's present tense'* and maintain an unchanging length in all inertial comoving frames, even though all such increments 'age' differently.

On the other hand, although the unit thrust medium does not (during acceleration) share a 'present tense' in inertial comoving frames, it does have a special 'NON-INERTIAL PRESENT' in each instantaneous 'proxy' non-inertial frame, wherein all increment own-times have the same own-time τ and accordingly age identically. These proxy frames are schematically represented by fixed-τ 'velocity cylinders' shown in Figure 19.3. Such 'simultaneities' of course *are differently shared* compared with *nonaccelerating* objects in inertial frames, in a manner which does not conform with conventional assessments of space and time. In fact the 'proxy frame', although we consider it as a 'reference frame', itself does not have constituent i.e. 'increment' observers who could share 'an inertial present tense' with other such observers on the medium.

This important paradigm spacetime scenario actually resembles an idealised *general relativity* case where each 'increment' of the medium would be identically accelerated in a *uniform* gravitational field, although even here *inter-increment* mass attraction forces would have to be viewed as negligible. We may invoke a gravity-free special relativity context however by imagining each 'virtually massless' increment to have its own 'minuscule' unit thrust rocket.

Just as we have seen in the chapter A Spacetime Odyssey for a point object such as a rocket and for the special rigor mortis extended medium case, we can now visualise relativistic acceleration parameters of *a homogenously extended medium*. Surface Υ may be considered as ' dynamically hosting' our continually changing proxy frames Π and is (one assumes) the 'missing link' needed to properly resolve the long fought over unit thrust medium expansion question. Unexpectedly perhaps, an external 'action principle' which would entail *asymmetrical* inter-increment forces and time delays, is actually *superfluous*.

20

A Relativity Cosmographicum's real spacetime metrics

"You are indeed the only person with whom I am really like to argue. Almost all the fellows do not look from the facts to the theory but only from the theory to the facts; they cannot extricate themselves from a once accepted conceptual web, but merely thrash about therein in a farcical manner."
Einstein, writing from Connecticut in 1935 to Erwin Schrödinger.

"Du bist faktisch der einzige Mensch mit dem ich mich wirklich gern auseinandersetze. Fast alle die Kerle sehen nämlich nicht von den Tatbeständen aus die Theorie sondern nur von der Theorie aus die Tatbestände; sie können aus dem einmal angenommenen Begriffs-netz nicht heraus sondern nur possierlich darin herumzappeln."

20.1   *Kepler's 16th century 'Mysterium Cosmographicum'*

[1]'STRETCH THY WITS HITHER MAN, TO GRASP THESE THINGS.'
Early in the 17th century Imperial Astronomer/Astrologer *Johannes Kepler* discovered three mathematical relationships governing orbital trajectories of planets around the Sun.[2] Worked out empirically from *Tycho Brahe's* extensive astronomical observations, these epochal laws later guided Isaac Newton's likewise landmark insights into mathematics and physics.

Kepler was inspired by his own earlier idea that Providence had confined the orbits of the (then known) six planets around our Sun along the surfaces of six concentric 'celestial' spheres in between which Euclid's five 'perfect' polyhedra—correspondingly scaled—would fit exactly. He was referring to the five unique flat-surfaced 'platonic solids': the cube's six squares, the dodecahedron with twelve pentagons, and the tetrahedron, octahedron and icosahedron, with four, eight and twenty equilateral triangles respectively. This *'Mysterium Cosmographicum'* itself however, ultimately proved a fantasy.

[1] 'MENSCH STRECKH DEINE VERNUNFT HIERHER UM DIESE DINGE ZU BEGREIFEN.'

[2] Kepler's laws of planetary motion:
  (1) Planets travel along respective ellipses all sharing one focus at the Sun.
  (2) Each respective planet's radial line to the Sun traces equal areas in equal time intervals.
  (3) Every planet's orbital period squared divided by its semi-major elliptical axis cubed, gives the same value.

Figure 20.1: Johannes Kepler's
'Mysterium Cosmographicum'
  in the *Kepler Museum* (and
house of birth) in *Weil der Stadt*.
    Hermann Bühler's 1930 model
shows the five perfect solids
encased in hemispheres.

Figure 20.2: Johannes Kepler,
1571-1630. Photographs taken by
the author by kind permission of
the museum curator

20.2   *The relativity helicoidal sextet*

This pinnacle chapter introduces a—nonfictional—'RELATIVITY COSMOGRAPH-
ICUM' which involves six *helicoidal* rather than six spherical surfaces and is
based on the unit thrust rocket 'ovoids' model of chapter 14, A Spacetime
Odyssey. We recall Figure 14.3's diagram containing a 'γ-distance ray' pivoted at the origin through unit radius-spherical hemix curve H and extend-
ing from the hemisphere's apex over an arbitrary colatitude velchronos angle
$\phi = \sin^{-1} v$, v being the rocket's increasing scaled velocity. The same ray
traces a planar 'gamma spiral' G along the -1 ovality plane, and a spiral F
on the $+1$ ovality unit diameter sphere. We now broaden that framework to
represent the parameters of a co-accelerating unit own-thrust *extended medium*.

In Figure 20.3, spirals ⑤, G and F are generator curves[3] of helicoids Υ, Γ and K[4] emanating together from an L-length line above the apex of unit radius hemisphere W and unit diameter sphere C.[5] As also shown for an arbitrary own-time τ, a radius $v = \tanh \tau$ velocity cylinder V intersects hemicoid Υ along a helix whose length reflects the medium's non-inertial own-length $\Lambda = L\sqrt{1 + \tanh^2 \tau} = L\sqrt{1 + v^2}$—equation (19.5).

[3] Rotated and elevated over equidistant intervals $0 \le l \le L$.
[4] Greek upper case *Upsilon, Gamma* and *Kappa* respectively.
[5] Unit radius hemisphere W and unit diameter sphere C appear with longitudinal angle cutaways.

Pseudo-expansion/pseudo-contraction helicoids Γ and K

Recalling (11.11)-i, spiral equation $G = {}_{Cyl}\left[t, \tau, 1\right] = {}_{Cyl}\left[\sinh \tau, \tau, 1\right]$ gives us:

'PSEUDO-EXPANSION' HELICOID $\Gamma = {}_{Cyl}\left[\sinh \tau, \tau + l, 1 + l\right] = \left[\sinh \tau \cos(\tau + l), \sinh \tau \sin(\tau + l), 1 + l\right].$

$$(20.1)$$

Tangents to Γ's fixed-l *increment curves* are:[6]

[6] Since $\frac{d \sinh \tau}{d\tau} = \cosh \tau$ and $\frac{d \cosh \tau}{d\tau} = \sinh \tau$.

$$\frac{\partial \Gamma}{\partial \tau} = \left[\cosh \tau \cos(\tau + l) - \sinh \tau \sin(\tau + l), \cosh \tau \sin(\tau + l) + \sinh \tau \cos(\tau + l), 0\right].$$

Γ's increment curve path lengths thus progress as ($\Rightarrow$(11.11)-ii,iii):

$$\left|\frac{\partial \Gamma}{\partial \tau}\right| = \sqrt{\frac{\partial \Gamma}{\partial \tau} \cdot \frac{\partial \Gamma}{\partial \tau}} = \sqrt{\cosh^2 \tau + \sinh^2 \tau} = \cosh \tau \sqrt{1 + \tanh^2 \tau} = \gamma \sqrt{1 + v^2}.$$

As fixed-l increment curves on surface Γ do not trace medium own-time τ, Γ is not a metric 'own-surface' of the medium. Instead, Γ's straight lines reflect home time $t = \tan \phi$—*radially* rather than by curve length progression.

Tangents to Γ's fixed-t/fixed-τ medium helices are

$$\frac{\partial \Gamma}{\partial l} = \left[-\sinh \tau \sin(\tau + l), \sinh \tau \cos(\tau + l), 1\right].$$

Γ's medium helices therefore expand as ($\Rightarrow$(11.11)-iii)[7]

[7] $\cosh^2 \tau - \sinh^2 \tau = 1$.

$$\left|\frac{\partial \Gamma}{\partial l}\right| = \sqrt{\frac{\partial \Gamma}{\partial l} \cdot \frac{\partial \Gamma}{\partial l}} = \sqrt{1 + \sinh^2 \tau} = \cosh \tau = \gamma. \qquad (20.2)$$

Surface Γ thus cuts a $L\gamma$ length helix on a home time fixed-t radius cylinder T of height L. Incidentally, many relativity textbooks *erroneously* take $L\gamma$ to be the medium's actually expanding length.

The 'pseudo-contraction' helicoidal surface K, which likewise is not a metric own-surface of the medium, is intersected by a (not illustrated) vertical cylinder of radius v/γ. As easily shown, its corresponding helix, which also plays a part in our relativity cosmographicum, has length $L\sqrt{1 + \frac{v^2}{\gamma^2}}$.

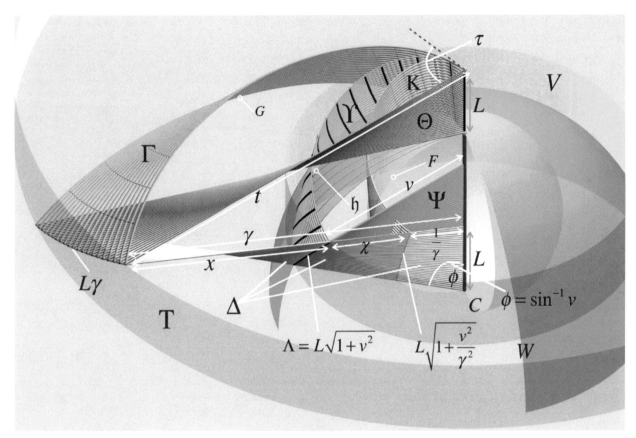

Figure 20.3: A relativity cosmographicum and its helicoid sextet

Ruled surface helicoids Θ, Ψ and Δ

[8] Upper case Greek *Theta, Psi* and *Delta*.

[8]For the arbitrary τ value, horizontal lines joining corresponding Γ and Υ helices to the vertical axis, form a HOME TIME HELICOID Θ and CHRONOSITY/VELOCITY HELICOID Ψ respectively. All three helices on the Γ, Υ and K surfaces may be connected by straight lines forming a ruled surface DISTANCES HELICOID Δ ending at a vertical height L line based at the model's origin point $[0, 0, 0]$. Figure 20.3's 'cosmographic' surfaces sextet $\Upsilon|\Gamma|K|\Theta|\Psi|\Delta$ is thus *a helicoidal protraction* of generator curves representing the relativistic parameters of the unit thrust rear rocket as established in chapter 14.

20.3 Extrinsic *and* intrinsic *parameters*

The three ruled surface helicoids Θ, Ψ and Δ corresponding to a chosen arbitrary τ value, reflect the medium's EXTRINSIC *inertial frame-related* parameters which are momentarily shared by all of the medium's increments: scaled velocity v, velchron angle $\phi = \sin^{-1} v$ and γ factor, home frame time t and distance x, and retrospective travelled distance χ.

Hemicoid Υ itself INTRINSICALLY portrays the spacetime history of the unit thrust medium as reflected by identical increment hemix own-time τ lengths[9] and the respective medium's helices' corresponding non-inertial own-lengths Λ. Each hemicoid's lateral medium helix forms the *quadruple* intersection of hemicoid own-surface Υ, velocity helicoid Ψ, distances helicoid Δ and velocity cylinder V which in a sense represents the 'proxy' non-inertial frame Π specific to own-time τ and velocity $v = \tanh \tau$. Also of significance, the medium's own-length Λ helix marks the boundary between retrospective distance χ segments and home frame distance x segments on distances helicoid Δ.

[9] As well as reflecting each hemix's path length, τ also equals longitude θ from the zero 'Greenwich' reference meridian.

20.3.

RULED SURFACE HELICOID Δ EVENT LINE SEGMENTS BETWEEN EVENT POINTS ON RESPECTIVE HELICES OF HELICOIDS Γ, Υ AND K, EQUAL INCREMENT TRAVELLED DISTANCES $x = \gamma - 1$ AND $\chi = 1 - 1/\gamma$ RESPECTIVELY.

20.4   *The unit thrust medium's gravity train*

Similar to the rigor mortis gravity train, we may imagine a series of *identically* accelerating 'compartment rockets' loosely joined together with flexible connecting chambers. Rocket passengers sensing a fixed unit gravity thrust would age identically, but more slowly compared with nonaccelerating home frame observers whose clocks relate, in accordance with equation (11.11), as $t = \sinh \tau$. Each compartment's passengers would experience adjacent compartments as gradually moving apart, *not, as propounded in many relativity texts, to an ever increasing γ factor separation extent*, but ultimately towards the square root of two times their home frame separation at launch. Of course should accelerations *suddenly cease*, things then happen as described in chapter 15.

20.4.

A UNIFORMLY ACCELERATING MEDIUM'S INCREMENTS DO NOT SHARE A 'PRESENT TENSE' IN EVER CHANGING COMOVING INERTIAL FRAMES EVEN THOUGH THEIR CLOCKS DISPLAY IDENTICAL OWN-TIMES. THIS FACT DOES NOT MAKE THE NON-INERTIAL 'PROXY FRAME' OWN-LENGTH CONCEPT ANY LESS 'REAL' THAN INERTIAL OWN-LENGTH.

Figure 20.4: Cylindrical coordinates differential

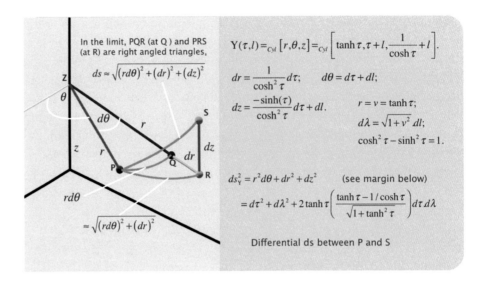

In the limit, PQR (at Q) and PRS (at R) are right angled triangles,

$$ds \approx \sqrt{(rd\theta)^2 + (dr)^2 + (dz)^2}$$

$$\Upsilon(\tau,l) =_{Cyl} [r,\theta,z] =_{Cyl} \left[\tanh\tau, \tau+l, \frac{1}{\cosh\tau} + l \right].$$

$$dr = \frac{1}{\cosh^2\tau} d\tau; \qquad d\theta = d\tau + dl;$$

$$dz = \frac{-\sinh(\tau)}{\cosh^2\tau} d\tau + dl. \qquad r = v = \tanh\tau;$$

$$d\lambda = \sqrt{1+v^2}\, dl;$$

$$\cosh^2\tau - \sinh^2\tau = 1.$$

$$ds_\Upsilon^2 = r^2 d\theta + dr^2 + dz^2 \qquad \text{(see margin below)}$$

$$= d\tau^2 + d\lambda^2 + 2\tanh\tau \left(\frac{\tanh\tau - 1/\cosh\tau}{\sqrt{1+\tanh^2\tau}} \right) d\tau.d\lambda$$

$$\approx \sqrt{(rd\theta)^2 + (dr)^2}$$

Differential ds between P and S

20.5   *The uniform thrust medium's real metric

Unit thrust own-surface (19.1)-i is (in cylindrical coordinates):

$$\Upsilon(\tau,l) =\ _{Cyl} [r,\theta,z] =\ _{Cyl} \left[\tanh\tau, \tau+l, \frac{1}{\cosh\tau} + l \right].$$

Total differentials $dr, d\theta$ and dz are easily written:[10]

$$dr = \frac{1}{\cosh^2\tau} d\tau; \qquad d\theta = d\tau + dl; \qquad dz = \frac{-\sinh(\tau)}{\cosh^2\tau} d\tau + dl.$$

[10] $\frac{d\tanh\tau}{d\tau} = \frac{d(\sinh\tau/\cosh\tau)}{d\tau} = \frac{\cosh\tau\cosh\tau - \sinh\tau\sinh\tau}{\cosh^2\tau} = \frac{1}{\cosh^2\tau}$; $\frac{d(1/\cosh\tau)}{d\tau} = \frac{-\sinh\tau}{\cosh^2\tau}$.

Recalling The rigor mortis 'real metric' section on page 139, we may express unit-thrust own-surface Υ's metric as $ds_\Upsilon^2 = dr^2 + r^2 d\theta^2 + dz^2$. Therefore, since $r = v = \tanh\tau$, $d\lambda = \sqrt{1+v^2}.dl$ and $\cosh^2\tau - \sinh^2\tau = 1$, the former equation becomes[11]

[11] $ds_\Upsilon^2 = \frac{d\tau^2}{\cosh^4\tau} +$

$\tanh^2\tau(d\tau^2 + dl^2 + 2d\tau.dl) +$

$\frac{\sinh^2}{\cosh^4\tau} d\tau^2 + dl^2 - \frac{2\sinh\tau}{\cosh^2\tau} d\tau dl$

$= \frac{1+\sinh^2\tau\cosh^2\tau+\sinh^2}{\cosh^4\tau} d\tau^2$

$+ (1 + \tanh^2\tau)dl^2 +$

$2(\tanh^2\tau - \frac{\sinh\tau}{\cosh^2\tau})d\tau.dl$

$= \frac{\cosh^2 + (\cosh^2\tau-1)\cosh^2\tau}{\cosh^4\tau} d\tau^2$

$+ d\lambda^2 +$

$\frac{2\tanh\tau(\tanh\tau-1/\cosh\tau)}{\sqrt{1+\tanh^2\tau}} d\tau.d\lambda.$

20.5.

THE UNIFORM ACCELERATION OWN-SURFACE METRIC

$$ds_\Upsilon^2 = d\tau^2 + d\lambda^2 + 2\tanh\tau \left(\frac{\tanh\tau - 1/\cosh\tau}{\sqrt{1+\tanh^2\tau}} \right) d\tau.d\lambda$$

Crucially, this homogeneously accelerating medium's real metric contains a VARIABLE COEFFICIENT MIXED DIFFERENTIALS EXPRESSION

$$2\tanh\tau \left(\frac{\tanh\tau - 1/\cosh\tau}{\sqrt{1+\tanh^2\tau}} \right) d\tau.d\lambda.$$

The awkward mixed differentials variable coefficient

Clearly, unit thrust own-surface Υ properly conforms to a formidable set of conditions conceivable for the homogeneous accelerating medium. Its metric (20.5) therefore definitely constitutes <u>a</u> solution to the homogeneous acceleration expansion problem. Proponents of Minkowski metric's general validity might argue that <u>another</u> actual solution may lie in *pseudo-Euclidean geometry*. After all, this book's rigor mortis case's real metric itself may be transformed just by replacing a real coordinate by an 'equivalent' imaginary one. Others, perhaps acknowledging that our hemicoid surface's properties may well reflect a *coincidental* solution, might insist, as claimed by Synge[12,13] in his well known 1956 classic and alluded to in the present book's *Prologue section An À LA CARTE Pandora's box, that *"a non-singular quadratic form"* metric equation *"appropriate to Einstein's [special] relativity"* such as metric (20.5) (if correct), should be somehow mathematically *equivalent* i.e. *reducible* by a 'coordinate transformation' to the quadratic form $ds^2 = d\tau^2 - d\lambda^2$ (in single spatial dimension metric form).

However, there is no way that metric (20.5)'s *nonconstant* mixed differential terms coefficient could be cancelled out by some conceivable transformation of coordinates. The nonzero mixed $d\tau.d\lambda$ term is *wholly incompatible* with the Minkowski spacetime interval $ds_{\mathfrak{M}}^2 = d\tau^2 - d\lambda^2$. Accordingly, either the unit thrust own-surface metric (20.5) or Minkowski's generalised metric must be wrong. Nevertheless, as discussed in the present author's *Results in Physics* 2016 and 2017 papers, where one might expect a cogent case for the obfuscating Minkowski approach to the extended accelerating medium issue to be presented, no consistent arguments are evident, either in textbooks or papers.

[12] Section §11, *The fundamental quadratic form*, page 17's equation (20):

[13] John Lighton Synge. *Relativity: The Special Theory*. North-Holland, Amsterdam, 1956

20.6.

CONTRARY TO GENERAL 'UNDERSTANDING' AMONG PHYSICISTS, MINKOWSKI SPACETIME DOES NOT APPLY TO A HOMOGENEOUSLY ACCELERATING MEDIUM. ACCORDINGLY, EXCEPT FOR RIGOR MORTIS ACCELERATION, IT IS <u>GENERALLY</u> INVALID.

In order to *further* underline this fact, the next chapter *Radar mappings from inertial home frame onto own-surface Υ shows how own-surface Υ trajectories of radar signals between the rear and front unit thrust rockets fully comply with predicted inter-rocket radar intervals and 'surfing' characteristics.

21

*Radar mappings from inertial home frame onto own-surface ϒ

'Regular surfaces in $\mathbb{R}^3$ provide a natural setting for two-dimensional calculus' Manfredo do Carmo 1976

21.1 Radar photon trajectories

[1]Figure 21.1 is a duplicate of the earlier Figure 16.1's unit-thrust medium's world-surface containing *home frame* hyperbolic world-lines (fixed-l increment curves), fixed-t vertical straight lines of home time simultaneity and outgoing and returning straight line radar trajectories. Figure 21.2 shows a one-to-one 'homeomorphic' mapping of these curves onto own-surface

[1] Manfredo Do Carmo. *Differential Geometry of Curves and Surfaces.* Prentice Hall N.J., Dover New York, 1976, 2016

$$\Upsilon(\tau, l) = \left[\tanh \tau \cos(\tau + l), \tanh \tau \sin(\tau + l), \frac{1}{\cosh \tau} + l \right]. \qquad (21.1)$$

Outgoing photon paths

For *an outgoing photon's radar equation[2]* ρ, we turn to radar transit equation (16.2) for an arbitrary photon's rear rocket emission own-time $\acute{t}$ and replace l with $-e^{-\tau} + e^{-\acute{t}}$ in (21.1):

[2] ρ is Greek *rho.*

$$\rho = \left[\tanh \tau \cos(\tau - e^{-\tau} + e^{-\acute{t}}), \tanh \tau \sin(\tau - e^{-\tau} + e^{-\acute{t}}), \frac{1}{\cosh \tau} - e^{-\tau} + e^{-\acute{t}} \right]. \qquad (21.2)$$

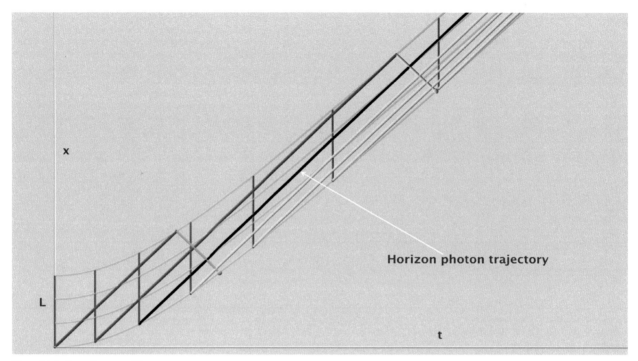

Figure 21.1: Home frame world-surface of a uniformly accelerating medium, with reflected and nonreflected radar trajectories and fixed velocity loci

For the chosen values of $L = 0.5548$ and $\Delta\tau = \frac{3\pi}{32}$, only the first two photons emitted are reflected. Their trajectories are shown in red. Recalling outgoing photon reflection equation (16.3)-i $e^{\hat{t}} = \frac{1}{e^{-\hat{t}} - L}$, for a photon whose emission time is $\hat{t} = \ln(1/L)$, equation (16.4) gives $e^{-\hat{t}} = L$, i.e. $e^{\hat{t}} = \infty$. As a medium's shared own-time τ approaches ∞, the 'horizon photon' trajectory (in black) thus tends to 'surf' the front rocket i.e. get ever closer to it at nearly zero speed, without ever reaching it. Later photons (coloured yellow) surf respective *intermediate* medium increments.

21.3.

A UNIT THRUST MEDIUM'S REAR ROCKET-EMITTED NONREFLECTED

PHOTON TRAJECTORIES 'SURF' Υ INCREMENT CURVES IN THE LIMIT.

Returning photon paths

The returning photon radar equation is obtained using chapter 16's *returning transit equation* (16.6) and replacing l with $L - e^{\tau} + 1/(e^{-\hat{t}} - L)$. Recalling equation (16.8): $\hat{\tau} - \hat{t} = \ln\left[L(e^{-\hat{t}} - L) + 1\right]$, if $e^{-\hat{t}}$ is very close to L, then $\hat{\tau} - \hat{t} \approx \ln(1) = 0$. In such a case, as τ approaches ∞ a *counter-directional* reflected photon would traverse the medium at a virtually infinite 'crossing rate'.

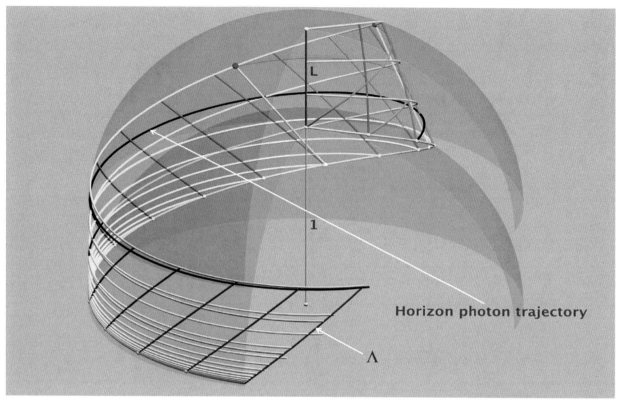

Figure 21.2: Own-surface increment and medium curves with
radar trajectories

21.4.

FOR AN EMISSION TIME $\acute{t}$ NEAR HORIZON VALUE $\ln 1/L$, A PHOTON'S RETURNING
UNIT THRUST MEDIUM'S TRAVERSING TIME TENDS TOWARDS ZERO. A REFLECTED
PHOTON WOULD TEND TO CROSS THE ENTIRE MEDIUM AT A 'SUPRALUMINAL' SPEED.

By *'supraluminal'* (on top of) we mean almost infinite, as opposed to *'super-luminal'*—faster-than-light yet *finite*, speed. We recall that the term 'speed'
here relates to *a medium's own-length crossings time-rated by an imagined third
party observer recording crossed medium increments' progressing own-time values.*
Of course both emitted and reflected photons always propagate at *unit scaled
limit speed* in the *inertial* home frame as well as in all other comoving inertial
frames.

21.2 *Shared radar curves' crossing angles and geodesic curvatures*

Finally we explore radar trajectories crossing medium helices. τ-differentiating radar curve (21.2) gives outgoing radar tangent vector ρ_τ and modulus $|\rho_\tau|$:

$$\rho_\tau = [\frac{1}{\cosh^2 \tau} \cos(\tau - e^{-\tau} + e^{-\hat{t}}) - \tanh \tau (1 + e^{-\tau}) \sin(\tau - e^{-\tau} + e^{-\hat{t}}),$$

$$\frac{1}{\cosh^2 \tau} \sin(\tau - e^{-\tau} + e^{-\hat{t}}) + \tanh \tau (1 + e^{-\tau}) \cos(\tau - e^{-\tau} + e^{-\hat{t}}), \frac{-\sinh \tau}{\cosh^2 \tau} + e^{-\tau}].$$

$$(21.5)$$

$$|\rho_\tau|^2 = \frac{1}{\cosh^4 \tau} + \tanh^2 \tau.(1 + e^{-\tau})^2 + (\frac{-\sinh \tau}{\cosh^2 \tau} + e^{-\tau})^2. \qquad (21.6)$$

Replacing l with $-e^{-\tau} + e^{-\hat{t}}$ in increment curve and medium curve tangent vector equations (19.2) and (19.4), we obtain for ρ_l:

$$\rho_l = \left[-\tanh \tau \sin(\tau - e^{-\tau} + e^{-\hat{t}}), \tanh \tau \cos(\tau - e^{-\tau} + e^{-\hat{t}}), 1 \right]. \qquad (21.7)$$

From (19.3) $|\Upsilon_\tau| = 1$ and from (19.5) $|\Upsilon_l| = \sqrt{1 + \tanh^2 \tau}$. Hence using (21.5), (21.6) and (21.7):

21.8.

RADAR TRAJECTORIES/MEDIUM CURVES EMISSION-INDEPENDENT CROSSING COSINE

$$\frac{\rho_\tau \cdot \Upsilon_l}{|\rho_\tau||\Upsilon_l|} = \frac{(1 + \tanh^2 \tau)e^{-\tau} + \tanh^2 \tau - \tanh \tau / \cosh \tau}{\sqrt{\frac{1}{\cosh^4 \tau} + \tanh^2 \tau.(1 + e^{-\tau})^2 + (\frac{-\sinh \tau}{\cosh^2 \tau} + e^{-\tau})^2}.\sqrt{1 + \tanh^2 \tau}}.$$

Expression (21.8) reduces to $\frac{1}{\sqrt{2}}$ (45 degrees cosine) for $\tau = 0$ and likewise as $\tau \to \infty$. As evident in Figure 21.2 also, radar trajectories are thus initially diagonal to fixed-τ medium and fixed-l increment curves, in accordance with unit limit speed in the rocket's launch home frame. As likewise expected, non-reflected photon trajectories ultimately 'surf' (overlap) increment curves, but, interestingly, cross medium curves at 45 degrees as $\tau \to \infty$, as at the beginning.

A particularly notable parameter is radar trajectories' *geodesic curvature* on surface Υ. [3][4]Geodesic curvature equals the dot product of Υ's *normal unit vector* $\frac{\Upsilon_\tau \times \Upsilon_l}{|\Upsilon_\tau \times \Upsilon_l|}$ with the cross product of the radar trajectory's *tangent vector* ρ_τ and it's *'acceleration vector'* $\rho_{\tau\tau}$ (not listed) divided by the tangent vector's modulus cubed. Hence, referring to equations (21.5) – (21.7)

[3] ⇒page 169:

[4] Andrew Pressley. *Elementary differential geometry.* Springer, 2010

21.9.

RADAR TRAJECTORIES EMISSION-INDEPENDENT GEODESIC CURVATURE $\kappa_g = \dfrac{\Upsilon_\tau \times \Upsilon_l}{|\Upsilon_\tau \times \Upsilon_l|} \cdot \dfrac{\rho_\tau \times \rho_{\tau\tau}}{|\rho_\tau|^3}$

$$= \frac{e^{10\tau} + 6e^{9\tau} - e^{8\tau} - 4e^{7\tau} - 34e^{6\tau} + 16e^{5\tau} + 10e^{4\tau} - 12e^{3\tau} - 31e^{2\tau} - 6e^{\tau} - 9}{4(e^{6\tau} + 2e^{5\tau} - 4e^{3\tau} + 5e^{2\tau} + 2e^{\tau} + 2)^{\frac{3}{2}} \sqrt{\cosh(\tau)^4 + 2\cosh(\tau)^2 \sinh(\tau) - 2\sinh(\tau)}}.$$

A 'retrospective' insight

Figure 21.2's radar trajectories cross fixed-τ medium helices initially and ultimately at 45 degrees, although they vary in between. Also, although radar trajectory *geodesic curvatures* tend towards zero in the limit since they 'surf' ultimately equatorial increment own-lines, *otherwise* such curvatures are nonzero.

A very significant 'retrospective' *physics insight* can be drawn from the above mathematical cosine and geodesic curvature expressions: Although vectors Υ_τ, Υ_l, ρ_τ and $\rho_{\tau\tau}$ each contain radar emission time expressions $e^{-\hat{t}}$, this term *is cancelled out* both in angle cosine equation (21.8) as well as in geodesic curvature expression (21.9).[5]

[5] The same applies to radar curves' *principle* and *normal* curvatures.

21.10.

SUCCESSIVE RADAR TRAJECTORIES ON OWN-SURFACE Υ CROSS EACH SHARED OWN-TIME MEDIUM HELIX AT RESPECTIVELY IDENTICAL ANGLES AND WITH IDENTICAL GEODESIC CURVATURES, INDEPENDENTLY OF THE PHOTONS' DIFFERING REAR ROCKET EMISSION TIMES.

On the other hand, own-surface Υ's *medium curves*, although helices, all have likewise nonzero geodesic curvature.

21.3 *Validations of the unit thrust medium's own-surface* Υ

- With no relativistic pre-assumptions, the unique laterally expanding $\lambda|\tau$ real metric 'own-surface' Υ *independently* emerges solely from expected characteristics of *uniformity*, *monotonicity* and *regularity*. Manifesting *initial* congruence with Figure 21.1's home frame's unit-thrust world-surface, Figure 21.2 surface's initially diagonal outgoing radar trajectories ultimately 'surf' increment curves which themselves are ultimately at 45 degrees to medium curves. Returning counter-directional radar trajectories tend to ultimately 'instantaneously traverse' i.e. practically overlap fixed-τ medium curves at near infinite crossing rate.

- Sharing own-time τ, surface Υ's helical medium curves feature several interesting characteristics. As geodesics on V_τ *'velocity cylinders'* which 'enshrine' comoving *non-inertial* frames, they are traversed by 'concurrent' radar paths of identical geodesic curvature and at identical crossing angles, *irrespective of differing radar emission times*. On the other hand, radar trajectory geodesic curvatures, which tend towards zero in the limit since they 'surf' ultimately equatorial increment world-lines, are otherwise nonzero.

- Inter-rocket radar intervals for $L = 0.5548$ and intervals $\Delta\tau = \frac{3\pi}{32}$ on Figure 21.1's home frame world-surface, give using rear rocket's radar interval (16.11): $\check{\tau}_0 - \acute{\tau}_0 = \frac{3\pi}{32} \cdot 3.497$ and $\check{\tau}_1 - \acute{\tau}_1 = \frac{3\pi}{32} \cdot 4.977$. *The exact same rocket radar intervals are metrically evident in Figure 21.2's own-surface* Υ.

In view of the importance of highlighting the generally unappreciated limitations of Minkowski spacetime, and of the proper solution to the Bell's string paradox, it seems appropriate to provide an account in the book's final Epilogue chapter, of some of the reactions of physics journal editors and reviewers encountered by the author when attempting to present the above insights.

22
Epilogue

MINKOWSKI SPACETIME'S 'POST-TRUTHS'

". . . they had succeeded in leading him up the garden path into one of their academic mazes, where a man could wander for eternity, meeting himself in mirrors. No, he repeated. Possibly they were all very nice, high-minded, scrupulous people with only an occupational tendency towards backbiting and a nervous habit of self-correction, always emending, penciling, erasing; but he did not care to catch the bug, which seemed to be endemic to these ivied haunts."

Mary McCarthy   THE GROVES OF ACADEME   1951

22.1   *"A glorious non-entity"*

[1] 'AN INVASION OF MATHEMATICS INTO PHYSICS' was the initial reaction of Einstein, himself ever wary of hallowed ivied haunts,[2] to *pseudo-Euclidean* 'Minkowski spacetime'. Yet he seemingly later came to terms,[3] as an approximation, with the imaginary variables metric of his earlier professor in Zürich, *Hermann Minkowski*. The latter, who had disparaged Einstein's apparent lack of enthusiasm for mathematics (but did later praise his ex-pupil's contributions to relativity), astonished the physics community at a legendary 1908 lecture in Cologne[4] by highlighting the *interconnectedness* of space and time.[5] His then also introduced *Minkowski metric* equation still plays a virtually indomitable role in special relativity, as—inappropriately—propounded in a 2006 treatise: *"...the geometry of Minkowski spacetime has been axiomatised in all rigour"*.[6]

A serious generally overlooked problem remains nevertheless. The garden paths of Minkowski spacetime, a *nonvisualisable* academic maze, only accommodate itineraries of point objects (*'particles'*) or groups of objects accelerating in 'rigid motion' mode, better labelled[7] *'rigor mortis' acceleration.*

[1] Mary McCarthy. *The Groves of Academe*. Harcourt, Brace, New York, 1951

[2] As satirised in his 1933 poem quoted (and translated) in the *Prologue.

[3] Alexander Blum, J Renn, D Salisbury, M Schemm, and K Sundermeyer. 1912: A turning point on Einstein's way to general relativity. *Annalen der Physik*, 524:A11–A13, 2011

[4] Actually first presented in Göttingen in September 1907.

[5] Described, using a different viewpoint, as 'CHRONOSITY'—distance-rated disparity of simultaneity—in chapter 1's An elegant spacetime underlay.

[6] Jürgen Ehlers and Claus Lämmerzahl. *Special Relativity - Will it Survive the Next 101 Years?* Springer, 2006

[7] To avoid confusion with differential geometry's 'rigid motion' theory.

Twistings and turnings

[8] J J Callahan. *The Geometry of Spacetime.* Springer, 2000

Questioning Minkowski metric's widespread deployment in *general relativity*, a 2000 textbook[8] stated *"Spacetime with gravity does not obey the laws of Minkowski geometry. . ."*. Yet this clear statement, an opinion not directly disputed in more recent physics literature, does not appear to have 'sunk in' among the community of physicists, judging by continual appearances of general relativity books which usually casually and without elaboration, adopt Minkowski's 4-vector method without further ado—in the time honoured traditional manner.

This book is concerned with the (mis)application of Minkowski's metric in the context of *special relativity*. Here indeed also, not everyone has been silent. In 2004 a paper by two Oxford physicists entitled *Minkowski spacetime: a glorious non-entity*,[9] took the high road by stating (somewhat tongue in cheek) in the *British Journal for the Philosophy of Science*: *"It is argued that Minkowski spacetime cannot serve as the deep structure within a "constructive" version of the special theory of relativity, contrary to widespread opinion in the philosophical community."* One might ask however, if this is true, *what might the consequences be* ?

[9] H Brown and O Pooley. Minkowski space-time: a glorious non-entity. *British Journal for the Philosophy of Science*, 2004

22.2 *Groves of Academe*

At the end of 2008, it became apparent to the present author that the 2004 discovered spherical geometric model for an accelerating object (described in chapter 14 A Spacetime Odyssey), if 'helicoidised', pointed to a resolution of the homogeneously accelerating extended medium problem commonly known as *Bell's string paradox*. Nevertheless, attempts to have this thesis accepted were not favoured by physics journal editors and reviewers.

The *American Journal of Physics* has a long tradition of relativity papers addressing the accelerating medium question, not least the very 1959 paper which brought the topic into prominence, yet that journal does not formally view itself as a 'research' journal. Accordingly, in reference to a related 2010 'off the beaten track' submission of the present author, its then editor kindly explained that *"... many papers need to be evaluated by research journals if they contain significantly new physics. I think that may be the case for your paper as well."*.[10]

[10] June 6th 2010 email correspondence on AJP manuscript MS23122.

Referring to the author's later published 2016 paper, the *European Journal of Physics* similarly stated: *'The tearing down of Minkowski space should at least begin in more specialised circles before making its way into the mainstream literature. I suggest that the author submits his (hopefully) profound insights to a journal such as Foundations of Physics.'* On the other hand, the New York *Journal of Mathematical Physics* declared that the paper's maths being *"at the level of elementary calculus'* excluded it being of interest to that journal and suggested: *"... Some of the discussions in the manuscript and arguments for new terminology seemed to point to a journal dedicated to Foundations of Physics as a possible place to submit this."*

A Dutch drawbridge

The globally deferred to Utrecht *Foundation of Physics* research journal posts a laudable if somewhat grandeur-laden policy:

> "Our views of the physical world are changing rapidly. Humanity's continuing search for coherent structures in physics, biology, and cosmology has frequently led to surprises as well as confusion. Discovering new phenomena is one thing, putting them into context with other pieces of knowledge, and inferring their fundamental consequences is quite something else. There are controversies, differences of opinion, and sometimes even religious feelings which come into play. These should be discussed openly. Philosophical issues that are of a nontechnical nature should be handled in the opinion pages of the news media, but when the discussed arguments become too technical for that, when peer review is needed to select the really valuable pieces of insight, only a distinguished scientific journal is the appropriate form."

This *"International Journal Devoted to the Conceptual Bases and Fundamental Theories of Modern Physics"* had already published a *related* paper in late 2013,[11] whose author's likewise related 2010 *European Journal of Physics* paper was partly endorsed but also partly criticised by the present author's paper submitted December 2013. The quite crudely aspersive refusal[12] by Foundations of Physics to even consider the paper for review therefore came as a surprise:[13,14,15]

> "This Journal's policy is one of severe restraint concerning theories that are well-understood and well-tested experimentally, such as the theory of special relativity. Regrettably, this fact places the current submission outside the scope of Foundation of Physics."

The later successfully peer-reviewed paper and its sequel published in the (likewise Dutch-based) *Results in Physics* journal, have so far attracted over two thousand downloads *in the U.S alone,* and a proportionate number in the FoP journal's Netherlands base. No dissenting comment has yet emerged.[16]

The Ante Portas 'invitation'

[17]The Montréal-based *Institute for Foundational Studies Hermann Minkowski*[18] received a copy of the author's January 2016 *Results in Physics* paper, with a request for comment. The institute's stated goals include *"To help change the present situation in fundamental physics and lead the research on the major open questions."* and *"To provide continual science education for the general public in order that scientific culture becomes an inseparable element of the common culture of*

[11] Jerrold Franklin. Rigid Body Motion in Special Relativity. *Foundations of Physics,* 43:1489–1501, 2013

[12] FOOP-D-13-00511 / FOOP-D-14-0048. The second submission remedied a minor blemish in the earlier submission.

[13] ⇒ A fallacy's domino effect on page 121.

[14] B.C. Minkowski spacetime does not apply to a homogeneously accelerating medium. *Results in Physics,* 6:31–38, January 2016

[15] http://dx.doi.org/10.1016/j.rinp.2016.01.001

[16] Nor has FoP responded to a subsequent formal request for comment.

[17] *Ante Portas* means *'Before the Gates'.*

[18] www.minkowskiinstitute.org

every individual.". Citing lack of time available to read the paper, a founder member[19] responded by mentioning a forthcoming *'Fourth International Conference on the Nature and Ontology of Spacetime'* sponsored by that institute, to be held at the end of May 2016 at the Black Sea Bulgarian city *Varna*.

The abstract of a *sequel* paper provisionally entitled *Bell's string paradox solved by real differential geometry* and explicitly containing this book's real metric equation (20.5), was thereupon submitted to the organizing committee, requesting a presentation slot but also emphasizing that a poster presentation alone would be inappropriate. The hope was for a live half hour dialogue with a challenging audience, an interesting, perhaps also enlightening prospect even though it would be a bit like 'going into the lion's den'. The previously forwarded already published paper was entitled *Minkowski spacetime does not apply to a homogeneously accelerating medium*, and an invited guest speaker was the same *Foundation of Physics* chief editor (after whom an asteroid is named) who had declined to even review that earlier paper.

Disappointingly, an invitation to the four thousand kilometres distant venue came for an 'ante portas' waiting-in-the-wings *poster presentation*, an option explicitly ruled out in the submission letter. An appeal to reconsider (made when several conference schedule slots had still not been filled) was not answered. Nor has any comment on the earlier emailed published paper been received. The intended presentation[20] sequel paper has now been successfully peer-reviewed and published in the same *Results in Physics* journal. (http://dx.doi.org/10.1016/j.rinp.2017.07.013)

Mistrodden ground

The *ex-cathedra* empty platitude of a major journal and the Minkowski Institute's likewise closed door policy—matters of record—suggest to the present author that not only have they coarsely misjudged the matter with respect to the metric topic, but also, contrary to their own self-proclaimed mandates, remain oblivious to other anomalies still prevelent in special relativity theory.

In addition to continually tolerated presentisms[21] and the quagmire of mathematical formalisms remonstrated against—to no avail—in Desloge and Philpott's 1987 AJP paper,[22] these include the literature's frequent overextension of the (unnecessarily postulated) limit speed principle, its cumbersome approaches to the 'rigor mortis'/rigid motion topic, and the many inadequate solutions put forward for the homogeneously accelerating medium scenario.

An outstandingly incriminating symptom of this oligarchic paralysis in spacetime theory[23] is the incredible *hitherto absence* in books and papers of the relevant straightforward but of course 'inconveniently' non-constant radar interval formulae.

[19] Author of *Accelerating spaceships paradox and physical meaning of length contraction* https://arxiv.org/pdf/0903.5128v1.pdf

[20] B.C. Bell's twin rockets non-inertial length enigma resolved by real geometry. *Results in Physics*, 7:2575–2581, July 2017

[21] ⇒ Prelude to a 2005 physics journal publication on page 60.

[22] Quoted at the beginning of chapter 19.

[23] ⇒ Equations that did not bark in the light on page 8.

22.3   Two Russian overtures

A 2009 correspondence with Russian physicist *Stanislav Podosenov* regarding the Bell's string expansion equation, led to his sincere proposal, with three of his colleagues, of joint collaboration. Surprisingly nevertheless, an assent to their interesting suggestion was not responded to. In a 2010 paper,[24] the same physicists appropriately asserted: *"The standard solution of Bell's well-known problem…must be revised"*. In 2014[25] they further aptly stated: *"The [Bell's] paradox is solved only when going out of [abandoning] the Minkowski [complex variables] space to the Riemann [real variables] space"*, and proposed (on their 2014 paper's page 24) a length formula equivalent to[26]

$$\Lambda(\tau) = \ln(\cosh L + \sinh L \cosh \tau). \tag{22.1}$$

Yet they unreasonably claimed that *"…all authors (except [own papers] [3-5]) connect the string rupture with the Lorentz shrinkages"*, without reference to the present author's 2009 communicated *non-presentism* equation:

$$\Lambda(\tau) = L\sqrt{1 + \tanh^2 \tau} = L\sqrt{1 + v^2/c^2}. \tag{22.2}$$

A January 2017 related paper[27] did not mention formula (22.2) which appeared in the web abstract of the present author's 2012 lecture in Göttingen[28], and also overlooked the simple radar approach to the 'rigid motion' acceleration topic expounded in the 2016 paper *Minkowski spacetime does not apply to a homogeneously accelerating medium*. Significantly, their 2017 paper (page 16) directly overruled their earlier equation (22.1): *"Although the formula…is correct both for large and low accelerations, it does not solve the Bell paradox in principle."*.

Stanislav Podosenov (who speaks only Russian) is one of the few physicists who have unceasingly been railing in earnest against the dismal Ptolemaic status quo of accelerating frames in relativity literature. Now, as this present book is 'going to press', he has repeated his initial 2009 (then not followed up) suggestion for joint cooperation, and has kindly undertaken to soon relate the present author's July 2017 paper *Bell's twin rockets non-inertial length enigma resolved by real geometry* in the context of his own April 2017 co-authored book[29]. This book's dedicated future website https://spacetimefundamentals.com is intended to encompass just such a dialogue.

[24] S. A. Podosenov, J. Foukzon, and A. A. Potapov. A Study of the Motion of a Relativistic Continuous Medium. *Gravitation and Cosmology – Pleiades/Springer*, 16(4): 307–312, 2010

[25] S. A. Podosenov, A. A. Potapov, J. Foukzon, and A. A. Menkova. Geometry of Noninertial Bases in Relativistic Mechanics of Continua and Bell's Problem Solution. *International Journal of Recent advances in Physics (IJRAP)*, 3(1): 23–37, February 2014

[26] L being the rockets' scaled 'launch' separation length, and τ the rockets' scaled own-time.

[27] S. A. Podosenov, J. Foukzon, and A. A. Menkova. Structure Equations, Permitted Movement of Relativistic Continuum and Sagnac's, Erenfest's and Bell's Paradoxes. *Physical Science International Journal*, 13(2):1–18, January 2017a

[28] B.C. Relativity Acceleration's Cosmographicum and its Radar Photon Surfings—A Euclidean Diminishment of Minkowski Spacetime, February 2012. URL http://www.dpg-verhandlungen.de/year/2012/conference/goettingen/part/gr/session/4/contribution/4

[29] S. A. Podosenov, J. Foukzon, and E. Menkova. *Difficulties in the Interpretation of the Einstein's Relativity Theory*. Lampert Academic Publishing, 2017b

22.4 The Emperor's New ~~Mind~~ Clothes

Fashionable devotion to Minkowski spacetime is epitomised by a sweeping statement on page 257 of *Roger Penrose's* best seller *The Emperor's New Mind*:[30]

> "...there is now an enormous amount of experimental evidence in favour of it."

[31,32]Perhaps the true reasons for this endemic overgeneralisation lie in observations made by the 'father of the atomic bomb', *Robert Oppenheimer*, to a poignantly receptive postwar Japanese audience.[33] As recounted on page 649 of a book by philosopher *Ray Monk*[34] (by coincidence using the same publisher), the American physicist vehemently criticised a certain physics elite as:

> " ...a small society because of its inherent snobbery [whose leading elite] go to the same colleges, they meet at the same clubs and they frequent each other and read the same things. [Their philosophers] are out of touch with science, they are out of touch with politics, they are out of touch with history. And what they are in touch with is themselves."

The unit thrust medium's real metric is firmly authenticated in chapters 19–21 as the sole possible solution to the six decades disputed and hitherto misconstrued Bell's 'string' paradox. Nevertheless, an inescapable consequence of this obviously still bewilders many physicists:

> *Minkowski's pseudo-Euclidean metric does not generally represent an extended accelerating medium, even in special relativity.*

In spite of (or actually perhaps *because of*) the relative simplicity of the issues dealt with in this writer's 2016 and 2017 papers, attempts to solicit comments and/or criticisms from established authors like Penrose and Naber or those of likewise mainstream books such as [35,36], have sadly fallen on deaf ears—an all too prevalent phenomenon succinctly documented in [37]. (http://www.bookpump.com/upb/pdf-b/9429934b.pdf).

Hopefully this book's dedicated website
https://spacetimefundamentals.com
will serve as a suitable platform for opening up discussions on the various issues raised in this book, both general as well as controversial, to a wider forum.

[30] Roger Penrose. *The Emperor's New Mind*. Vintage, 1989

[31] A notable other example being:
[32] Gregory L Naber. *The Geometry of Minkowski Spacetime*. Springer, 1992, 2010
[33] *'An Afternoon with Professor Oppenheimer'*—unpublished 1960 talk to the Tokyo *Society of Science and Man*.
[34] Ray Monk. *Inside the Centre - The Life of J. Robert Oppenheimer*. Vintage, 2013

[35] Ta-Pei Cheng. *Relativity, Gravitation and Cosmology*. Oxford Universtiy Press, 2005, 2010
[36] Matthias Bartelmann et alia. *Theoretische Physik*. Springer, 2015
[37] Martín López Corredoira and Carlos Castro Perelman, editor. *Against the Tide: A Critical Review by Scientists of How Physics and Astronomy Get Done*. Universal Publishers, Boca Raton, Florida, 2008

Glossary

apocalyptic equations Relativity acceleration differential identities—a missing link which yields core interrelationships between relativistic forces.

chronosity An inertial frame's distance rated disparity of simultaneity for two spatially separate events which are simultaneous in another inertial reference frame.

home frame world-surface A surface formed by an extended medium's where-lines and when-lines in a single home reference frame.

inertial own-length A nonaccelerating or 'rigor mortis' extended object's length in comoving inertial frames.

medium-timed non-inertial own-length's photon crossing rate A third party's observation of a photon's rate of crossing of 'non-inertial length', rated by (imagined) increments' own-time clocks.

non-inertial own-length A homogeneously accelerating extended object's own-length in comoving *non-inertial frames*.

own-surface An extended medium's 'metric' surface containing increment curves progressing with own-time τ, and fixed-τ medium curves.

own-time An object's (or particles') own clock time.

proxy non-inertial frame A homogeneously accelerating extended object's comoving *non-inertial frame*.

retrospective separation The accelerating rear rocket's momentary distance in the front rocket's (not shared) comoving inertial frame.

signal response ratio The ratio of two consecutive signal responses.

spatial momentum Mass by an object's own-time rated change of an observer's distance.

temporal momentum Mass by an object's own-time rated change of an observer's own-time.

when-line A line of simultaneity of one frame in a dual spacetime chart.

where-line A straight world-line in a dual spacetime chart representing a fixed position in one frame.

world-line A trajectory on a single or dual spacetime chart representing the history of a point object or of an 'increment' of an extended object.

Bibliography

B.C. A dual first-postulate basis for special relativity. *European Journal of Physics*, 24:301–313, May 2003.

B.C. An elementary first-postulate measurement of the cosmic limit speed. *European Journal of Physics*, 25:L31–L32, 2004.

B.C. Special relativity dynamics without a priori momentum conservation. *European Journal of Physics*, 26:647–650, 2005.

B.C. A five-fold equivalence in special relativity one-dimensional dynamics. *European Journal of Physics*, 27:983–984, 2006.

B.C. Relativity Acceleration's Cosmographicum and its Radar Photon Surfings—A Euclidean Diminishment of Minkowski Spacetime, February 2012. URL http://www.dpg-verhandlungen.de/year/2012/conference/goettingen/part/gr/session/4/contribution/4.

B.C. Orbiting Particles' Analytic Time Dilations Correlated with the Sagnac Formula. *Vixra.org*, May 2015. http://vixra.org/pdf/1505.0041v8.pdf.

B.C. Minkowski spacetime does not apply to a homogeneously accelerating medium. *Results in Physics*, 6:31–38, January 2016.

B.C. Bell's twin rockets non-inertial length enigma resolved by real geometry. *Results in Physics*, 7:2575–2581, July 2017.

John Bell. *Speakable and Unspeakable in Quantum Mechanics*, chapter How to teach special relativity (1976), pages 67–68. Cambridge University Press, 1987.

George Berkeley. *De motu: Sive; de motu principio et natura, et de causa communicationis motuum*. Berkeley's Philosophical Writings, New York: Collier (1974), 1721.

Ambrose Bierce. *The Devil's Dictionary*. Neale, New York, 1911.

Alexander Blum, J Renn, D Salisbury, M Schemm, and K Sundermeyer. 1912: A turning point on Einstein's way to general relativity. *Annalen der Physik*, 524:A11–A13, 2011.

David Bohm. *The Special Theory of Relativity*. Routledge, 1965, 1996.

Max Born. Die Theorie des starren Elektrons in der Kinematik des Relativitätsprinzips (The theory of the rigid electron in the kinematics of the relativity principle). *Annalen der Physik*, 30(1-56), 1909.

H Brown and O Pooley. Minkowski space-time: a glorious non-entity. *British Journal for the Philosophy of Science*, 2004.

J J Callahan. *The Geometry of Spacetime*. Springer, 2000.

Manfredo Do Carmo. *Differential Geometry of Curves and Surfaces*. Prentice Hall N.J., Dover New York, 1976, 2016.

Ta-Pei Cheng. *Relativity, Gravitation and Cosmology*. Oxford Universtiy Press, 2005, 2010.

Brian Coleman. *Raumzeittheorie Elementar Neu Begriffen*. BCS, 2018.

James Cushing. *Philosophical Concepts in Physics*. Cambridge University Press, 1998.

Olivier Darrigol. James MacCullagh's ether: An optical route to Maxwell's equations? *The European Physics Journal H*, 35:133–172, 2010.

T. S. Davies. On the equations of loci traced upon the surface of the sphere, as expressed by spherical co-ordinates. *Transactions of the Royal Society of Edinburgh*, XII:259–362, 379–428, 1834.

D A Desloge and R J Philpott. Uniformly accelerated reference frames in special relativity. *American Journal of Physics*, 55:252–261, 1987.

E Dewan and M Beran. Note on stress effects due to relativistic contraction. *American Journal of Physics*, 27:517–8, 1959.

Lewis Carrol (Charles Lutwidge Dodson). *Through the Looking-Glass, and What Alice Found There*. Macmillan London, 1871.

Conan Doyle. *The Memoirs of Sherlock Holmes*. George Newnes, 1894.

Denis Weaire (Editor). *George Francis FitzGerald*. Living Edition Austria, 2009.

Jürgen Ehlers and Claus Lämmerzahl. *Special Relativity - Will it Survive the Next 101 Years?* Springer, 2006.

Albert Einstein. *Dokumente eines Lebenswegs/Documents of a life's pathway.* WILEY-VCH, 2005.

Louis Essen. *The Special Theory of Relativity: A Critical analysis.* Clarendon Press Oxford, 1971.

Matthias Bartelmann et alia. *Theoretische Physik.* Springer, 2015.

Richard Feynman. *Six Not So Easy Pieces - Einstein's Relativity, Symmetry, and Space-Time.* Addison-Wesley, 1997.

George FitzGerald. The Ether and the Earth's Atmosphere. *Science,* 13(328): 390, 1889.

Jerrold Franklin. Lorentz contraction, Bell's spaceships and rigid body motion in special relativity. *Eur. J. Phys.,* 31:291–298, 2010.

Jerrold Franklin. Rigid Body Motion in Special Relativity. *Foundations of Physics,* 43:1489–1501, 2013.

A.P. French. *Special Relativity.* Chapman and Hall, 1968.

Hans Freudenthal. Lie groups in the foundations of geometry. *Advances in Mathematics,* 1:145–190, 1965.

Galileo. *Le Opere di Galileo Galilei,* volume XI. Firenze, Tip. di G. Barbera, 1900.

Georg Galeczki and Peter Marquardt. *Requiem für die Spezielle Relativität.* Haag and Herchen Frankfurt, 1997.

R H Good. Behind the event horizon. *European Journal of Physics,* 8(3):174–175, 1987.

Christoph Gudermann. *Theorie der Potential- oder Cyklisch-Hyperbolsichen Funktionen.* Crelle's Journal der Mathematik 6, 7, 8, 9, 1833.

Bruce Hunt. *The Maxwellians.* Ithaca: Cornell University Press, 1991.

Vladimir Von Ignatowski. Das Relativitätsprinzip. *Arch. Math. Phys.,* 17/18: 1/17, 1910.

Michel Janssen. The Trouton Experiment and E = mc2.

Regiomontanus / Müller Johannes. *De Triangulis Omnimodis - On Triangles of All Kinds.* Published in Nuremberg, 1464/1533.

James Joyce. *Finnegans Wake.* Faber and Faber, 1939.

Arthur Koestler. *The Sleepwalkers.* Hutchinson / Penguin, 1959.

John B. Kogut. *Introduction to Relativity: For Physicists and Astronomers*. Harcourt, 2001.

Marc Lange. *An Introduction to the Philosophy of Physics*. Blackwell, 2002.

Joseph Larmor. *Aether and Matter, Adams Essay*. Cambridge University Press, 1898/1900.

Joseph Larmor. *The Scientific Writings of the Late George Francis FitzGerald*. Hodges Figgis Dublin, 1902.

Enrique Palumbo Loedel. Aberración y Relatividad. *Anales de la Sociedad Científica Argentina*, 145:3, 1948.

A A Logunov. Henri Poincaré and Relativity Theory, 2005. URL http://arxiv.org/pdf/physics/0408077.pdf.

Martín López Corredoira and Carlos Castro Perelman, editor. *Against the Tide: A Critical Review by Scientists of How Physics and Astronomy Get Done*. Universal Publishers, Boca Raton, Florida, 2008.

Wesley Mathews. Relativistic velocity and acceleration transformations from thought experiments. *American Journal of Physics*, 73:45–51, 2004.

Mary McCarthy. *The Groves of Academe*. Harcourt, Brace, New York, 1951.

W.D. McComb. *Dynamics and Relativity*. Oxford U.P., 1999.

David Mermin. Relativity Without Light. *American Journal of Physics*, 52:119–124, 1984.

Ray Monk. *Inside the Centre - The Life of J. Robert Oppenheimer*. Vintage, 2013.

T.A. Moore. *A Traveler's Guide to Spacetime: An Introduction to the Special Theory of Relativity*. McGraw-Hill, 1995.

Gregory L Naber. *The Geometry of Minkowski Spacetime*. Springer, 1992, 2010.

Gary Oas. On the Use of Relativistic Mass in Various Published Works, 2008.

Lev Okun. The mass versus relativistic and rest masses. URL http://isites.harvard.edu/fs/docs/icb.topic1214842.files/11lev-okun-on-mass.pdf.

Lev Okun. *Energy and Mass in Relativity Theory*. World Scientific, 2009.

Lev B Okun. The concept of Mass in the Einstein Year. pages 31–36, June 2005.

Roger Penrose. *The Emperor's New Mind*. Vintage, 1989.

S. A. Podosenov, J. Foukzon, and A. A. Potapov. A Study of the Motion of a Relativistic Continuous Medium. *Gravitation and Cosmology – Pleiades/Springer*, 16(4):307–312, 2010.

S. A. Podosenov, A. A. Potapov, J. Foukzon, and A. A. Menkova. Geometry of Noninertial Bases in Relativistic Mechanics of Continua and Bell's Problem Solution. *International Journal of Recent advances in Physics (IJRAP)*, 3(1):23–37, February 2014.

S. A. Podosenov, J. Foukzon, and A. A. Menkova. Structure Equations, Permitted Movement of Relativistic Continuum and Sagnac's, Erenfest's and Bell's Paradoxes. *Physical Science International Journal*, 13(2):1–18, January 2017a.

S. A. Podosenov, J. Foukzon, and E. Menkova. *Difficulties in the Interpretation of the Einstein's Relativity Theory*. Lampert Academic Publishing, 2017b.

Henri Poincaré. *La Science et l'hypothèse*. Flammarion, Paris, 1902.

Henri Poincaré. Sur la dynamique de l'électron. Académie des sciences, Paris, 1905.

Andrew Pressley. *Elementary differential geometry*. Springer, 2010.

Edmund Purcell. *Electricity and Magnetism*, volume 2. McGraw-Hill, 1985.

Dragan Redžic. Note on Dewan&Beran Bell's spaceship problem. *Eur.J.Phys.*, 29:N11–9, 2008.

Dragan Redžic. Relativistic Length Agony Continued. *Serb. Astron. J.*, 188:55 – 65, 2014.

Hans Reichenbach. *The Philosophy of Space and Time (Philosophie der Raum-Zeit-Lehre)*. De Gruyter Berlin, 1928.

Wolfgang Rindler. *Introduction to Special Relativity*. Oxford Universtiy Press, 1982, 1991.

Wolfgang Rindler. *Relativity, Special, General and Cosmological*. Oxford Universtiy Press, 2001, 2006.

Thomas Ryckman. *The Reign of Relativity*. Oxford Universtity Press, 2005.

Leo Sartori. *Understanding Relativity*. Univ. of California Press, 1996.

Bernard Schulz. *Gravity from the ground up*. Cambridge University Press, 2003.

Peter Schuster. *Moving the Stars - Christian Doppler, His Life, His Works and Principle and the World After*. Living Edition Austria, 2005.

F Sears and R Brehme. *Introduction to Special Relativity*. Addison Wesley, 1968.

Albert Shadowitz. *Special Relativity*. Dover, 1988.

James H Smith. *Introduction to Special Relativity*. Dover, 1965, 1996.

Aleksander Solzhenitsyn. *The Gulag Archipelago*, volume 2 p.296. Westview Press/Harper & Row NY, 1973.

Arnold Sommerfeld. Über die Zusammensetzung der Geschwindigkeiten in der Relativitätstheorie (On the composition of velocities in relativity theory). *Physikalische Zeitschrift*, 10:826–829, 1909.

Hans Stephani. *An Introduction to Special and General Relativity*. Cambridge U.P. Cambridge U.P., 3rd edition, 2004.

Georg Süssmann. Begründung der Lorentz-Gruppe allein mit Symmetrie- und Relativitäts-Annahmen. *Z. Naturforscher*, 24a:495–498, 1969.

John Lighton Synge. *Relativity: The Special Theory*. North-Holland, Amsterdam, 1956.

John Lighton Synge. *Relativity: The General Theory*. North-Holland, Amsterdam, 1960.

Rudolf Tomaschek. Über das Verhalten des Lichtes ausserirdischer Lichtquellen. *Annalen der Physik*, 378(1-2):105–126, 1924.

Scott Walter. Minkowski, Mathematicians, and the Mathematical Theory of Relativity. *Einstein Studies*, 7:45–86, 1999.

Nicholas Whyte. *Science, Colonialism and Ireland*. Cork University Press, 1999.

Nicholas Woodhouse. *Special Relativity*. Springer London, 2003.

Robert C. Yates. *A Handbook on Curves and their Properties*. J. W. Edwards - Ann Arbor, 1947.

Index

A 'retrospective' insight, 163
A Dutch drawbridge, 167
A fallacy's domino effect, 121
A five-fold equivalence, 77
"A glorious non-entity", 165
À la recherche du temps perdu, 111
A Russian overture, 169
A simple question, 144
A Spacetime Odyssey, 101
A unit thrust medium's expansion limit conditions, 122
absolute time, 21
Abu'l-Wafa, 88
accelerating 'proxy' non-inertial frame, 148
accelerating courier, 85
accelerating medium's increment, 122
accelerating rocket scenario, 61
acceleration hemix, 95
acceleration phase, 110
action equals reaction, 71
aether, 14
Also Spuke Zerothruster, 70
Ambrose Bierce, 4
American Journal of Physics, 108, 147
American Journal of Physics, 5, 60, 121, 142, 166, 168
angle supplement, 90
'apocalyptic' relationships, 81
apocalyptic acceleration identities, 65, 66
arbitrary active signal return interval ratio, 50
arbitrary fixed own-acceleration relationships, 125
arbitrary frame spatial momentum sum is conserved, 76

arbitrary frame temporal momentum sum is conserved, 76
arbitrary signal speed Doppler factor, 50
Aristotle, 67
Astronomy Ireland Dublin lecture, 102

background rear rocket acceleration phase, 113
background space, 17
Bell's string paradox, 109
Bell, John, 9
Berkeley, George, 29
Big Bang, the, 58
Borel, Emil, 80
boundary speed, 20
boundary speed rescaling, 22
Buridan's ass parody, 68
Buridan, Jean, 67, 68

cascaded relativity tetrahedra, 95
celestial bodies, 67
celestial spheres, 151
CERN 2011 experiment, 53
characteristic light spectra, 58
chronocity, 26
chronosity, 18, 21, 29, 35
chronosity angle, 22
chronosity-velocity relationship, 23
chronosity/velocity ratio, 26
classical force, 68
classical momentum, 68
collison particles force relationships, 76
common sense, 29
comoving frame, 69, 108
comoving frame variables, 110
comoving frame's distance dispersal, 129

comoving inertial frame, 81
comoving reference frame, 62
constancy of light wave speed, 45
constant thrust rocket, 106
contagious limit speed, 46
'contracted' length, 143
'contraction' surface curve, 102
convention, 21
coordinate relationships, 39
cosines and sines laws in global navigation, 93
cosmic boundary speed, 20
cosmic boundary speed limitation, 74
cosmic limit speed, 20, 49
curved spacetime, 15
cyclic velocity, 26
cylindrical coordinates, 102

De Triangulis Omnimodis—Regiomontanus' 1464 book *On Triangles*, 87
definitions of length and time, 109
Descartes, 67
destination spacestation, 111
determination by indeterminacy, 49
The Devil's Dictionary, 4
diagonal trajectories of photons, 118
differential relativity spherical triangle, 97
dilation, 103
direct portrayal of relativity velocity composition, 92
dispersal distance, 112, 129, 144
dispersal time, 112, 144
dispersals triangle, 111
dispersed solo gap distance, 112
distance ray, 102, 106
distances helicoid, 155
diversifying momentum and force, 67
Doppler equation, 6
Doppler relationships, 55
Doppler standard velocity formula, 57
dual reference frames chart, 24, 29, 39

$E = m\gamma c^2$, 73
Einstein, 3, 15, 68
elastic collisions, 75
elastically colliding particles' relativistic forces, 76
electromagnetic constants, 27

electromagnetism, 43
emitted photon transit times, 116
emitted photon's horizon excess, 118
emitted photon's asymptotic horizon, 118
energy, 70
energy is conserved, 74
epistemological problems, 109
errors perpetuated in relativity literature, 143
Essen, Louis, 4
establishing the boundary speed, 43
Euclidean metric own-surfaces, 133
Euclidean own-surface, 146
European Journal of Physics, 19
European Journal of Physics, i, 5, 7, 11, 14, 43, 54, 60, 73, 118, 166, 167
European Mathematical Society, 49
event, 18, 25, 30
event horizon, 8, 108, 113, 118
evidence of an expanding Universe, 57
evidence unwittingly 'withheld', 120
existential background, 15
expanded length, 143, 144
explicit signal response ratios formula, 53
extrinsic and intrinsic parameters, 154

final separation distance, 143
final shutdown dispersal time, 113
FitzGerald, George, 42
fixed own-acceleration home frame hyperbolic relationship, 83
fixed thrust, 81
fixed velocity loci, 118
fixed velocity rigor mortis world-surface loci, 131
flat spacetime, 15
flat spacetime continuum, 27
force, 67
forward 'rigor mortis' radar interval, 128
forward acceleration, 64
forward general radar equation, 128
forward transit equation, 127
forward velocity equation, 41, 43
Foundation of Physics journal, 167, 168
four forces of the apocalyptic identities, 71
four relativistic force forms, 71
Freudenthal, Hans, 27
front rocket's 'retrospective' inter-rocket

separation, 114
front rocket's radar interval, 120
frozen times, 19

Galileo, 8, 67, 68
gamma surface curve, 102
general inter-rockets' radar intervals, 125
geometric model, 150
Girard spherical triangle area theorem, 92
'good in spots' bad egg, 131
gravity-free inertial frames, 43
great circles, 87
Groves of Academe, 166
Gudermann connection, 82
Gulag Archipelago, The, 54

Heidegger, Martin—*Being and Time*, 15
helices and hemices, 147
helicoidal pitch m, 145
helicoidal sextet, 151
hemices, 106
hemicised rigor mortis own-surface, 137
hemicoid own-surface, 147
hemispherical hemix, 99
hemix, 7, 95, 106, 137
hemix 'distance ray' projections, 102
hemix arc length, 103
hemix path lengths, 106
hemix vector coordinates, 99
hemix vector equation, 100
hemix: a transcendental history-line, 98
home distance, 103, 155
home frame, 148
home frame acceleration, 64, 103, 115
home frame chart, 26
home frame distance, 115
home frame hyperbolae, 109
home frame hyperbolic equation, 84
home frame hyperbolic world-line, 84, 159
home frame time dispersal, 129
home frame world-surface, 116
home frame's rigor mortis medium's world-surface equation, 130
home reference frame chart, 84
home time, 103, 106
homogeneous acceleration velchronos angle, 82

horizon photon, 118
horizon photon's emission time, 118
Hubble, Edwin, 58
hyperbolic functions, 82
hyperbolic world-line, 126
hypothesis, 21

Ignatowski, 5
Ignatowski constant, 53, 54
Ignatowski's tragic fate, 54
impetus, 67
implicit signal response ratios formula, 52
In search of lost time, 111
increment curve surfing, 160
increment curves, 146
Increment curves and medium curves, 134
increment of an idealized 'co-accelerating' medium, 116
individual increment hemices, 147
inertial object, 43
inertial reference frame, 43, 62
inertial spacestations, 84
initial launch separation, 148
initial shutdown time dispersal, 111
instance of the boundary speed, 43, 45
inter-rocket acceleration radar intervals, 120, 126
inter-rocket comoving frame retrospective separation distance, 114
intermediate comoving frames, 110
intermediate world-lines, 116
intrinsic own-surface criteria, 144
intrinsic spatio-temporal 'length' characteristics, 150
intuition, 21
Islamic spherical geometry, 87

Johannes Müller, Regiomontanus, 87

Kepler, Johannes, 151
key distance parameters, 118
kinetic energy, 103
kinetic energy increment, 70
kinetic energy increment formula, 73

Larmor time dilation fcator, 34
Larmor, Joseph, 14, 39, 42

Larmor-Lorentz transformations, 23, 39, 40, 111, 129, 143

lateral expansion factor $\epsilon(\tau)$, 147

lateral medium helices, 147

lateral thinking, 43

launch separation distance, 118

Leibnitz' rule, 66

length 'contraction', 32

light photon, 43

light waves, 43

limit speed, 6, 20

limit speed ratio's explicit signal response ratios formula, 53

limit speed ratio's implicit signal response ratios formula, 52

lines of home time simultaneity, 159

lines of time simultaneity, 16

Loedel chart, 111

Loedel, Enrique, 39

logical relationship, 43

Lorentz, Hendrik, 39, 42

loxodromes, 100

MacCullagh, James, 42

MAPLE, 52

mathematical reasoning, 21

mathematical relationships, 113

Maxwell, James Clerk, 42

Meaninglessness of the present tense, 34

Measuring the Cosmic Limit Speed, 49

Mecca, 87

medium curves, 134

medium helices, 146

medium's 'lengths' in four reference frames, 148

medium's 'non-inertial own-length' defined, 144

medium-timed photon crossing rates, 121

Mercator projection, 102

meridian arc length, 103

meridian great circles, 87

meridianal inclination, 94

Michelson, Albert, 14

Minkowski chart, 26

Minkowski metric, 131

Minkowski spacetime, 8

Minkowski spacetime's 'post-truths', 165

Minkowski, Hermann, 43

mirage, 32

mirages of 'length' and time, 29

momentum, 67

monotonic, 19

'Mysterium Cosmographicum', the, 151

Nature, 17, 26, 46

Newton's second law of motion, 68

Newton's 3rd law reformulated, 70

Newton's Principia, 67

Newton, Isaac, 7, 67

Newtonian physics, 5

non-elastic collisions, 77

non-inertial 'present tenses', 150

non-inertial accelerating 'proxy' frame, 144

non-inertial expansion, 147

non-inertial objects, 43

non-inertial own-expansion factor, 145

non-inertial own-length, 145, 150

non-inertial own-length from the medium's rear end, 145

non-uniformly accelerating medium, 143

non-unit fixed own-thrust relationships, 125

Nuñes, Pedro, 100

nuclear energy, 74

object-frame force, 69

observer-frame force, 70

observers' agent, 70

obtuse angle, 90

Occam, 21, 67

Occam's razor, 21, 43

Okun, Lev, 6

On Triangles, Regiomontanus' 1464 book, De Triangulis Omnimodis, 87

outgoing and return spacetime itinerary, 104

outgoing and returning photons, 121

outgoing and returning radar trajectories, 159

outgoing photon equation, 117

outgoing photon paths, 159

outgoing photon reflection equation, 117

outgoing transit photon equation, 117

ovality factor, 102

own-acceleration factor, 81

own-distance, 155
own-length, 30, 143
own-length measurement criterion, 114
own-space, 24
own-time, 24, 30

Pandora's box, 10
parallel helicoids, 151
Persian astronomers, 87
Philoponos, Johannes, 67
photon crossing rates in the limit, 122
photon's associated arrival time, 117
Plato—*Sophistes*, 15
platonic solids, 151
Podosenov, Stanislav, iii, 169
Poincaré, Henri, i, 3–5, 21, 27, 45
post-shutdown phase inertial frame, 143
'present tense' in non-inertial frames, 155, 157
present tense, 18, 34
primary acceleration relationships, 63
Providence, 20
pseudo 'contraction' factor, 103
pseudo-Euclidean Minkowski metric, 140
pseudo-expansion/pseudo-contraction helicoids, 153
ptolemaic accelerating medium, 125

Qibla, the, 87
quadruplet velocities ratio, 46
quality of movement, 67
quantum mechanics, 15

radar curves' crossing angles and geodesic curvatures, 162
radar intervals, 115, 116
radar mappings, 159
radar photon trajectories, 159
rate of change of momentum, 69
re-emitted reflection equations, 119
re-emitted transit equations, 119
re-synchronization event, 111
re-synchronization of the rear rocket, 113
re-synchronization onset time, 113
re-synchronization period, 114
re-synchronizations, 113
real spacetime metrics, 151
real variables metric surface, 9

rear rocket's radar interval, 120
rear rocket's time dispersed solo gap distance, 111
redundant 2nd postulate, 5, 45
reference frame coordinates, 39
reference frame intervals, 30
reference frame observer, 29
reference frame velocity triplets, 96
reference frames, 17
reference frames quartet, 46
reference frames triplet, 41
reference home frame point, 96
reference origin, 25
reflected photon, 118
Regiomontanus, Johannes Müller, 87
Reichenbach, Hans, 61
relative motion, 21
relativistic acceleration, 81
relativistic velocities, 41
Relativity Cosmographicum, the, 151
Relativity Cosmographicum's helicoid sextet, 152
relativity Doppler factor, 55
relativity Doppler polyhedron, 96
relativity signal speed Doppler factor, 56
relativity spherical triangle's volume and area relationship, 92
relativity spherical triangles, 95
relativity tetrahedra, 95
relativity triangle's longitudinal criterion, 90
relativity's real spherical triangles, 87
Requiem für die Spezielle Relativität, 4
rest mass to energy ratio, 27
Results in Physics, 10
Results in Physics, 11
retro-acceleration, 64, 98, 103
retro-distance, 62, 83, 103
retro-perceived acceleration, 63
retro-separation, 109
retrospective inter-rocket separation, 108
return transit equation, 127
returning photon paths, 160
returning photon transit equation, 119
returning photons, 118
returning transit equations, 119
reverse 'rigor mortis' radar interval, 129
reverse general radar equation, 128

rigid motion, 9
'rigor mortis', 9, 128, 143
rigor Mortis acceleration, 125
rigor mortis accelerations condition, 131
rigor mortis gravitational field, 139
rigor mortis gravity train, 138
rigor mortis home frame world-surface, 130
rigor mortis medium's own-surface, 135
rigor mortis own-surface vector equation, 137
rigor mortis radar intervals ratio, 129
rigor mortis real metric, 139
rigor mortis scenario, 128
rigor mortis space and time dispersals, 129
Rindler, Wolfgang, 34
rocket acceleration parameters, 103
rocket and spacestation world-lines, 110
rocket arrivals time-dispersed, 111
rocket comoving frame's retro-distance, 83
rocket own-time, 82, 103, 106
rocket own-time intervals, 116
rocket's return journey, 104
rocket's world-line, 126
rockets' home frame asymmetric hyperbolae, 110
rockets' asymptotic horizon, 118
rockets' own-time intervals, 116
rockets' rendez-vous with two spacestations, 109
ruled surface helicoid event line, 155
ruled surface helicoids, 154

Süssmann, Georg, 27
Sagan, Carl, 101
Saint Augustine, 101
scaled boundary chronosity, 22
scaling times and lengths, 81
Science and Hypothesis, 21
second postulate invalidity, 120
separation, 150
separation length, 113
shutdown frame, 110, 114, 148
shutdown frame re-synchronization, 113
shutdown frame retrospectively perceived solo gap distance, 114

shutdown frame rocket arrivals' time dispersal, 111
shutdown frame ultimate distance dispersal, 111
shutdown speed, 110
signal return interval, 50
simple nonaccelerating own-surface, 134
Slipher, Vesto, 58
Solvay Conference, 3, 80
Solzhenitsyn, Aleksander, 5, 54
Sommerfeld, Arnold, 80
spacestation inertial clocks, 111
spacestations, 17, 51
spacetime chart's 'reference origin, 110
spacetime charts 'where-lines' and 'when-lines', 16
spacetime charts and world-lines, 21
spacetime diagram, 151, 161
spacetime theory, 109
Spacetime's and (Geometry's ?) missing 'hemix', 95
spatial homogeneity, 27
spatial isotropy, 27
spatial momentum, 26, 69, 76, 103
spatio-temporal symmetry, 22
special relativity, 15
special relativity velocity composition, 91
special relativity's scope, 5
speed of light, 26
speed of time, 26, 69
speeds above the limit speed, 46
spherical triangle, 87
spherical triangle cosines law, 80, 89, 93
spherical triangle relativity acceleration composition, 97
spherical triangle sines and cosines laws, 88
spherical triangles' hitherto missed relativity connection, 91
staggered dual frame charts, 85
surface ovoids, 102
surfed photon, 122
symmetric curved world-lines, 110
symmetrical dual reference frame chart, 110
Synge, John Lighton, 10, 11

tandem response time ratios, 51

temporal divergence, 21

temporal momentum, 26, 69, 76, 103

The Ante Portas 'invitation', 167

The Emperor's New Mind Clothes, 170

The Inverse Larmor-Lorentz Transformations, 40

the missing own-surface Υ, 145

thermodynamics, 75

Thought experiment, 22

thrust reversal tunnel, 105

time dilation, 33, 64, 69, 83

time disparity, 18

time dispersal, 109

'time gap' inertial frame, 113

time gap transition, 109

Time lost and gained, 7

time machine, 101

time scale, 22

time schism, 14

time travel, 35

time travel odyssey, 80

time travel ovoidal projections, 102

time travel relativistic parameters, 102

total energy, 74, 103

triad ratio equation, 52

triad velocities formulae, 41

triple gamma relationship, 90

triple gammas velocity formulae, 90

triplet reference frame velocities, 92

ubiquitous backwards traversing, 122

ubiquitous home frame observers, 109

ultimate synchronisation spatial separation, 111

uniform thrust medium own-surface, 151, 161

uniform thrust medium world-surface, 109

uniform thrust medium's real metric, 156

uniform thrust own-surface equation, 145

uniform time travel, 101

uniformly accelerating extended medium, 153

uniformly accelerating medium's 'non-inertial own-length', 150

unit acceleration, 103

unit acceleration medium home world-surface, 116

unit acceleration velchronos angle's rate of change, 82

unit limit speed, 81, 103

unit mass, 103

unit own-acceleration, 81

unit own-accleration parameters, 82

unit scaled boundary speed, 22

unit scaled limit speed, 116

unit sines law ratio spherical triangles, 89

unit thrust medium own-surface, 143

unit thrust medium's gravity train, 155

unit thrust rocket, 81

unit thrust rocket's equations, 86

unit thrust times and distances, 83

universal constant, 26

velchronos angle, 30, 31, 96, 101, 103, 106

velchronos angle differential, 82

velocities, 43

velocity angle, 22, 103

velocity composition equations, 41

velocity composition visualised, 87

velocity signal response function, 51

velocity triads, 43

velocity–signal response function, 51

verifying the explicit limit speed formula, 53

versed sine, 101, 103

what Alice found, 95

when-line segments, 30

when-lines, 16, 18, 40

where-line, 22

where-line segments, 30

where-lines, 16, 18, 40, 43, 50

world-line angles formula, 41

world-line trajectory, 126

world-lines, 25, 43, 50

world-surface, 109

Made in the USA
Columbia, SC
18 April 2021